Sunrise to Wind

Other Sailing Classics

SUNRISE TO WINDWARD

Miles Smeeton

GRAFTON BOOKS

A Division of the Collins Publishing Group

LONDON GLASGOW
TORONTO SYDNEY AUCKLAND

Grafton Books
A Division of the Collins Publishing Group
8 Grafton Street, London W1X 3LA

First published in Great Britain by Rupert Hart-Davis Ltd 1966
Reissued by Grafton Books 1987

British Library Cataloguing in Publication Data

Smeeton, Miles
    Sunrise to windward.
    1. Voyages and travels   2. Yachts and
    yachting
    I. Title
    910.4'5   G540

ISBN 0-246-13171-3

Printed in Great Britain by
William Collins Sons Ltd, Westerhill, Glasgow

TO CLIO AND ANN

Contents

Aden Protectorate

Socotra

Seychelles

Comoros

Mozambique

Madagascar

Inhambane

Rodrig

Mauritius

Reunion

Lourenço Marques

Durban

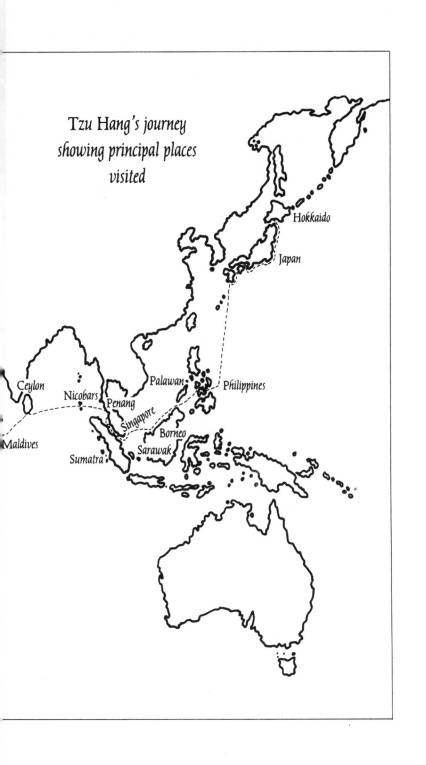

Tzu Hang's journey
showing principal places
visited

Hokkaido

Japan

Ceylon

Nicobars   Penang   Palawan   Philippines

Maldives   Singapore

Borneo

Sumatra   Sarawak

1   *A Start from Paris*

THE leaves were gone from the trees. The rain blew up the river in gusty squalls and over the bridges. It rattled on the roofs of the cars and assaulted the passers-by, who leant forward, clutching their coats about them, as they hurried towards the shelter of the streets beyond.

Beryl and I stepped on to the wooden planking of the *passerelle* and looked across the Seine to where *Tzu Hang* was moored on the right bank, above the Palais de Chaillot, between several motor yachts and barges. Her masts were in Le Havre, where we had left them at the end of a cruise that had taken us from Ireland, round by the Shetlands to Norway, to Sweden and the Baltic. The river had left several dirty waterlines on her white hull. She was not looking her best, but she was still beautiful. The curve of her bow, her strength, and her lovely sheer showed that this was no boat of the inland waters and that her home was the wide sea. She was home for Beryl and me anyway—home for the winter in Paris, or wherever else she might take us.

The dog that Clio had bought as a puppy, nine years ago in Madeira, hurried ahead of us with the strange 'dot-and-carry' gait that one of his scraps had left him. His name was Popa after a compatriot on a Portuguese yacht that had lain next to us in Lisbon, who was ordered '*a popa*' or '*a proa*' as the decks were being washed down. We had just recovered him from one of his love affairs.

'I wonder why he always chooses the left bank?' Beryl asked.

'Perhaps now that he's getting old he finds it easier there. Less classy than on our bank,' I suggested.

The Siamese cat was the only member of the crew who was not fully enjoying her winter in Paris. She had spent a night in one of the sewers into which she had fallen during a hunting expedition, and had lost her taste for the life ashore. Not so Popa. He was off all the time. We had joined a society for the protection of animals in Paris, and Popa wore their medal on his collar with his address on the reverse side. If he had been missing for a night we walked up the bank to the Touring Club de France and usually found a message to say that he was waiting in someone's apartment on the *rive gauche*. Our trips to recover him took us to all sorts of places: to a single room in a garret occupied by an old lady, where he and a bull-terrier were waiting for the bell, tied to chairs in opposite corners; to the elegant flat of a Guards' officer, a military attaché in Paris.

We crossed the *passerelle* and went down the steps to the far bank, past a group of fishermen impervious to the weather, past a Norfolk wherry lying far afield, past the big white barge of the Club Nautique, and jumped down on to *Tzu Hang*'s deck. The Seine was still low. 'Wait until the flood season comes,' we were told, 'and you may find yourselves on the pavement.' There were two seasons hanging over our heads. The flood season and the suicide season, which was supposed to be worst at the time of the *baccalauréat*. Monsieur Berthelot, the taciturn watchman of the Club Nautique barge, told us that there was not much to be made out of pulling them out.

A yacht permits you to meet people that you would not ordinarily meet as a tourist and hardly a day passed without a new visitor. It might be a yachting enthusiast, or someone just curious about yachts, a member of the Siamese Cat Club, a member of Popa's society, or a friend of Clio's from London in search of a cheap bed. Very rarely it was someone who had read about *Tzu Hang* in the Southern Ocean, and once we heard voices calling 'Clio!' softly from the quay, a diffident little French couple who had remembered her name from that story, and had a yacht themselves in La Rochelle. Amongst our visitors we had one very strange person.

Early one morning, just as daylight was beginning to filter through the skylight above our bunks, we heard the sound of someone stepping lightly down on to the deck. I looked through the skylight and saw a dapper little man, in tight trousers and a short overcoat, moving gingerly aft along the deck. I followed the light footsteps above me silently through the main cabin and into the doghouse. The hatch was closed and the bottom weatherboards in place against the rain, leaving only a narrow gap at the top for fresh air. I felt like a cat stalking a mouse. A pair of knees appeared at the gap, and a moment later the young man squatted down and looked inside. He found my face immediately opposite his, and I could not resist the temptation of saying 'Boo!' Still with his umbrella over his head he sailed on to the quay in one shocked bound, so that he looked like the film of a parachutist landing down in reverse. He then took off down the quay as fast as his pointed shoes and his tight trousers would let him.

Christmas passed with the cabin full of cards and decorations, and a small tree on the locker by the stove. Presently the flood season arrived with no high levels, and the suicide season came with two attempted suicides from the *passerelle*. Soon the chestnuts were in bloom. We went climbing on the practice rocks at Fontainebleau, and fell off without damage and without much shame, as the holds were never far from the ground and sometimes very difficult. There were children there who climbed as if they were weightless and had suckers on their feet. I wondered how many of France's great climbers had started on those rocks. Beryl and I played our annual game of golf at Compiègne, and all too soon it was time to leave for England, to fit a new engine and to set off somewhere if we were going anywhere.

'We can't go back to Canada the way we went before,' said Beryl. 'Can't we go east about this time. To Japan?'

It is part of her character. Steps must never be retraced, one must always go forward, the Matterhorn must be traversed. My first reaction was to do with difficulties although I know that this is not the way to deal with my wife. The more that I produce the easier she thinks it is going to be. I remembered a Red Sea passage at the beginning of the war, blacked out, in September, and the oppressive heat.

'That means a summer Red Sea passage and a following wind. Desperately hot it will be.'

'I long to be hot again. Good for the rheumatism.'

'And then the typhoon season, an average of twenty-five a year.'

'Yes, but they must have a free season. In fact I know they do. When I was in Hongkong—'

'It will take us two years at least.'

'But I don't want to rush back to Canada,' she said, 'I want to stop in places, take a house perhaps, and see something of the people. We could have Clio out to join us from time to time,' she added, her mind leaping ahead to all sorts of possibilities and forestalling my next objection. Soon I began to have visions of white-walled patios drenched in Spanish sun, of revisiting old friends in India, of an elegant Japanese house and wonderful maids, of industrious, skilled, and inexpensive workmen for *Tzu Hang*. Of course I know that it won't work out like this. That the industrious workmen will be ourselves, and that our houses, if we have them, will be about as comfortable as an igloo, but anyway it is worth trying, and if much falls short of the dream much will exceed it.

We had never been in the Mediterranean before, and if we were to see something of it now, we would be too late to go down the Red Sea. The favourable wind blows down the Red Sea from July to September. We decided to go to the Mediterranean, winter there, and to do the Red Sea trip the following year. Although parts of the journey to Japan had been done by various yachts, none that we knew had gone the whole way from England, or even Europe, and this, like an unclimbed mountain, was an added attraction.

It was May before we started. We idled down the Seine in lovely summer weather. As the reaches of the river unfolded between wooded hills and rich fields they revealed something of beauty or interest, a turreted castle, an old château, a ruined abbey, or another lock with piles of foam floating beyond it from the detergent in Paris washtubs. By day the cuckoos called, and by night the nightingales sang over our anchorages. At times we managed to station ourselves on the quarter of a barge and were carried along on the edge of its wake at about eight knots, until some mistake in steering or upcoming traffic made us fall behind and revert to our customary four or five.

At one lock the barge *Annette* tied us alongside, and for a whole day we were passengers on board her. There never was a more spotless cabin than *Annette*'s, nor brighter brass than in the wheelhouse above. The crew consisted of a man and his wife, with a son at school somewhere on the riverbank. Both were paid, and they got three weeks' holiday a year. They worked from seven in the morning until seven at night, when the locks closed, but if they had to continue beyond these hours to reach a tying-up place, they got overtime. We were very taken with all the river people. They gave us a wave as we passed and were ready to help with our lines at the locks, or to interpret the strange noise that issued from the loudspeaker as we approached, the only intelligible words to us being '*le yacht anglais*'. But then the whole impression of what we saw in France was one of friendliness. At that time an article appeared in one of the leading English papers, saying that our relations with France could hardly have been worse, but as far as ordinary people were concerned they could not have been better.

At one halt a Frenchman came over from the opposite bank and asked us to come to his summer cottage where he and his family were spending the weekend. We were talking about the extraordinary wealth of France, so obvious on either hand as one comes down the river. It was at the beginning of the de Gaulle era. 'I think,' he said, 'that we are the only country in the world that could afford such bad governments as we have had recently.'

We took the Tancarville canal to Le Havre. On one side there were enormous oil installations with flares roaring up into the sky, on the other were green fields and cattle grazing, not much changed since English archers marched from there to Agincourt. As we slid through the canal late in the evening the gas flares were reflected in the water on one side of the bow, and on the other a fox slipped down through the reeds to the water's edge, and only interrupted his lapping to give us a casual glance as we passed.

We shipped our masts in Le Havre where they had been lifted out, stored under cover by the yacht club, and replaced for a total cost of seven pounds. For the passage of the locks and the long stay in Paris we had not been required to pay a sou, but the cost of living had been higher than in England.

We spent the next two weeks at Deauville and left in June, pitching into a rough sea left by strong winds of the day before. The cat, the dog, and we ourselves after the long spell ashore felt seasick. We were able to lay a course for the Isle of Wight and next morning were off Shanklin. Beryl had spent some years as a girl in Shanklin and whenever I talk of settling permanently in England she recalls its horrors. Useless to speculate where we might be if it hadn't been for Shanklin. When I saw the rows of houses on a grey morning from the sea I felt that I understood.

In the afternoon, off the Needles, we found that we had a leak but were unable to discover the cause. The pump, after its long disuse, refused to work, and we bailed out the bilges with a bucket, hoping that it would not be necessary to do it again before we arrived at Dartmouth. During Beryl's second watch she woke me to say that we would have to do something as the water was over the floorboards. I had just got to sleep and got up feeling that fortune was treating us very unkindly. I knew that I should have fixed the pump but was all too ready to blame anything or anyone other than myself. Having emptied the bilges again we had another search with a flashlight as we were now making water badly. This time I could hear the leak, and we found that part of the exhaust fitting had broken away. We put *Tzu Hang* on the other tack, caulked the leak from inside and thereafter had no more trouble.

In the morning we were off Portland Bill and remained there for the best part of a contrary tide. By then the sea was down, and we had a light wind from the south, so that we had a quiet sail in the sunlight towards Dartmouth.

It was long after dark when we arrived. As we motored up the narrow channel we were hailed by a loudspeaker from the harbour office. This time we could understand it.

'Hello, that yacht over there,' it said. 'What ship are you and where are you from?'

'*Tzu Hang*. From Deauville.'

'All right. You can anchor. We'll be over in the morning.'

'Wonderful to be back in England,' I said to Beryl, as soon as the anchor was down. 'They are always so efficient and reasonable.'

'And they make you pay for it too,' said Beryl. She has never forgotten Ramsgate, the first port that we ever made. When we cast off from the quay to leave, the motor stopped. I hooked on to a buoy with the boathook and made fast there while I got the engine going again, but not soon enough to avoid the arrival of a port official who cheerfully extracted buoy dues from us although we had paid harbour dues the day before.

We found a boatyard a few miles up the river where we could get the new diesel engine installed, and where we would be able

to paint *Tzu Hang* on the tide. The owner of the yard, his
foreman Donald, and an engineer came down to see what had
to be done. In *Tzu Hang*'s cabin, the talk for some reason
turned to Corfe Castle. Donald was an excellent workman,
quick and accurate and full of ideas. 'They ought to take the
edges off,' he said, 'and make it look neater.'

We moved up the river next day, with *Tzu Hang*'s designer,
H. S. Rouse, piloting us. He had never been on *Tzu Hang*
before, at least not since he supervised her construction in
Hongkong.

'What do you think of her now?' I asked.

Tzu Hang's mast is five feet shorter, and she has no bowsprit
and a single headsail since the sea swept her clean in the
Southern Ocean. Now her doghouse is lower, with curved sides
to the roof, her mizzen boom does not project over the stern,
she has roller reefing instead of the reef points that she used to
have, and she has a good pulpit at the stern and bow. All her
masts and spars are painted white instead of being varnished,
and her jib stay is set up on a lever so that it can be released and
taken back to the shrouds, allowing *Tzu Hang* to tack under the
genoa, which goes to the masthead. Her working sail which
used to be 915 square feet is now 800, and in exchange for a
more compact and easier rig we do not seem to have lost a great
deal of speed. Downwind with the twins set we have a slightly
bigger sail area than we had before. To windward we usually
have enough, and in very light airs no sailing ship has enough
sail. *Tzu Hang* is not a racer, and our object is to get there in
maximum comfort and with the least exhaustion. Above all
anyone who has handled a headsail, or even a mizzen, on a
black night will appreciate the great benefit of a strong pulpit
fore and aft for a shorthanded crew. I am always glad when I
have got myself safely wedged into it.

Rouse looked as if he did not like the changes.

'Come on,' I said.

'Well, I must say that I think you have spoilt her,' he
answered.

I wish that he could have sailed with us and seen how well
she goes in her new rig. At any rate we owe him a big debt for
the way she was designed and the strength of her construction.
He told us that she had been dropped from her slings on to the

quay, when being loaded in Hongkong, and that the only damage that was done was a slight flattening of her lead keel.

As we approached the boatyard *Tzu Hang*'s movement slowed and her stern rose until she stopped altogether, still some way from the yard. Rouse was unperturbed. 'It looks as if we are a little short of water,' he said. We fixed boards to our spinnaker poles so that they would not sink into the mud and fastened the other ends with handy-billies to the pinrails in order to hold her upright. At low tide there was a long furrow behind us that she had ploughed in the mud. Higher tides were coming, and the next day we put her alongside the quay without any difficulty. The new engine arrived and Donald installed it.

I had arranged with a firm in London to take the old Gray Marine, but now a customs officer had something to say about the transaction. 'If you put it ashore,' he said, 'we'll have to charge you import duty based on the cost price, and that'll be more than you'll get from a dealer.'

'When I'm buying a new British engine?'

'Can't help that. Those are the regulations. If I was you,' he added, 'I'd take it to sea and dump it.'

'But it's still a good engine,' I said, horrified at the waste as well as at such cavalier treatment of an old friend. 'I can't possibly go to sea with a bloody great engine on the deck. Surely there's someone who'll find it useful, a fisherman or someone to whom I might give it?'

'If you put it ashore I shall have to come and smash it,' he said with a cold look in his pale eye. We put it ashore and he smashed the cylinder block with a hammer. I began to revise my opinion about reasonable customs officers. Provided the battery was charged and the fuel clean it had always started, but it had never quite recovered from its adventures in the Southern Ocean. It deserved a better fate. We had blessed it many times and cursed it too, but always with a guilty feeling that the fault was really mine if it did not go.

Clio joined us in Falmouth, and our crew was complete. When the three of us had first left England, all of us novices, we pursued only battleship courses and approached land with diffidence. Now we were a little more experienced and prepared to come within the five-fathom line if there was something worth seeing and the weather permitted. We sailed from the Helford River on the first leg of our long journey on 2 August 1960, with our plans only half formed, except that we would go east. *Tzu Hang*'s voyages are governed by the minimum of planning, times, and rendezvous, but we had promised to meet Nicole and Michel, the young couple with the yacht in La Rochelle, and to pick up Norah Kasteliz in Bilbao, where Señor Ignacio de Abando, whom we had also met in Paris had promised to meet us and to drive us to the caves of Altamira.

2 *To Ilha Berlenga*

ON our first day from the Helford River, the wind came lightly from the northwest, the sea was calm, the sun shone, and to sail the English seas seemed to be all that man could want. At lunchtime we were close off the Lizard, and in the evening we anchored west of the small and shallow harbour of St Michael's Mount.

We launched the dinghy and rowed ashore. The last bus had left, and the streets of the village at the foot of the Mount were deserted. A pub stood cold and closed, with a sign-holder but no sign, and the Island Café was closed also. There was a feeling of the corners of window blinds being lifted and hostile eyes following our progress; of some stern and unseen presence who spent his time issuing orders and notices and pinning them in archways. We imagined two lives that were lived here. One when the island was open to tourists and another, a secret one into which we were intruding, after the causeway was closed. Perhaps the villagers were busy counting their gains, perhaps they were gambling and drinking in some hidden hall, or perhaps they were all in bed. It felt as if no joy and little love were there.

At three in the morning I was awoken by a feeling that something was wrong. I went on deck to find that it was only the tide that had changed, and *Tzu Hang*'s motion with it. Beryl, who had heard me moving on the deck, joined me. As we looked at the dark pile above us, high in a narrow window a light went on. If we had then heard a faint voice crying, 'Help, help, for God's sake get me out of here!' we would not have been in the least surprised.

In the morning Clio took Popa ashore for a run on the rocks, but they were chased away by a man in a mackintosh who, impervious to youth and beauty, flourished his stick at her. This impressed Popa more than it did Clio and he led the flight to the boats. As soon as they were on board we set sail for the Scillies.

The weather report for Plymouth and Sole was that the winds would be light westerly. We were favoured by another summer's day and sailed north of Wolf Rock to Crow Sound, off the north shore of wind-brushed St Mary's Isle. We walked over to Hughtown and got our clearance to La Rochelle, and a customs officer, a reasonable one, took us back to *Tzu Hang* in his launch.

We sailed next day in a rainstorm across the flats to Tresco and anchored in the narrow sound close off Hangman's Island. This is one of the few places where there is shelter. All the islands show signs of the long winter battle against the winds. The trees are few and leaning away from their attack, and except in sheltered parts everything that grows links arms with its neighbour in order to hang on to its patch of soil. Where there is shelter there is splendid growth, and the garden of the Lord Proprietor is full of flowers as exotic as his title. There also is a collection of ships' figureheads, from those that have been wrecked on the Scillies, very well restored and shining in new paint. It was on St Mary's that Sir Cloudesley Shovel's squadron was lost, when the *Association*, the *Romney*, the *Eagle*, and the *Firebrand* went down in 1707.

Popa, who, after his winter in Paris should not have been ashore at all, disappeared. Clio took one way and I another in search of him, and presently I heard his peremptory bark and found him waiting for us at the dinghy. Since we had first sailed from England Clio had grown up and Popa had become old, but her voice as I heard her calling him sounded absurdly young. She came striding back, her hair blowing, looking as free as the wind itself. 'Oh Popa, where have you been?' she called. It is a chant that comes back in memory from many foreign shores.

From Tresco we had an easy sail with the coast of France in sight for most of the way, until we sailed between the twin towers that guard the entrance to the old port of La Rochelle. On the midnight weather forecast there had been gloomy talks of strong winds in the Bay, but a fresh wind brought us spinning down the Pertuis Breton in brilliant sunshine and just in time to catch the high tide through the lock gates into the crowded little harbour.

We found Nicole and Michel, who wears a glossy beard like a spinnaker, in a corner of the harbour, where we had to leave them after a day or two, burning with enthusiasm to do a long cruise one day, with *Tzu Hang* enriched by the gift of a ship's clock, and ourselves by their warmth.

We beat out past the Ile de Rey into a southwesterly wind and a steep short sea. A big Polish schooner was going out on the same course under her engine. She was lifting her bow and then plunging it into and sometimes under the sea, and making very slow progress. We passed close under her stern on one tack and well ahead on the other, a most satisfactory feeling. She was shamed into getting up some sail, but before this was accomplished we were off for Bilbao, averaging over six knots for most of the passage.

Bilbao seemed huge, bleak, and deserted after the intimate little harbour of La Rochelle, but Spanish charm and hospitality were much in evidence, from Señor Churruca, the Commodore of the Club Maritimo del Alva, to the club boatman who lent us 300 pesos until we had succeded in cashing some money. An ancestor of Señor Churruca had commanded the *Nepomuceno* at Trafalgar and had sent a signal to his family before the action, 'If my ship is taken you will know that I am dead.' He was killed, and his ship was taken. She was one of the four prizes that reached England after the battle.

Norah arrived from Paris where she had been one of the pillars of the house of Plon. She brought grace, good looks, and four languages, three of which she speaks so naturally that it is impossible to tell which is her own. Popa and I were now in a minority of two to four, but Popa was a broken reed anyway. We had arranged with Señor Ignacio de Abando that he would pick us up in Santander. From there we set off for the caves of Altamira.

We drove to Santavilla, which is a wonderfully preserved example of an old Spanish town. The sun beat down on the square, but the narrow streets were cool and shady. Within the walls of the houses, many of which had an old family's crest above the door, within the small patios and courtyards, and under the tall arches of the church, all was cool and restful, and infinitely pleasanter than modern air conditioning could make it. The caves were spendid, and the best part about them was that no one had had the bad taste as yet to introduce organ music. They were dimly lit by electricity and, though they had steps and handrails to keep tourists on their feet and their hands off the drawings, they were seen in approximately the same light in which they were drawn. Bushmen's paintings should be seen surrounded by the clear Rhodesian sunlight, caveman's scratchings in something approaching the light of a burning fire or a primitive tallow lamp.

At the hotel where we had lunch Norah pocketed an ashtray. I was shocked that anyone so high principled should stoop to petty theft. Norah was surprised at my reaction, and Señor Ignacio assured me that I was out of date and that ashtrays were there for tourists to snitch as souvenirs. If I had thought of Norah's character it had only been in relation to the highest and almost intimidating standards. Now I wondered if there were not some interesting depths as well.

From Santander we sailed along the north coast of Spain, always in sight of the mountains. We made various stops in harbour or behind a headland, anywhere where we could find shelter from the westerly swell that rolled into the bay. Cape Ortegal sent us a blast, and we struggled round with some difficulty and put into Cedeira, a long narrow sound with a fishing village at the end. There we celebrated the turning of the corner of Spain with a bottle of wine and an enormous crab.

The harbourmaster at Cedeira had been fishing on the Newfoundland Banks with Emilio Boras, an old friend of our first visit, whose farm at Punta Capitan in Arosa Bay stretches down to the sea. From him we learned that Emilio was at home and decided that we must see him again. He is the most colourful character, bubbling with an immense *joie de vivre,* with three fingers missing from one hand. Because of his beret, his lean Spanish face, and his vigour, one assumes that he lost them in some bloodthirsty affray in the Civil War, but in fact it was an affair of fish and dynamite. I had received a postcard from him in British Columbia to say that he was putting in to Halifax and would like to come and see us for the weekend.

On our way there Cabo Villano and Cabo Torinana, with its

jagged island close off the point, were both in sight. We were sailing inshore, too close according to those deepwater sailors Beryl and Clio, but far enough offshore, I thought, to weather the buoy marking a shoal patch off Cabo Torinana. As we approached the position where I expected to discover the buoy, we had the wind dead aft, the main boom to starboard and a preventer guy rigged. Once round the buoy we would have the wind once more on our quarter, and I was hoping to get round without a jibe.

A fishing boat was coming up the coast and I thought that I could pass astern of it without altering our course. It altered course towards us, but I still thought that I might be able to pass behind it. There was no sign of the buoy. We were racing along, with Beryl and Clio forward handing the useless jib, which was blanketed by the sail. I saw now that the boat had stopped and was taking up a lobster pot, several men hauling as she came up over the position. I was aiming to pass as close as possible under her stern, when I heard Beryl and Clio shouting 'The buoy, the buoy!' and saw them pointing close ahead on the starboard bow, where it was lying on its side, rusty and half awash. It was a question of a jibe all standing or squeezing past just inside the buoy. Beryl and Clio were looking at me with no confidence at all, and at this moment there was a bray of alarm from the fishing boat, whose crew were lining the rail. '*Piedras!*' they shouted '*Piedras!*' A man in the bow made a gesture of diving overboard, and a man amidships pulled his coat over his head. I heaved on the tiller, the boom shot up into the air, the sail came over with a mighty thump and everything held except a ringbolt on the rail through which the preventer guy passed. *Tzu Hang* leapt across the bow of the fishboat, and in a moment was clear of danger and on an easier course. There was no excuse. Since I had not picked out the buoy, which might have been missing altogether, I should have jibed away from the danger long before. The sea doesn't often give you that sort of chance. Badly shaken by this, but with a crew who kindly refrained from saying, 'I told you so,' we went on to anchor behind Punta Sardiniero opposite a small sandy beach.

We made sail at three in the morning, and by two in the afternoon, after showing a marked tendency to battleship courses again, we let go the anchor off Punta Capitan. A picnic was in progress on shore, just as it had been when we arrived ten years before. Emilio, a tall lithe figure leapt to his feet. 'Señor Miles!' he shouted, as if it were only yesterday that he had last seen me, and a moment later was pulling a dinghy out to the boat.

Nothing had changed, and no one looked a day older except ourselves. In fact Señora Boraz, Emilio's mother, who gave us brandy and Brazas del Gitanos at the farm, had shed her sombre black and was looking younger and infinitely gayer than before. The eyes of Señor Calvo, on holiday from Madrid, darted as mischievously as ever, but now they were directed at Clio and Norah. Ten years ago Clio and I had gone ashore to a fiesta at the village behind the farm.

'Where is your mother?' Señor Calvo had asked Clio.

'She's staying on board. She wants to be alone,' Clio answered.

'Impossible,' he said, 'I shall go and get her,' and putting on his yachting cap, he rowed the dinghy with some difficulty out to *Tzu Hang*. He found Beryl buried in a book and revelling in her temporary peace. No protest of hers would turn him from his purpose and Beryl eventually told him to wait while she changed into a dress.

The door of her clothes locker served also, when opened as a temporary door for her cabin. In this role, although it fulfilled all the normal requirements of privacy, it did not fit closely. She closed the door and had just started to change when she saw a small black object, about knee height, slipping up the crack made by the ill-fitting door. 'Oh dear,' she thought, 'a rat,' fearing that it had escaped from the locker and was running up the crack. She bent down quickly to examine it more closely and found herself gazing at point-blank range into the beady black eye of Señor Calvo.

At Punta Capitan we met the Marquis of Matonte. Tall and aristocratic, he arched over Beryl's hand, but as he raised it to his lips he became as rigid as a pointer over a partridge. Beryl's gracious little smile froze on her face. She thought that he had been transfixed by the sight of her hands, which after days at sea showed signs of hard work with ropes. Then she remembered the onions that she had cut up for lunch. 'Ah,' he said at last, breaking the suspense and completing the salute, 'a Midou.'

'I must explain,' said his pretty Contessa to Beryl, who wears her watch on her right wrist, 'He's mad on watches.'

The misfortune in the Marquis' life is that he was born a Marquis. He should have been an engineer. By teatime Clio's watch, which she had worn swimming, was in pieces in a cupful of water, he had already fixed the automatic change in a car that the local mechanics refused to face, and was very soon eyeing my radio set in an ominous way.

Clio and Norah were due to leave for London and Paris and Emilio for Madrid on the following morning. It was decided that they should go together, but first there was the question of cashing some cheques. It was now after five in the evening, but in Spain the day was just recommencing. Emilio had a friend in Villa Garcia on the other side of Arosa Bay who was a bank manager and who would cash cheques for a friend no matter what the hour. The whole picnic party was embarked on *Tzu Hang*, and we arrived at Villa Garcia, nineteen of us, at ten-fifteen. The bank manager was in bed with influenza. We were back empty-handed by two in the morning and as on a previous expedition to Villa Garcia, '*el Scotch*', had been in great demand. Fortunately this time it did not alternate with a skin of wine, and I had greater confidence in Emilio as a pilot since he had taken his ship to the Newfoundland Banks and back. Our crew left early next morning. Emilio, in his Madrid clothes, still looked like some gay maquisard as he whirled them away. His younger and larger brother, the fair-haired Gonzales, and the Marquis of Matonte decided to accompany us to Bayona.

We left at three in the morning in order to take the tide out of Arosa Bay. While I was attaching the snap shackle to the mainsail peak, Gonzales heaved on the halyard with his vast strength and pulled it out of my hand. We hooked the bosun's chair on to the genoa halyard, and I went up to the masthead in pursuit, but so quickly, with the eager Gonzales hauling, that the first part of the journey was made upside down. The anchor was obviously a job for Gonzales, but the chain came in so fast that the shackle jammed in the hawse-hole, and it was with difficulty that we managed to knock it out. Eventually we got him safely lodged in the cockpit and, since he knew the bay backwards, he conned us out, while Beryl and I relaxed in the knowledge that our gear was temporarily safe.

As soon as we were out of the bay and began to feel the Atlantic swell, both he and the Marquis succumbed to seasickness. It was rotten weather for two visitors, with very little wind and a big oily swell that emptied the genoa and filled it again with a crack. We soon got tired of this and took down all sail. Beryl took over and I passed the prostrate Marquis in the main cabin, on my way forward to get some sleep. I found Gonzales in my bunk, smoking a large cigar. 'I feel a little sick,' he said cheerfully. I lay down in Beryl's bunk and as the ship rolled and the smoke swirled over me soon began to feel a little sick too.

As soon as we had the anchor down under the walls of the fort in Bayona they both recovered, and, while Beryl and I tidied up below, we heard them on deck talking to the holidaying visitors, who surrounded us in small boats.

'Where have you come from?'

'Just down from Bayona.'

'In so small a boat?'

'That's nothing. This yacht has sailed round the world.'

Although *Tzu Hang* has sailed from England westwards to 145° East and from England eastwards to 142° East, there is still an uncovered gap of 180 miles, but we did not object to this exaggeration.

'Was it very rough outside?'

'Ah, nothing you know. But it can be terrible out there. There was little wind today.'

Having impressed everyone within earshot, and thoroughly enjoyed their new role, they came below to celebrate 'My first trip in an English cruiser,' as the Marquis wrote in the guest book. I told him how much we enjoyed Punta Capitan where there always seemed to be a holiday atmosphere.

'In Spain,' he said, 'there is a saying—"If work is life, then viva the tuberculosis".'

They left in the afternoon, the husky farmer and the lean aristocrat, and both of them with a philosophy that seemed to give them intense pleasure in each moment of the sunlit day without any awareness of the pressure of its passing. They had even seemed relaxed when they were seasick.

One hundred and sixty odd miles south of Bayona and a few miles off the coast of Portugal is the Ilha Berlenga, and outside it some smaller rocks known as the Os Farilhoes. Most yachts, on their way south to Lisbon, swinging along in the Portuguese trades and with a favourable current under their stern, give them a wide berth and see them by day showing dim and grey in the coastal haze, or watch the Berlenga light come out of the sea ahead and fall behind during most of a summer's night.

We had done so the last time that we had come down the coast, making almost the best run of *Tzu Hang*'s career, but this time we decided to go and have a look at them. Again we had a good run, so good that we thought the state of the sea would not allow us to find shelter in the Farilhoes. As we approached them we saw a fishing boat snugged in behind Farilhoe Grande so guessed that we could also find shelter there. We anchored southeast of Farilhoe Grande, between Farilhoe Nord Este and Farilhoe da Cova. We found it fairly well sheltered with the wind in the north—one of the most romantic anchorages that *Tzu Hang* has made, in the bosom of a small and rocky group of islets, thrust out and braving all the great Atlantic. The wind soughs between them and gusts down over the bare back of Farilhoe Grande, making the anchored yacht heel and pluck at her chain. It makes the crew pop their heads out of the hatch during the night, only to see the light blinking slowly above them and the cloud shadows chasing across Farilhoe da Cova close astern, and, since the holding ground is good, no closer than before.

In the morning we climbed up to the lighthouse, and when we got down found a boat, the *Berlenga*, over from the main island. They signalled us to come on board. A Portuguese Naval officer, Antonio de Andrade e Silva and his sister Miuska, and some pretty señoritas, who raised languid hands from the cushions on which they were lying. Señor Antonio and his sister were of rather a different stamp and one had a glimpse in them of the old Portuguese adventurers who carried their flag so far and so boldly round the world. They were both expert skin-divers and Miuska was an international skier as well. They persuaded us to move over to the main island, where we anchored off a small cove on the eastern side, containing a few fishermen's white cottages.

They arrived next morning with a boat full of large dogfish which they had speared, and arranged to take us round the island. With a small outboard engine we dodged in and out of rocks where the swell sucked and groaned. We stuttered through echoing passages of red rock decorated by green fern. The cliffs bulged above us and closed to make tunnels through which we passed, while the cormorants on ledges above the arches vomited at us in alarm as we went by. They were absolutely at home in their cockleshell amongst the rocks and breakers, diving deep to shoot and struggle with great fish amongst the dragging currents and the changing pressures of the swell.

Miuska had an oval face and high broad cheekbones, lovely wide eyes and clearly drawn eyebrows, and a little bit of pink new skin showing on the end of her delectable nose. Beryl and I loved being with two such vital young people. They were the first Portuguese that I had met in any intimacy and banished forever a lingering idea that had found root somehow in my boyhood, that the Portuguese were dull, not particularly beautiful and not very brave.

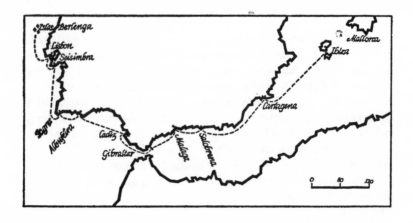

3 *Winter in Ibiza*

AFTER delaying a day because Berlenga was wrapped in fog, we left in thicker fog than ever, hoping to keep the line of the Farilhoes as a protection until we were clear. The fog was more persistent than we had expected, and after an hour or so ships' foghorns were blowing all around us, while the grey fingers clutched tighter, holding us almost stationary and as bemused as a cub in cover when the hounds are out. We could hear the steady beat of a ship's engines approaching, and the bearing remained steady. If we started the engine to give us some ability to manœuvre we could not hear the noise. We sat peering through the threatening wall around us, pointing repeatedly over the compass, as in the Chinese game, 'paper wraps stone'. Soon we began to hear the hiss of a bow wave ahead of us. 'My God,' I said to Beryl, 'I think the bastard's coming straight for us. Better start the engine.' In the moment that followed, the hiss of the bow-wave sounded a little to starboard. A quick look at the compass to find that we were still on the same course. The noise definitely drawing to starboard, and then a sudden soul-shattering roar over our heads. The wall of fog was so thick that I could not even see the white line of the bow-wave as she passed.

A moment later the sun showed a white disc above us, and

suddenly we were released, while the ship that had passed us trumpeted her fading warning away to the north. We understood now why she had not been sounding her foghorn as she approached, and wondered, as all small boat sailors wonder, whether she had seen us on her radar or not. Perhaps the greatest danger to ships in fog is from those who have not yet entered it.

During the night the fog came down again, and again we heard the ominous soughing of a bow-wave as a ship came up from astern and passed without a light to be seen. Soon another was coming up close behind us, but this time there was a diffused glow on our quarter and a moment later she burst out of the fog like an exploding rocket, her lights clear and bright. That was the last of the fog.

Daylight showed a pipit squatting on the deck by the winch. I have never known a bird forced on to *Tzu Hang* by the wind or fog to take anything to eat. Even if we saved them from the cat they never survived until we reached land. They lost heart and, when at last they were warm and in safety, the will to live. This little bird sat on the deck until the sun was up and then struggled off. Twice it fell into the sea and twice managed to get off again, but the third time it stayed there. Beryl dived in in her clothes and swam after it. She brought it back alive while I held *Tzu Hang* into the wind. It only had to wait an hour or two and we could have put it ashore, but it died.

Presently, our quaking moments in the fog forgotten, we found ourselves sailing up the wide river, the Tagus, and approaching Fort St Juliao. Jorrocks found hunting analogous to war. So in some ways is sailing. In fog and storm it certainly provides its moments of fear, and the sweet relaxation after it is over. It is just as uncomfortable and it brings its unforgettable rewards. The one I like best is when a passage is over, but the port not yet made, when there is no longer any doubt that you will arrive, but the time of anchoring under critical eyes, the visits of customs officers and other officials, the mixing again in the multitude, is still in the offing.

So now we anchored in a small bay, watched the traffic of the river go by, soaked up the sun, ate our lunch and drank our wine. There was still plenty of time to moor up in Belem, in Bom Successo yacht harbour. *Jolie Brise* was there, still beautifully kept up, *Foxhound*, with tall masts and clean lines all glittering in the sun, and several other yachts to which *Tzu Hang* now added her own type of vagrant beauty. There was also a great change of attitude in the customs officers and police, who in days gone by had been offhand and officious. Now they were positively welcoming—due, we were told, to a new minister who was also a keen yachtsman.

It was the fifth centenary of the death of Henry the Navigator. It seems strange to celebrate deaths rather than births, but perhaps, like the gloomy fadoes, it's part of the Portuguese character. Flags were flying everywhere, and there was a special exhibition which included a large collection of old charts, some inscribed on leather, many of them of the seas in which we were to sail, although heaven knows where we would have ended up if we were to use them. From Bom Successo many a sailing ship had left for the Far East, but few with so small a crew. For us it was the beginning of a journey which over several years and various deflections kept the Far East as a target—the beginning, because hereafter, as far as *Tzu Hang* was concerned, everything was new. Here was the monument to Henry the Navigator, here was the church where the old voyagers had prayed before they made their journeys and here for a few days were we.

When the day came to leave, Beryl decided that we must go to Sagres to see the Navigation School founded by Prince Henry. I imagined great buildings and ancient astrolabes, but, since Seisimbra was on the way and only a day's sail away, we decided to go there first. We had a splendid run with a fresh northerly wind, rounded the sheer cliffs of Cabo Espichel and headed in for the bay. A powerful sports fisherman came up to us closely pursued by a lifeboat. They came alongside and asked us if we wanted any help. We were absolutely unable to understand their eager offers of assistance or, as they became more disappointed and excited, what they were saying at all. In the end they dropped us and rushed away in the direction of the Cape. We anchored in the harbour and later met the coxwain of the lifeboat, a huge jovial man dressed entirely in black. He told us that they had had a signal from the lighthouse to say that a yacht was in distress, but it had turned out to be a German yacht, fourteen miles offshore, which was in need of

assistance, and that a minesweeper had succoured it before
they arrived.

The fishing village at Seisimbra was brilliant with the
colours of fresh paint on the boats which were drawn up on the
shore or being built in open-air yards, from which they were
trundled along the road on rollers to the launching site. It was
also tied together with nylon line. There were men baiting lines
with salted sardines, there were men stretching lines along the
sands, men untangling lines, and there were men wrapping lines
round white-painted gourds, with a red cross fixed to the top;
lines that would be laid by a green boat with a red star and
crescent on the bow. There was one small boat that rested on
the sands against the night, when they would all go out in
glittering array, that was named 'Dios es mi Comigo.' At night
the little boats put to sea, each with a paraffin torch burning
at the bow. From both sides of the long beach the flares crept out
until they linked and formed a complete line which encircled
the bay. At night the land was dark and deserted—the bright
village was on the sea.

When we arrived at Sagres we anchored at the head of the
bay which is open to the south, but safe enough in offshore
winds. We walked up the hill and through the white wall of the
fort that cuts off the head of the peninsula, but we found only a
compass rose laid out on the gravel, one or two noticeboards
that directed tourists to a blowhole, and a large expanse of
bare rock. At the top of the cliff two fishermen were fishing with
rod and line from a point at least a hundred feet above the sea.
They had caught nothing, so it was impossible to tell what sort
of fish they hoped to winch up from below.

On our way the next day we saw a Portuguese Navy patrol
boat fire some blank cartridges at a big Spanish fishing vessel
and then lie alongside and board. They were soon under way
again with the Spanish ship obviously under arrest. As they
passed *Tzu Hang* we dipped our ensign. They both answered
the salute, the Portuguese austere, the Spaniards waving merrily
as they did so.

The south coast of Portugal is bare and inhospitable, and
there is no port of refuge from southerly winds. We put in at
Albufeira. As if to make up for the parched monotones of the
landscape behind, the colours in the small villages, the white

and blue houses, the sands, and the brilliantly painted boats on the beach, are as lovely in contrast as alpine flowers on the edge of a moraine. At Albufeira I saw a beautiful girl get out of a car by the beach. She looked immensely haughty and tired. A little maid in khaki trousers and a red scarf fussed about her, smoothing her sleek hair and tying something about her head. I thought that she must be a Contessa at least, and so beautiful that after a turn through the boats I had to come back for another look. She was as removed and unattainable as before, still gazing haughtily beyond the horizon, dressed in a peacock blue bathing-dress, a turban, and a beach coat. She was leaning against the bow of a boat, and a man with a Rolleiflex was busy photographing her for some fashion magazine.

We sailed into Cadiz Bay and then took *Tzu Hang* round into the inner harbour, but it is crowded and made disgusting by the slime that covers its walls. Still it is well worth going to see the treasures in the Cathedral, the gold and the silver; to buy the juiciest olives from the stalls in the narrow streets, to walk on the sea front and to think of Nelson's frigates on the horizon, to imagine Villeneuve's thirty-three ships all making sail to leave the bay, or of Drake sailing in—seven days out from Plymouth—with thirty sail to tackle a hundred.

We sailed for Gibraltar, but were soon hove-to in a filthy levanter which blew itself out in the night. Next morning found us entering Gibraltar harbour. A Royal Navy boat, paint immaculate and brightwork glistening, hailed us: 'What ship are you?' And, as soon as they had our name, 'Follow us. You have permission to enter the inner harbour.'

From Gibraltar we made various calls along the south coast of Spain, a bare rocky coast backed by naked hills where one would think a goat would be hard pressed for a living. We anchored off the beach at Salobrena late one evening and hurriedly put on some respectable clothes to go ashore in to see the castle on the hill, to buy some bread, and to do some other minor shopping. *Tzu Hang* was rolling her underwater paint a foot or so out of the water when we left, and when we got to the beach we saw that a landing would be tricky. We were just about to try when a fisherman pointed down the beach. We supposed that he was pointing to a better place, but noticed as we set off in the direction that he pointed, that a small green Guardia Civil, his polished hat glinting in the setting sun, a carbine across his arm, was hurrying towards us. We chose our spot and were just preparing to come in when he started shouting to us to stop. By then I was rowing frantically on the front of a wave and there was no chance of doing anything about it. As we grounded and pulled the dinghy hurriedly out of reach of the breakers, he arrived, breathless and excited.

'Go back to your ship and leave immediately,' he ordered.

'It's quite all right,' I answered in bad but understandable Spanish, 'we have visas and can come ashore. We have been ashore in many ports in Spain.'

'You heard what I said. Get back to your ship.'

'We only want to come ashore to buy bread and something to eat,' Beryl put in, in her half-starved voice.

'That is of no consequence,' he shouted. I began to feel angry at the thought of no eggs for breakfast.

'On what authority are you doing this?' I asked.

'This is my authority,' he screamed, besides himself with rage, tearing the cover off his carbine and banging a round into the breech.

'Get his name,' Beryl suggested.

'Then you will give me your name and I shall report you to the Chief of Police at Malaga,' I said, hoping to recover some of our lost dignity.

He gave it and Beryl started to write it down on her shopping list with a blunt pencil.

'Give it to me,' he said as she faltered over the spelling and, taking a pen from his pocket and tucking his carbine under his arm, he signed with a flourish. 'Now get back to your ship,' he said, with an ominous jerk to his carbine.

There was nothing else to do. You cannot ignore even small policemen with loaded rifles. It is hard to embark in a small dinghy in breakers with any dignity. We tumbled in together with six inches of water and rowed stiffly back to *Tzu Hang*. A large factory chimney was smoking away at the end of the beach.

'I'm sure there is something funny going on,' Beryl said as soon as we were on board again. 'Perhaps that's where they dispose of political prisoners. I think you always make little men worse,' she added, 'with that supercilious look on your face.'

'I suppose you think you'd have managed better by yourself.'

'Perhaps,' she said smugly.

In Cartagena three frigates and H.M.S. *Tiger* were in. We were asked to lunch on the flagship.

'Is there anything at all that I can do for you?' asked the tall Admiral.

'Oh yes, please. Can I have a bath?' asked Beryl.

The Admiral never faltered, and in no time she was splashing in his private bathroom. Soon afterwards in the beautiful stern cabin she was sitting surrounded by the Chief of Staff and the three frigate Captains. They were leaning forward eagerly and dwelling on her words as she talked about the sea, their own element. I thought what a lovely compliment it was—and how well deserved.

When *Tzu Hang* first entered Puerto Ibiza it looked as if she would have to spend the winter lying to two anchors at the head of the harbour, with long lines to the sea wall that fronted a dusty road. On the port hand as she passed the lighthouse at the head of the breakwater, the quay and the jetty were occupied by trading schooners and an inter-island steamer. To starboard the only deep water was already reserved by a fan of big yachts with their sterns converging at a small jetty. They stirred uneasily as we entered, like passengers in a railway carriage when a late and unwanted arrival opens the door. Further to starboard we could see the masts of smaller yachts showing over the low protecting wall of the yacht harbour, too shallow for us to enter. By a stroke of good fortune a combination of wind and current soon after our arrival raised the level sufficiently for *Tzu Hang* to squeeze in. There she settled comfortably on a mud berth for the winter and even seemed prepared to stay when the time came for us to leave.

South of us the old town rose in tiers c. narrow houses crowned by a cathedral and a fort of such massive construction that the hill seemed overburdened with its weight. The city is built on a promontory and the outer walls of the fort enclose the older part of the town and dominate the only approach not already protected by the cliffs and the sea. To the west and north the land sloped gradually upwards to the distant hills.

Bare stony land crossed and counter-crossed by stone walls, dotted by white farms and cottages, by grey trunked olive trees, green algarobas, and by fig trees with such wide spreading branches that they had to be propped up with posts. Behind us was a shallow bay and to the eastward the sea.

A day or two after our arrival Beryl clattered on board *Tzu Hang* with excitement in her step. 'I've found the most marvellous house,' she said, 'right on top of the hill—an old Moorish house with huge rooms and a domed ceiling and a bridge across the street to a sort of garden—splendid for the animals. It will be absolutely frigid in winter. You must come and see it now.'

We climbed up the hill along a narrow cobbled road that grew narrower as it got higher. At the bottom it went through an old archway which had been widened to allow General Franco's car to pass through when he had paid the town a visit. At the top it went through a tunnel, frequently used as a latrine. Just before we reached the Bishop's Palace, the highest building except for the cathedral and the fort, we turned to the right along a narrow lane. A hundred yards up the lane was our house. It was a dirty lane because the rubbish man, who came every day with two mules, always had their panniers full by the time he reached it. Even if they were not the dogs and cats had already had a dig in the garbage bins and scattered the choicer fishes' backbones up and down the path. We entered our house through a large double door into a stone floored hall, from where a wide staircase led up to the door which was the entrance to the living part of the house. In the hall on either side of the staircase there were two doors leading into rooms which appeared to be occupied.

'Whose are those?' I asked Beryl.

'Oh. Those belong to the squatters,' she replied. 'Apparently when you take a house in Spain and someone is already occupying part of it, you cannot turn them out unless you provide other accommodation. We are all upstairs and I don't think that they'll bother us.'

It was a most romantic house, and since it had been occupied by a Dutchwoman who had just left for Holland, we inherited a splendid Spanish maid, Catalina, and sufficient furniture for our needs. The most extraordinary of the fittings that went with the house was an electrical apparatus in the bathroom, known as the *calefacción*. When switched on to heat the bath, besides an obvious tendency to blow up, it gave an electric shock to anyone who, yards away, turned on the cold water tap in the kitchen.

Catalina was broad and motherly. She took us under her wing and gave us her love as if we were part of her family. I loved her particularly because she laughed at my jokes. 'Caramba,' she'd say, 'you are a one!' and I soon began to think that I was a bit of a wit. Beryl loved her because Catalina chattered Spanish to her all day long, told her all that was going on and who was sleeping with whom amongst the foreign residents on the hill.

If she spoke of the Civil War she involuntarily looked behind her before she spoke. Ibiza had changed hands twice and there had been some grisly shootings, particularly within the secret walls of the great fort.

'Masks may not now be worn in Spain on Mardi Gras,' she told us, 'too many old scores would be paid off. Why, that man who keeps a store down the street, everyone knows that he is a murderer many times over, but no one can do anything about it.'

'And what were you doing then.'

'Caramba! What do poor people know about anything? All we did was to run for shelter in the tunnels when they were bombing, and to pray when someone came to the house and called our men outside.'

'El Obispo' was her chief interest. El Obispo's sermon was too long. El Obispo had pruned his trees and just thrown the cuttings in the street. One should see El Obispo dressed all in red—'Caramba, what a beautiful sight!' She lived in a spotless little flat at the top of one of the tall old houses, and was as good a person as one could hope to meet.

We could not see inside the fort, but it was a forbidding place. A short way above the entrance to our lane was the top of the cliff, where there were some gun emplacements and a small area of ground in front of the fort. Here an untidily dressed sentry lounged, looking over the sea-pitted rocks far below. Every day a sweating mule hauled the ration cart up from the town, with an occasional push from any of the ration party who had managed to stay with it. Sometimes we saw officers, their waists too wide, their feet too narrow and their caps too flat, breathing heavily on the ascent, or hurrying down at midday. Ibiza must be the deepest backwater that any military man could fall into.

We were lucky in the artists because the better they were the higher—in altitude—they lived. Beryl and I know nothing of abstract art and we may have judged them more on their qualities as people, but at least the ones at our giddy height were able to sell their work. One was showing us his pictures. 'I like that,' Beryl said, 'it looks to me like a ship.'

'Oh hell,' he said, 'now you've ruined it for me. I shall always see a ship when I look at it.'

There was another time when we were looking at an artist's work as he tossed his pictures out in front of us.

'What on earth's that?' Beryl asked.

'That,' he replied, 'is supposed to be an expression of my joy and satisfaction, you know, when I got this house, and my wife, and all that.'

'And what is that?' she asked, pointing to another.

'Oh that,' he looked at it doubtfully. 'I really don't know. It looks like a design for oilcloth.'

The artist who lived higher than any of the others had forsaken a home in England and a well-paid job as a cartoonist on a leading English newspaper, in order to settle in Ibiza and paint the things that he wanted to paint. He was a little satyr with a short grey beard, his eyes twinkling with humour and the delight of living, a father confessor to many mixed up young people who sought his aid, his spare bunk a psychoanalyst's couch, although he liked to imply that advice was not the only treatment that he gave them. Talking about artists and their proficiency, he said to me once, 'At least I have trained my hand to do what my eye tells it.' And in Ibiza this seemed to me to be an outstanding quality.

If the city had been the only place on the island, with bearded foreigners forever talking at the coffee tables round the square, our stay of four months would have been far too long. As it was I began to feel that I should have earrings in my ears and a bearded chin wagging about the things that we were going to do, while *Tzu Hang* mouldered in her berth. Fortunately there was the country and good walks through the farmland and into the hills, where the hard-working peasant people were still in Ibizenko dress, the women with black scarves on their heads under wide straw hats. Fortunately, too, there was Gordon Sillars with a yacht that he had sailed from England in the harbour and a small farm in the country, making a reappraisal of his life, since he had recently retired from the marines, but, like us, he was really as out of place in Ibiza as a Scotch thistle in a greenhouse. On Sundays Beryl and I used to hire Mosquitoes, pedal bicycles with a motor operating on the rear tyre which made a high-pitched keening noise. We vibrated over the country roads, the motors popping and humming, pedalled furiously up the inclines, or wobbled anxiously down. We usually ended up at Gordon's farm.

When we were in Canada Clio had a friend called Ann who used to spend her holidays with us. Now Ann was in London and sharing Clio's flat. They were both due to join us for the Christmas holidays. No longer awkward and tousled, in muddy jodhpurs and with unbrushed hair, but polished and manicured, efficient and assured—or so I imagined them—I pictured myself with a radiant young beauty on either arm. Their room was prepared, huge stocks of food laid in, and Catalina fluttered as excitedly as Beryl and I, until the day arrived. The boat came in after dark and as the passengers poured off, our heads turned excitedly this way and that in order to be sure not to miss them.

'They always come out last,' I said to Beryl, as I felt the first twinges of anxiety. Our smiles faded as the flood of passengers slackened to a dribble and finally stopped all together. The years descended on our shoulders and we climbed slowly up the hill. The next boat arrived and the next. By now all gossipy Ibiza was interested and watched our quick steps descending and our slow return. In the end they arrived, but Ann's face confirmed some of our fears. She had a black eye and a nose slightly out of true.

'Oh, we hit a car leaving London in a fog so I had to get my nose fixed, and it has made us a week late,' she said. The black eye might have been a handicap anywhere, but not in Ibiza. A bearded young man with unbrushed long hair sidled up to me. 'Is that your daughter?' he asked.

'Which one?'

'The fair one with the black eye. I'd like to meet her. I want her to be my girl.'

It was a good Christmas, with reels and games in the big central room of such vigour that the squatters complained to Catalina that we would have the roof down on their heads. New Year came and thoughts of where the next New Year would find us, and about this time a letter arrived from a person I did not know called June Kay from Southern Rhodesia. 'I have read *Once is Enough*,' it said, 'and I wonder whether you would not like to come sailing for a change in a DKW exploring the Okovango.' She went on to describe their life in the swamps of Bechuanaland and the wealth of game to be seen there. I replied cautiously and asked to hear more. The finger of fate was moving and for a moment pointed at Ann's fair head.

Clio and Ann left a few days later, having failed by a whisker to persuade Gordon Sillars to drive them over the Pyrenees to England in his model T Ford. Gordon had done one of the early small-boat crossings of the Atlantic in a boat called *Buttercup* whose captain had had the unlikely but soldierly name of Major Major. It was just big enough to accommodate the two of them. Clio's proposition was turned down perhaps because the car was too old, or perhaps Gordon had reached the age when he garnished his dash with a little common sense.

The Spanish boat pulled away from the wharf. Two tangled heads appeared for a short time on the windy boat deck, one brown, one fair, and disappeared as the ship turned. Ibiza became a dull place, but the list of things to be done on *Tzu Hang* was growing longer, and, almost before we were ready for it, March arrived.

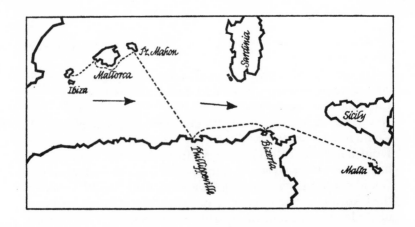

4   Minorca to Malta

On 7 March we started the engine to leave the yacht harbour but our waterline was six inches above the water at high tide and *Tzu Hang* refused to budge. Although the *Pilot* warns that the water level may be a foot and a half below normal during January, February, and March, the local inhabitants had 'never seen anything like it before.' We hoisted all sail to a fresh breeze and *Tzu Hang* remained a splendid but stationary sight. It was not until we had enlisted the aid of a fishing boat that we were able to leave. With engine roaring, all sails drawing, colours flying, and a tug pulling, we ploughed a deep furrow through the mud and out into the harbour, bound for Mallorca and Minorca.

Ella Maillart joined us in Mallorca. There was a day when everyone knew of her, sailor, skier, hockey player, an international performer in all three, a famous traveller and a writer into the bargain. Ella is indestructible, but if there are degrees in indestructibility, she is perhaps a little less so than she used to be. She had recently snapped her Achilles tendon skiing on Mont Blanc with Monsieur Lambert of Everest fame. Now she arrived like a fresh north wind, a little lame on one leg, an Afghan hat on her head, a mountaineering ruscksack on her back, and a nomad's bundle in her hand. It was twenty-odd years since she had stayed with us in India, but she had changed very little. 'The three musketeers are together again,' she announced dramatically.

She and Beryl know each other very well; both travellers, both enormously well read, they had once been in Tibet together. Ella was fresh from one of her visits to India where she had met, as she always did, her friend Pandit Nehru. They were soon deep in details of what was going on in Tibet and Bhutan. When we arrived at the yacht Ella sank down on the doghouse roof. 'Ah, my God, it is terrible,' she said, rubbing her ankle, 'I don't think that it will ever be the same again.'

I was still shaken by my new musketeering rôle but forgot my embarrassment in my anxiety for a woman in distress.

'We'll have to watch Ella's ankle,' I said to my hardy wife, as soon as we were alone.

'Oh, nonsense,' she said. 'You know Ella. She's as bad as you are. It will get worse if you make a fuss about it. She'll forget about it in a day or two, and anyway she was talking about Tibet.'

We made various calls up the east coast of Mallorca, and so early in March had perfect sailing. We found the island too full of tourists. Of course, we are tourists ourselves, but it's not so much the tourists that we dislike as the prices that go with them. Minorca we liked better than all the other islands, and if I was to stay anywhere in the Balearics it would be Minorca that I'd choose. It is a colder, harder and tighter island than the others, with tall and broad stone walls to shelter the small fields, and the trees leaning to the south. We toured the island with Ella sitting bravely on the back of my motorcycle, and Beryl, her windproof parka inflated by an updraught, sped along on her Mosquito like a blue balloon. The Minorcans look back with pride to the long British occupation, a strange and welcome feeling these days for the visiting Briton. Perhaps also there is something inherited from the time when the masts and spars of British warships stood like an avenue of elms in winter, down both sides of the long harbour. They do things when they say they'll do them and finish at the time they have promised.

In Port Mahon there was a splendid little slip where we hauled *Tzu Hang* out with the help of a 5 h.p. electric motor. It was clean, had a high wall all round it, and a door that could be locked. This privacy was much appreciated by the cat who was up and down all the time, an expert on any shipyard ladder. Popa would have preferred access to the street and further investigation of a dog's life in Minorca. He could climb up a ladder but had never mastered the art of going down. He was a truculent little sailor and had a fight in almost every port that he visited. He used to spend the first few days of every voyage licking his wounds until the worms that he picked up as regularly started him scratching instead.

On 25 March we set sail for Philippeville in Algeria, our principal object being to restock with wine. It was high time to leave Port Mahon. The town had some of the most delicious smelling *pastelarias* which Beryl was quite unable to pass by. Everything was cheaper than in the other islands and the chocolates—Beryl's only weakness—far better than anything since Paris. I began to wonder if there was not something more than the breeze filling her parka.

The wind was blowing straight down the long harbour. We got away under sail and tacked out in short tacks, pointing high in the calm water, but as we reached the two pairs of black and red buoys at the entrance, a big swell began to roll in, and the three musketeers to look a little seedy. When the wind dropped during the evening it left an unpleasant sea, and soup was all that we felt we could face with assurance for dinner.

On the morning that we arrived in Philippeville, daylight found a French frigate, the *Frondeur*, approaching. 'Heave to. We are going to board,' they ordered, and launched a small black rubber life-raft in which a young officer and several sailors paddled over. They clambered on board *Tzu Hang* and, disappointed by her middle-aged crew, gave her a perfunctory look over. We felt sorry that Clio and Ann were not there to make their journey worth while. They all wore heavy shore boots, inappropriate to a yacht's deck and left oily footprints all over the ship. It was during the time of the Algerian war and they were looking for illicit arms for sale to the rebels.

We had a friendly reception in Philippeville by all except the Harbourmaster who asked us to leave on the following day. There was nothing to stay for. It was a drab little town overrun by soldiers, both Paratroopers and the Foreign Legion. Most of the Foreign Legion that we saw were Germans. They admired themselves in the shop windows as they passed. The Paratroopers looked hard and ruthless killers, the sort of soldiers that one would prefer to have on the same side in a war. They looked unscrupulous, efficient, fit, and their morale was obviously high.

We left against a head wind, well stocked with wine, but made slow progress up the coast. It was a lovely coast to sail up, with bold capes, strange rock formations and islets. Off Cap de Garde we got a fair wind at last and came spinning down to Cap Rosa. On the beach there was a picnic party and some smart cars drawn up, while above them two flights of twin-engined bombers circled as they formed up and soon set their course to the south. A perfect moonlight night followed with a light north wind, and next day we had the west wind again as we sailed close inshore. We rounded Cap Serrat which runs down to the sea like a dragon's backbone, sailed inside Fratelli rocks and anchored after dark in Bizerta road.

Next morning we tied up to a small jetty. As soon as we were made fast a bearded Arab, in a hooded burnous with small tufts of wool sewn on in odd places, swept up to greet us. He shook hands with great formality and stepped on board. I had no idea who he was or how to treat him, but on the supposition that he might be a local dignitary, we seated him politely in the cockpit. After a time he left. It turned out that he was the local idiot.

Everyone who came to see us was at pains to point out a hill behind the harbour, a French base, which they said contained a fabulous and secret underground city. In contrast to this was the ancient Arab town, inside a great stone wall by the old port, a fascinating place. It was a rabbit warren of narrow streets and low arches, and thousands of children followed us, dancing and shouting till we felt like the Pied Piper and must have looked like a riot. In contrast to Philippeville and its feeling of war and occupation, Bizerta was clean and prosperous and promises one day to be a thriving tourist resort. There were many French still there and many Maltese, all of whom were eager to show us their British passports. One Frenchman came on board with his family. Presently Popa arrived on the deck and then came down the ladder, the only one that he can manage, into the cabin. There was a cry of dismay and

then of laughter. They had already met Popa, who had lifted
his leg against the Frenchman's trousers on the wharf. There is
really no stopping him when he gets ashore.

We anchored next day under the shelter of Cap Carthage,
off the ruins of the old port, where we arrived after dark. Next
morning we rowed ashore and walked up to a little village to
do some shopping and have a look round. We were picked up
by two students who spoke French well and who cut their
class in order to show us the Well of the Thousand Amphorae.
We went down what appeared to be a drain at the side of the
road, and it turned out to be an old vaulted chamber full of
the village refuse. We dreaded what we might tread on, but the
students encouraged us by calling, '*Passez, passez. Mais prenez
garde pour les serpents.*'

Having escaped the Well of the Thousand Amphorae I
very nearly replaced an old Carthaginian when I just avoided
falling into a deep and narrow tomb. It was on a hill which
overlooks the summer palace that was then being built for
President Bourguiba; an imposing affair with a roof of green
glazed tiles. A stout man in the uniform of the National Guard
now appeared and warned us that we should not be there.
Ella turned her sparkling charm on to him, and before he knew
what had happened he was showing us round the old Roman
reservoir which used to supply Carthage and has now been
repaired and provides fifteen day's water for Tunis. He had
been a political agitator since his student days, but at the
beginning of the war had made things so hot for himself that
he had been forced to escape from Tunis and had found sanctu-
ary in Switzerland. The Swiss had been kind to him—one of
the reasons that Ella found it so easy to get round him—but
since it was wartime they had decided that he must work for
his keep and had made him into a cowman. This was altogether too much for him, and, backed by bracelets of Swiss
watches all the way up his arms, he had worked his way through
Italy to the Americans and then managed to stow away on a
ship bound for North Africa. Unfortunately it was bound for
Algiers and the French soon had him under lock and key again
for the duration.

When the war was over he went back to Tunis and was
rewarded for his revolutionary services by a commission in the

National Guard. He had married a pretty little wife, whom we met later, had two children, and unless he lost a lot of weight it looked as if his days of adventure were over.

We said goodbye, but he turned up again in a car while we were wandering about the ruins of Carthage, and carried us off to see some Punic remains with sad rows of carved stones marking child sacrifices to Tanit. He was bored by ruins and as soon as possible took us to his home. His wife gave us coffee and green almonds. We ate them as they were in their soft green shells.

'Do you always eat almonds like that?' he asked.

'Never. But we thought that perhaps you did.'

'No. Always dried. But that was all my wife had to offer you.'

Tunisia, or what we saw of it, had a good feel about it.

The people whom we met were enthusiastic and thought a lot of President Bourguiba. To our concern they were inclined to ask what we thought of him too. Up till then I had hardly thought of him at all, but I hope that our enthusiasm was convincing when we replied that he was very well thought of in England and Canada. In our immediate surroundings a big cast was being made to bring in the tourist trade. Concrete hotels, swimming pools and other buildings were going up, but in their rough and unfinished state it was difficult to imagine their final attractions. Much was already there: lovely beaches, a good climate, ancient ruins, the contrast between the desert and the town, and attractive people. They should be successful. Unlike many of the new African nations, they have a long history of successive civilisations to build on.

Best of all there was this feeling of youthful enthusiasm, as if the world was before them, and maybe in their case it was.

We had a fast trip to Malta, in three days, but when we attempted to enter Marsamascetto in the dark we were confused by the paraffin lamps of the fishermen just within the harbour entrance. We stood away, and this brought a volley of swift Morse on our heads from the Lloyd's signal tower. We tried again and were again showered with Morse, so that we stood off until daylight when we found that we could go in without any more questions. We sailed in, but at the entrance to Lazaretto Cove took down our sails and motored up, looking this way and that in search of a suitable anchorage. There were some yachts at the head of the cove on the port hand. We slowed down and turned towards them. It was still very early, but a tousled figure in pyjamas appeared on the deck of the nearest.

'Here you are,' the figure shouted. 'There's a mooring buoy here that you can use. Wait a minute and I'll take your line.' He hurried aft, jumped into his dinghy, and rowed hastily over. Just as he arrived he caught a crab. Two white legs encased in purple and brown pyjamas rose skywards as he went flat on his back in the bilge.

'I feel a perfect fool,' he said as he struggled up again.

'Well, you don't look it,' I said. 'Anyone who takes a line and tells us where to go at this time in the morning looks just the job.'

His yacht was called the *Alano*, and he was an American businessman who, in middle age and due to illness, had suddenly given up everything to start with his wife a new and adventurous life. Nothing that they had undertaken before could have prepared them in any way for what they had undertaken. As they told us of their mistakes and their adventures, Beryl and I, without their having any idea of it, were enthralled by the tale of their courage.

Malta swarms with people and has little soil to feed them, so that one wonders where the food will come from in the end. Whatever the story of our relations with the people of the island, the mistakes that may have turned into bitterness, the good that may be forgotten, there are two things for which England must take the blame. The first is the introduction of the British bun of the worst railway station variety, which flourishes to the exclusion of all lighter forms of pastry, and the second is the aspidistra in the seaside lodging-houses. In spite of this we never met a Maltese outside Malta, and we met them all over the place, who did not flourish his British passport with pride.

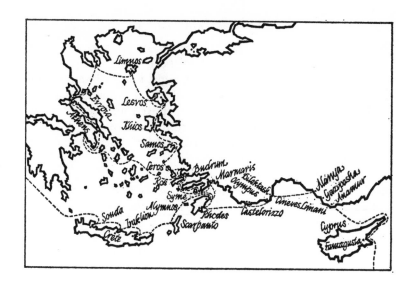

5 *Round the Aegean*

GOING eastward in the Mediterranean there is usually a wind from a westerly quarter, but in the Aegean the Melteme blows from the north from half way through June until the end of August. We decided to go eastward, first to Rhodes, then up the Aegean until the Melteme arrived in force, then down to Athens to pick up Clio and Ann, then eastward along the Turkish coast to Cyprus. We hoped to haul out there and to start for the Red Sea at the beginning of September. In this way we expected to have an unhurried cruise in the Mediterranean, take a fair wind down the Red Sea when the weather began to cool off, and the Northeast Monsoon down the African coast, for we were beginning to think more seriously of the invitation to the Okovango Swamps. This plan worked very well, and for most of the time we had fair winds and good sailing.

We left Malta, St Paul's Bay, in the afternoon with a Force 5 wind from the south. Strong gusts sent *Tzu Hang* speeding out of the bay with the anchor still at the hawse-hole for she was off the moment it broke out. Up went the jib and the water began to hiss at the bow while Beryl hoisted the mizzen. 'This is the way to leave a harbour,' I thought until a bump at the bow reminded me that it wasn't, and that the anchor was not yet inboard. By the time that it was stowed and lashed down on the deck, we had altered course to the east.

'I think we're going to need a reef,' Beryl called to me from the helm.

It was better to reef now while we were still under the shelter of the island and before dark. I walked aft, collected the reefing handle from its pocket just inside the hatch, went forward again, rolled down a short reef, and stood back to admire my handiwork. Satisfied that it would do, I made my way back towards the cockpit. 'Reefing handle, reefing handle!' Beryl called, seeing that I had forgotten it. I went back, pulled it out of the gear, and returned to the cockpit again.

'How's she doing now?'

'Fine now. Tea time.' We changed places and she went down to make it. It was good to be off again, the two of us, for three or four days at sea. The cat arrived on the deck, wrinkled her nose to windward. A trickle of water ran across the deck at her feet. She shook a paw and disappeared below again. We were bound for Souda Bay in Crete.

Three days later and with four hundred miles on the log, a light came winking suddenly out of the night: two flashes and the loom of a third as the crest of a wave intervened. Three flashes. The Antikithira light which marks the passage between Greece and Crete. *Tzu Hang* was swinging along in a troubled sea with a dark overcast sky above. Her main boom was wide to port with the preventer guy set up, and the headsail giving a lazy flap as the ship rolled. Until I saw the light the sixteen-mile-wide southern passage had been shrinking to a third of its size, the cliffs on each side had been extending their jagged teeth underwater, and visibility was only a mile or two. As the reassuring light flashed out again in the right place anxiety fled, *Tzu Hang* steadied on her course, the sea moderated and the visibility improved. All was well. With the light to watch the remainder of my spell passed quickly, and I pointed it out abeam to Beryl with satisfaction as we changed.

By the time my watch below was over it was daylight again,

but the coast of Crete was hidden in haze and low cloud. Looking aft, however, fine on the starboard quarter we could see a vertical shadow, a thin line of darker shading, hanging from the grey sky. It was the end of the great promontory that thrusts out to the north from the west end of Crete. We altered course slightly to starboard and soon discovered the cape that marks the entrance to Souda Bay. The mountains shook the clouds from their shoulders, the sea lit up, and in brilliant sunshine with the snows above us *Tzu Hang* raced round the point and headed back into the long bay. The squalls avalanched off the cliffs and Beryl needed both hands to the tiller as I struggled to get the jib down and the storm jib set. Just as we were wondering whether it would not be prudent to roll a reef as well, the squalls eased in the wider waters of the bay.

The bay is about ten miles long and three miles wide, running between harsh grey hills covered with boulders and scattered scrub. It is easy to see how in wartime a resistance could have thrived, for the ground is difficult to move over, and a man could hide almost anywhere. We beat up through the bay, tacking smartly between the ships of the Greek fleet which were assembled there for an inspection by the late King. When he arrived a day or two later, his launch altered course to pass close to our stern. We had dressed up for the occasion and he saluted as we dipped. We had a good look at him—and so did the cat: a fine, tall, and kingly man.

We stayed in Souda Bay for several days waiting for a friend to arrive from London. During one night the wind, which every day hit us with tremendous blasts off the mountains, excelled itself. *Tzu Hang* staggered all over the place, and we hanked on the storm jib in case we had to slip our cable. We were sheltered from the sea since we were behind a breakwater, but neither of us had much sleep. On board a big freighter, high in the water, every one was asleep. She coasted past us sideways, dragging her anchor on too short a cable, until she fetched up right at the head of the bay, having made a trip of a mile without anyone on board knowing it.

Norrie arrived from her Chelsea home, her eyes as blue as the sky on the day she came, her speech dramatic, her laughter bubbling as merrily as a spring. 'Isn't this terrific? Don't you remember?'—many memories. We climbed the stony hill with the scrub and gorse close-cropped by goats and we walked to the war cemetery, in beautiful surroundings, very well kept up, and with many unknown soldier's graves. Before we left we motored over the mountainous spine of Crete to Sphakion. The road goes through the green village of Vrieses, alight with running water, where the best yogurt in the world is made. It climbs through a dark valley, still stained with blood feuds, and up between rocky hills, where the boulders crouch along the ridges like Pathan tribesmen in ambush. At the top, balanced on the stony ridge, we looked down on the beach from where the last British and Australian soldiers had been evacuated twenty years before. All over the Aegean islands the signs of war remain. The bomb craters still march over old German or Italian gun emplacements, and houses destroyed by bombing have never been repaired. In the village below us there were several without roofs and the bomb craters scarred the edge of the cliff.

We left Souda Bay in a light westerly wind on our way to Heraklion. Bobby Somerset had arrived with his *Thanet* from Puerto Andraitx and we arranged to cruise together for a few days. *Thanet* left some time after we did, and we watched her sail growing bigger all morning as she came slowly up to us. As soon as we were out of the bay we found a big swell rolling in from the west although the wind was still very light. The glass was falling rapidly, and it looked as if we were in for a blow. We went too close to the cliffs at Panormos, which sucked the wind up and over leaving us wallowing in the vacuum below, while the waves cannoned off the cliffs and came rolling back to us. All order went from the sea and *Tzu Hang* lurched and bounced, her empty sails filling again with a smack as she rolled, until eventually she rolled herself into the wind again. *Thanet* was doing much the same shortly afterwards, and we could see her sail turning itself into a figure of eight as she lolloped about. Norrie, who had been prostrate with seasickness for some time, was now really ill and lay empty and cold in one of the bunks.

'How's Norrie?' I called to Beryl. She disappeared for a moment and then reappeared at the hatch.

'She looks absolutely ghastly—but she's still breathing.'

Thanet overtook us off Akra Panagria, and it was a lovely

sight to see such a big yacht go past at almost nine knots now that the wind had freshened, lifting and thrusting forward on the front of the big swell. As darkness fell we could see the great triangle of her sail gliding along behind the breakwater. The wind was rising all the time as we followed her in later. We saw her moored stern to the breakwater with a boat in the water to take our stern line. Lucky *Tzu Hang* to have a friend already in port. We lowered the dinghy and made another line fast astern and then, since the sea was already coming over the wall behind us, transferred the dinghy to the bow and went below for supper. Norrie was still very weak, but she was speaking again, not very often and not very loudly. Next morning we decided that we had better get her ashore, but there was no question of using the dinghy and we got a fishing boat up to the bow which took her ashore to an hotel. 'There goes someone who will never sail again,' said Bobby, seeing the still corpselike figure taken away.

In harbour was the right place to be that day. The inner harbour was packed with small craft, but *Tzu Hang* and *Thanet* remained behind the breakwater in a wet isolation. The spray flew to the masthead of a cargo ship moored up to the breakwater, and thundered on to our deck so that we had all the impression of being at sea in a gale and none of the danger. An oilskinned shore party made its way along the breakwater, crouching under the shelter of the wall, to meet an American destroyer that was coming in. She got a nylon hawser on to a bollard, but the moment that she stopped her way the wind set her back so strongly that the hawser stretched and broke. As if in disgust at this turn of events she backed out of the twisting channel, into the sea, and off to shelter behind some island.

We spent the next day at Cnossus and were glad to find Norrie completely recovered. 'I've found a terrific drink,' she said, 'Ouzo. The barman tells me that it is just the thing for seasickness. I'm absolutely going to live on ouzo and drama-mine.'

We set off next morning in a calm sea to Agio Nicolas further down the coast. Norrie placed herself in the cockpit, in one hand a bottle of ouzo and in the other the dramamine, the light of battle in her face. After a preliminary slug she declared that cruising was absolutely wonderful, and towards the end of the day, her blue eyes in no way dimmed by the lethal brew, she was ordering us to 'Crack on, or whatever you say. Faster, faster.'

There are various fascinating anchorages on the way to Rhodes, but the most exciting one was Tristomon in Carpathos, which has a narrow entrance opening into a mile-long sound. It is difficult to spot, as the entrance looks like no entrance at all from outside, for it turns to port and it is not until you are round the corner that the sound is revealed. We might not have found it, but *Thanet* had been there since the evening before, and Bobby was out in the dinghy to pilot us in. There was a swell running, and the cliffs at the entrance are so high that they dwarf everything else, so that for some time we thought that Bobby's well-covered grey head above the dinghy was a seagull ruffling its feathers on a log.

There is a small tumbledown village at the head of the sound. Above it the steep and narrow valleys are terraced by huge stone walls, dwarfing the little fields that they protect. The ridges in between, running up to the backbone of the island, are rocky and scrub-covered. Old women in Greek dress drive the goat flocks here, whistling on their fingers or through their teeth like a Scotch shepherd, and pitching a stone at the leader or a laggard goat with the accuracy of a baseball player. Lying in the water at the edge of the village was a slender Greek column to which a boat was tied, and there were other cut stones lying about, showing that the village, now on its last legs, had once known better days.

In the Aegean the next harbour is usually in sight or round the headland and rarely is it necessary to go more than thirty miles to find it. The land is poor, and life is hard in the Dodecanese, the 'Twelve Islands' which stand like frontier posts close off the shore of Turkey and were once occupied by the Knights Hospitallers of St John. In Carpathos, Cos and Rhodes there are fir trees, but on most of the others, except for a few olives, the hills are covered only with rock and scrub, burning hot in summer, cold, windy and wet in winter. They must breed a hardy race to have survived not only the struggle with poor earth and strong winds, but the occupation by the Turks, the Knights, the Germans and the Italians—and the ravages of earthquakes as well.

Alymnos was one of the poorer ones, but it had a good little bay, which had been an Italian M.T.B. base during the war, with empty barracks and a short pier still standing, and a good walk to the remains of an old Moorish fort on the hill above. From there we went on to Rhodes, where the walls of the old port, the fortifications down to piles of catapult balls, the Street of the Knights, and the old town, are so well preserved that it takes no effort of the imagination to picture life as it was there five hundred years ago. Although Rhodes was not yet trying to stem the tourist flood that inundates it later in the year, it wasn't the sort of place that *Tzu Hang* likes to stay in for long, and we were eager to get off to the Turkish coast.

Except in Rhodes, which has its tourists to feed on, we had never been very far away from poverty, the sort of poverty that pinches the cheeks of children and tightens the skin about the eyes. Now suddenly we were to run into signs of wealth. Just round the southwest corner of Turkey eastward of the point, is the great cliff and mountain enclosed bay of Marmaris, lying on a dog-leg which finally opens out into a wide deep bay. As we sailed up the sound, the bay still closed to us, we saw what looked like a reef extending right across the channel.

'What on earth's that?' I called to Beryl. 'It looks like a reef.'

'Well, where am I to go then?'

I slipped down to have a look at the chart.

'Nothing here,' I called. 'Better try and go round, though.'

We approached most cautiously and found that it was no reef at all but a floating shoal of loaves of bread, grapefruit halves, empty tins of orange juice, cartons and crates. New York harbour could hardly have sent out a bigger collection, and when we opened the bay we found that it was part of the Sixth Fleet that was at anchor there.

They were putting on a show for the inhabitants of this remote little port. Amphibious tanks were giving a landing demonstration, a band, almost entirely Negro, was blowing in the town, a large party of carpenters and sailors were banging an old wooden quay straight, and a cinema screen was being erected on the sea front. In the evening when the film started we could see something of it from *Tzu Hang*. It was a fast-talking, hard-kissing, swift-shooting affair. We wondered which of the fleet's activities could have surprised the inhabitants most and decided that it must undoubtedly have been the straightening of the pier. The Negro band was the most popular.

From Marmaris, having filled in five different forms five times in front of five different officials for the second time in two days, we left for Buyuk Limani, the ancient city of Cnydus, westward along the coast. Two breakwaters once enclosed the harbour made of large square-cut stones, but one is now awash or under water. A narrow neck of land forms the head of the harbour, and divides it from a similar but shallower harbour on the other side. On each side of the one that we had entered the hill rose steeply, and terraces followed its curve, covered with cut stones from the tumbled ruins of Cnydus. When the two bays were full of shipping they must have looked like a busy stage to the people in the town above.

Now there were only ruins and some dilapidated soldiers who refused to allow us ashore. They were primitive and rude and lived at a police post at the head of the bay. When we insisted on a short walk, they came with us, smoking our cigarettes and clambering about with loaded rifles held in a most unprofessional way. Unfortunately they were all too common on the otherwise attractive Turkish scene. They always appeared in pairs but fortunately did not frequent the more out of the way places, nor were they evident in the more civilized.

A yacht can go north from here along the east coast of Turkey or east along the north coast. We went north to the grey castle of Budrum, with the crests of the Knights of St John who had held it carved in marble looted from the Mausoleum, the tomb of Mausolus, let into the walls. This was a real N.A.T.O. affair with an English tower, a French tower, an Italian tower, and a Snake tower. Whose, I wonder, was that?

North again to Gumusluk, with a camel outlined on the point against the evening sky, to see if there was anything remaining of the ancient city of Myndus, but we found only doorsteps made from the pedestals of Greek columns. Across to the Greek islands again, to Leros and lovely landlocked Partheni Bay, where the fishermen's wives sang to us one morning for the tape recorder, and when we played it back on deck, late in the evening, every door on the hillside flew open and fishermen were dragged out to hear the beauty of their wives' voices screeching across the water.

From there to Patmos with its white monastery like a tented camp upon the hill and steep stone steps leading up to it. In the village we found a young American girl, fresh and breathless. She and her mother had come to visit their homeland.

'We thought we'd stay six months,' she told us. 'Mother has been in the States twenty-four years, and although we always speak American she has never learnt to speak it. Now we are in Greece she says that she can't speak Greek. We don't know what to do. She understands it, of course, but our relations just talk and talk and go to church. We've only been here a week and I guess I've been to church ten times. Say, there isn't even a drugstore on this island. Mom has been looking forward to this visit for years, and now she can't talk, and we're both fed up. I guess we'll be off to the States again in a week or so. I wish I was like you. Do you mean you put your whole house on your boat when you say you live in it? I'd like to go to Australia. What sort of language do they speak there?'

She was eighteen.

From Patmos to Samos to the port of Vathi, where the houses cascade down the hill like a waterfall, white and clean at the top, muddy and spreading at the bottom; and from there to Chios.

One of the common sights in the Aegean is a string of small fishing boats being towed out of harbour late in the evening or returning with the first light of the morning. In the harbour at Chios a tow was getting ready to leave and a fisherman signalled me to go with him. A tug-boat with a net-boat in tow came up to the six small flare-boats bobbing at the wharf, lines were thrown from one to the other and quickly made fast, and in no time we were away. It was just getting dark when we reached the fishing ground and the flare-boats were dropped off at half-mile intervals. The fisherman lit his paraffin lamp and hung it over the stern, and then with the aid of a bottle of wine, a loaf of bread, and a pack of cigarettes, composed himself for a long wait. We could see the other flare-boats like buoys marking a long channel. The Turkish coast showed dark and mountainous a few miles away, with never a light showing. The life of a fisherman seemed not so bad.

Some hours later the fisherman decided that there were some fish under the boat, attracted either by the light or whatever the light attracted. He lit a flare made by a bundle of rags soaked in paraffin on the end of a wire and waved it to call the tug. Presently its lights appeared as it came up to us. The net-boat was rowed round us casting the net and both ends brought in to the tug-boat, and, as they began to haul, we escaped over the net floats to one side. The fisherman rested on his oars outside the closing circle. From the remarks of the handlers and the lack of disturbance within the net it was soon obvious that we had got nothing. 'That's the way it goes,' said the fisherman. 'One outfit the other night made a hundred dollars a boat. It doesn't often happen. More often we're lucky if we get sufficient to feed ourselves.'

As daylight came the flares went out, and soon the string of boats was retracting as the tug picked them up. They steamed close past us, a line was thrown, the fisherman whipped it round a pin, let it slide as the boat heeled, and then made fast as she started to tow. He sat down with his back to the tug, hooked his coat over his head, and lit a cigarette. We had nothing to show for the night, but 'That's the way it goes,' he said.

From Chios we went north to Lesvos to the inland lake of Kolpos Yeras, where the olive trees and rhododendrons grow along the steep shore, and we were woken every morning by the fishermen drumming on the bottoms of their boats with their heels to frighten the fish into the net. We anchored off the hot baths of Sultan Hamid and bathed there every day. Norah joined us here again, and on that evening we heard two young girls singing as they wandered along the shore. They waved and beckoned to us and one of them sang so prettily that we rowed in with the tape recorder and asked her to sing to us again. She was about fifteen and beautiful, in rags pinned together, but when we started the recorder she opened her mouth and no sound came. Norah then sang her a Greek song that she had learnt in Paris and after it was played back, her confidence returned and she sang for us to the accompaniment of the waves breaking on the beach, barefoot and in rags, while the mountains and the trees seemed to listen to Chloe by the lake. I asked her to come back next morning so that I could take her photograph, and she came, but in a poor little dress and shoes. She was still beautiful, but the glory had gone.

From Lesvos we went north again to Muros which was a great army base during the Dardanelles campaign, where many people still speak some English, and where there are more fair-haired people than we saw anywhere else in Greece. Norah collected an extraordinarily gay and naughty wink from an old fisherman, who we were told was ninety-seven years old, and who still had a boat and went fishing.

By then the Melteme had arrived, so we cut across close hauled to land-locked Porto Koufko, then to Skiathos and down inside Kolpos Evoikos to Athens, where Norah left us, and Clio and Ann, with a friend called Jenny, joined us. We now had a superfluity of youth and good looks on board, and of sun oil with which the deck was soon covered. We set off eastwards to Sounion and through the windy Cyclades to Nisi Levitha and Kos. From there racing on a strong Melteme round Akra Krios to Simi to hear the Paniero monastery bells ring out in welcome as we ran between the heads of the harbour. They ring for every boat that enters or leaves, a sudden short peal, which we could just hear above the sound of the wind and the waves and the movement of the ship. To Rhodes again with an East German and a Soviet tourist ship in the harbour, and square, solemn and aloof people, duly attentive to their guides; then to Lindos where *Tzu Hang* anchored over a pile of broken amphorae in lovely St Paul's Bay, beyond the port, where the entrance is so narrow between rocks that it looks as if the crosstrees will touch if the ship should roll. We climbed up to the Acropolis by a path that took off from the beach over the local rubbish dump and from the top could look down on *Tzu Hang*'s deck, sweltering in a little rock-enclosed bowl.

An Englishman, a woman and a small child rowed out to us. They were on holiday in Lindos and asked us how we had liked Ibiza. 'Not much,' I said. 'Everyone living together and none of them married, at least if they were they weren't living with their wives.' Even as I said this I began to feel prudish and silly, in fact showing some of the cheapness I objected to in Ibiza, but at any rate, I thought, I surely haven't put my foot in it here, with an upstanding child of two as a guarantee of respectability—or had I?

The man cleared his throat. 'As a matter of fact we're not married actually,' he said.

We sailed east again to Castelorizzo, the last and most distant of the Dodecanese and within the arms of the Turkish shore—a dying island. It had been heavily bombed during the war and its flattened houses never rebuilt. Many of its inhabitants, of which there used to be twelve thousand, had emigrated to Australia. There were only four hundred left now, kept going by money from Australia, and for such a small population an extraordinary number of little shops, buying and selling from each other. We climbed up the cobbled hills in search of eggs and milk and were asked into one little farm as clean and as empty as a swept cupboard, where the only food seemed to be algarroba beans, which we were given to eat.

We entered Turkey at the port of Kas in the Gulf of Caste-lorizzo and then sailed up to Bayindir Liman to anchor. There was no house to be seen. In the cliffs above were Lycian tombs and the shore was rocky and scrub-covered. There were tracks of wild pig and jackal on the shore, and no sooner was the anchor down than we heard the nostalgic sound of chikor chirruping amongst the rocks. This was our sort of country. That night a wolf howled on the hill, and jackals tossed their shrill keening along the shore. The moon shone on hot rocks and ancient ruined walls, on the tumbled seats of an amphi-theatre and broken steps. Only the animals were astir here, but above us two sputniks cut their swift way across the familiar pattern of the stars. Next day we climbed up to a saddle and found a shallow valley where a field of grain had recently been harvested. As we came upon it there was a whirr of wings and hundreds of chikor flew off. When we saw the thin stubble on the baked earth, the brown hills behind, the steep shoulders of the saddle with the twisted bushes in the rocks on each side, and the birds vanishing up the valley, Beryl and I found it hard to believe that we had not slipped back in time and were walking once more the hills of Baluchistan.

Of all the places on this wild Turkish coast that we visited Deliktash was the best. Deliktash is a small village in Cirali Liman and there are two anchorages. The first is Cinovese (Genoese) Liman, with tall cliffs overshadowing the small bay, which has a curved beach and a salt marsh at its head. The other is west of Deliktash village in the corner of the bay where a rocky point provides some protection. On the spur of this point are the grey stone walls and towers of an old Venetian fort. Within the point a clear river runs into the sea. It has pushed up a sand bar across its mouth, making a freshwater pool in which to bathe. In the pool and all up the river are many small turtles. This is the site of the old city of Olympus. There are landing quays along the river bank made of cut stone, a wide arch that has survived a rock fall from the hill above, a theatre and many smaller ruins. A little way up the valley which curves between stony hills, we found some nomads encamped with their sheep and donkeys, among the ruins. They had patched up the roofs and some of the gaps in the walls with wattle. An old man was just setting off up the valley with a long-barrelled rifle like an Afghan jezail on his shoulder, a couple of dogs at his heels.

Further round the bay, and a mile or so inland, burns the 'eternal flame' mentioned by Pliny, on the Yanar volcano. We set off to see it early in the morning, before the heat of the day, but our march was interrupted by various discoveries: a hole in a rock in which there was drinking water reached by a long handled scoop and which Popa defiled by plunging in; a donkey about to foal for Clio; an old man whom Jenny had to photograph; and a young camel with enormous eyelashes that Ann fell in love with. It was blazing hot before we left the valley and began to climb the stony path where the rocks smouldered in the sun and the walls of the valley imprisoned their heat. Popa, always game in spite of his lame leg, panted from patch of shade to patch of shade until we took it in turns to carry him.

At the top the flame still burned, leaving a smoky scar on the rock above. Near it were the remains of a small Byzantine church and of a little Greek temple, where water from a spring dribbled into a stone bowl, soon occupied by Popa. No man, no animal, no litter, not even a carved initial was there, nor a signpost on the way up. Like so many of the ruins on this coast they were quite uncared for, unrestored and rarely visited, so that we felt almost as if we had discovered them.

From Cirali Liman we went on to Gazi Pasha, but seeing a number of bathers, we anchored some way from the village. A party of men swam out to us and Beryl hustled the bikini-clad girls below since she was unsure of the degree of the Turks' sophistication in this part of the world. The leader turned out to be the mayor and asked us to dinner in a small town about a mile inland. The local sessions were on, and we had dinner with the mayor and two judges none of whom were over thirty. Afterwards we all walked back to the beach in the moonlight. As we walked Ann kept leaping forward and then taking another place in the line, while Beryl and the two judges performed a series of intricate sidesteps until Ann leapt forward again. At one time, as she arrived rather breathlessly beside me, I asked her what on earth she was doing. 'It's the judges,' she gasped, almost hysterical with suppressed laughter. 'They're pinching.'

We were unable to see Trajan's tomb at Gazi Pasha owing to the arrival of some more uncouth soldiery, so we left for Alanya and the long formalities of a larger port. Alanya has a large octagonal tower guarding the port and a double wall running up from this bastion to a fort on the hill above. We had no history of the coast and were unable to tell whether these forts were of Genoese, Venetian or Byzantine construction. They appeared to be fortified trading posts, protected from both land and sea attack.

Anamur, a little way up the coast, is the most impressive, with three-storeyed walls and two keeps, one of them opening on to the sea. We anchored off it to go ashore, but the anchorage is fit only for a short visit, and anyway it was now 17 August, time to get on to Famagusta, to arrange a haul out, and to start off for the Red Sea. The Taurus mountains, the rugged backdrop to the Turkish shore, to the poor little villages, the ruined cities and the austere and deserted forts, faded slowly into the evening as *Tzu Hang* stepped over towards Cyprus. As she sailed we thought of all that we had seen: of the wildness of the shore and the jackals calling; of the ruins of elaborate tombs and temples and all the marks of a high and wealthy civilization tumbled and ignored; of the poverty of the little ports and villages; of the troublesome and ignorant police-soldiers; of the fathoms of red tape; of the bank manager who said, 'We must change all this, we must change it,' and of the friendliness of many people that we met. No doubt it is already changing, and the coast road that was being built will help, and then I should say that the south coast of Turkey will be an infinitely more interesting place to visit than the Grecian islands.

Early next morning *Tzu Hang*, who had been wandering idly through the night, gave herself a shake, heeled to a new wind, and set off for the Cypriot coast. We hit the coast well south of Kyrenia, and by the time we were off the harbour it was dark again. There was now a strong wind blowing, the harbour looked narrow and confined, and the lights of the town behind were confusing. We decided to carry on to Cape Andreas, the eastern end of Cyprus, and when daylight came it was in sight.

Round Cape Andreas there is a small cove beneath a monastery, where the water is so clear that the anchor can be dropped on sand between patches of rock. We anchored there and then had a siesta to recompense us for a night at sea. Afterwards, while the three girls bathed, Beryl and I went ashore to a building marked as 'Customs House' on the chart. It was the wrong sort of customs house, but I thought that we might be able to enter by telephone pending our arrival in Famagusta.

The customs officer was not at home, but after a time he arrived by boat and was obviously very distressed at our being there at all. 'It is most irregular,' he kept saying, but he telephoned to Famagusta, and in the end told us that we might remain where we were for the night, but should not come ashore again until we had entered at Famagusta. He said that he would tow us back to the yacht.

While I had been waiting for him Beryl had rowed back to the ship and brought the girls ashore. Now they had vanished.

'I'm afraid that we've lost the girls,' Beryl said as we arrived at the beach.

'Lost the girls?' the customs officer echoed in alarm.

'Yes. I'm afraid they've gone.'

'But they can't have gone. It's impossible.' He looked anxiously up and down the beach to see where we had mislaid them.

'They've just gone for a walk. They'll be back soon.'

'But this is really most irregular. We can't leave them like this.'

We gave them a call, but, since there was no answer, persuaded him to come out to *Tzu Hang* and have some tea. He brightened up at this suggestion, but still looked anxiously shoreward as he towed us out. We had just started tea when a big police launch rumbled alongside, up from Famagusta, fifty miles away, to investigate us. They wanted to know who we were, why we had anchored in the cove, and what the rest of the crew were doing. All but the last being easily answered, they settled down to some tea, and to await the missing crew, whom the customs officer had decided, were now in the hands of the white slavers. They were efficient and well-mannered, and presently, after a call from the shore, looked as if they thought their journey had been worthwhile. They decided to stay the night in the bay, and, almost before they knew it, the girls had extracted a promise for a large exchange of paperbacks and many assurances that our paths would be made straight in Famagusta.

We left before the police launch was astir next morning, making long tacks up the coast. For the first part, up the panhandle of Cyprus, there was hardly a village or a house to be seen, but only bare brown hills and scrub and an occasional truck on the coast road. As we approached Famagusta bay the villages on the plain began to appear. We anchored off Borghaz in a nasty swell and sailed into Famagusta next day. A few days later Clio, Ann and Jenny left for London, the patches of sun oil began to disappear from the decks, and *Tzu Hang* was hauled out and painted on an old-fashioned wooden slipway. By 8 September we were ready to sail, and by now we had decided that we would make for Mombasa and probably do a trip to the Okovango swamps the following year.

I cannot say that we liked Cyprus, although I was lucky enough to have a niece there, the wife of a soldier, and they made our stay a happy one. The taint of bitterness, the shadow of evil, hang too closely about its villages and roads. Over the villages flew Turkish or Greek flags and here and there on the side of the road a wooden cross, a tattered Greek flag and some dead flowers, showed where some wretched ambusher had been too tardy in slipping away.

In Famagusta Beryl showed an empty milk bottle to the Turk who kept the store at the entrance to the harbour in explanation of what she wanted. He looked at the bottle in disgust and then spat out two words—'Greek milk.' The milk that he got us tasted just the same. I could never forget the words of the Greek Cypriot girl, whose husband, a Greek Cypriot policeman, was murdered by the so-called patriots, also Greek Cypriots. 'This used to be a happy land,' she cried.

A little magnanimity on the part of the Greek Cypriots and it might be happy again, but the long years of Turkish misrule have burnt into the Greek soul. Whatever political use is made of Enosis in Greece, in private it must be an embarrassing question for a people who are unable to allay the poverty in their outer islands. Not that there is any sign of wealth in the Turkish shore just across the way, but anyone who looks north from the hills above Kyrenia cannot help remarking that Turkey is very close and Greece a long way away, and anyone who has visited Castelorizzo, Alymnos, or Carpathos might be chary of moving too fast towards Greece.

One place we found completely free from this aura of unhappiness. We spent almost our last day and night at anchor off Salamis. That was a happy place—but no one had lived there for a thousand years.

6 Suspect in Suez

THE early sun struck over the roofs of the dockyard at Famagusta, lighting *Tzu Hang*'s white topsides and shadowing her new bottom paint, as she slid down the old wooden slipway into the sea. It was the smoothest launching from the most old-fashioned way that we had ever experienced. The water splashed at her stern, her bows lifted, and with her own momentum she slid clear of the cradle and floated again.

I started the engine, and we took her out past the end of the quay, where we saw a young couple sitting, their legs hanging over the edge. They waved to us as we passed. The man had a red beard and was wearing a checked shirt, and the lumpy girl at his side was filling blue jeans and wore a bush-hat. I had seen them before about the wharf and been unable to place them. As soon as we were at anchor I rowed the dinghy back to the quay, to collect one of our lines that had been made fast there.

'Will you give us a lift?' asked the man.

'Where to?' I asked, thinking that they wanted to be taken somewhere in the dinghy.

'To Port Said or Durban?'

'I'm so sorry,' I said, and saw that the girl was hanging on my answer, 'we really don't need a crew.' They didn't look like the sort of couple one would ask to come, even if a crew was needed.

'All right,' the man said, 'have it your own way.' And they stood up and walked away as if I had turned down a favour. Next morning we heard that a small sailing yacht with a Volvo Penta engine was missing from the harbour, but we were too involved with our own preparations for leaving to think much of it.

We got away about midday. The long quay was empty of

ships which usually blanked off the offshore wind so that we were able to ghost along it and out of the harbour entrance, then merrily along the inside of the reef until we reached the buoy that marked its end. Here we went about and came back outside it. The sun was warm, the sea calm, and the wind light. We passed the harbour and the tall new buildings along the beach, blocks of flats for the accommodation of soldiers and their families, or of civilian personnel attached to the forces. We have come to recognize expensive-looking new accommodation for soldiers as a sign of flowering before death—perhaps that is why Gibraltar still looks so durable. We sailed quietly down the coast and gradually the lovely bitter island veiled itself in the midday haze.

Beryl took the first watch in order to soak up as much sun as possible while the wind was light. She was in the cockpit, buried in book and sun and I was half asleep below, when I heard the hum of a big outboard engine and the steady crunching of a motorboat's bow. A moment later there was an indignant exclamation from the cockpit and a scuffle which showed that Beryl was not dressed for visitors. As I came on deck the motorboat arrived alongside.

'Excuse me,' said the young man at the wheel, who had the sort of girl one would like to have as crew beside him, 'we heard that a couple in Famagusta, a man with a red beard and a girl who wore a bush-hat, asked you for a lift yesterday. Could you tell me where they were going?'

'They asked for a lift to Port Said or Durban,' I said, thinking how little is missed on a waterfront. 'Why? What's the matter?'

'We are the insurance people for the yacht that has been stolen, and we think that they may have taken it. Thanks so much. That's just what we wanted to know.' They turned and bounced away again towards the indistinct shore.

'Well I'm damned,' I said. 'What happens now if we overtake them?'

'It doesn't look as if we are going to overtake anything in this wind,' said Beryl, who never bothers about possible eventualities. 'Anyway, surely they won't try to make Port Said in that little boat unless they know something about sailing. I should think that they'd try for Beirut or the coast somewhere near.'

'They could do that easily,' I said, 'on their engine. They'll use it anyway if they want to get away.'

The wind was very light, and what there was of it blew directly from Port Said. We went about on the starboard tack, which seemed to be the most profitable, and kept on until we saw Beirut on the following day. About again, and next day found us only sixty-four miles on our course after forty-eight hours' sailing, set back by the circular current which seeps round the end of the Mediterranean. Then the wind freshened from the west, and, after two days of hard, wet, sailing, we raised the lights of Port Said. We tacked slowly up during the night under reduced sail and against a two to three knot current, so that by morning the entrance to the channel was still far enough away to make us wish that we hadn't shortened sail. By morning also the wind had dropped so that we motored slowly against tide and current, a brown flood of Nile water, towards the entrance buoys. As we closed them the big pilot boat waiting off the entrance to the channel, turned and steamed authoritatively towards us.

We were approaching Port Said in doubt as to what sort of reception we might have, for there had been reports amongst yachtsmen of policemen posted on yachts in harbour, of damage caused by rough handling by pilot boats and police launches, of petty annoyances and extortionate charges. We watched the advance of the pilot boat with some anxiety. As she drew near we could see that we were being studied through binoculars by a group on the bridge. She turned and placed herself across our path, forcing us to slow down and turn up alongside. We throttled the engine back, put the gear in neutral and rolled slowly beside her.

'Where are you from?' we were hailed.

'From Famagusta.'

'Where are you bound?'

'To Aden.'

'Do you want a pilot?'

'No thanks, we're quite all right.'

There was a short discussion on the bridge, heads bowed together, and then with a swirl of water at her stern, the pilot boat drew off and returned to her station. A moment later, as if on second thoughts, she turned again and hurried past us towards the harbour as we laboured slowly, crabwise against the current, between the first two buoys.

We watched her hurry down the five-mile stretch to where a dun-coloured landless city grew suddenly out of the sea. Just outside the harbour she met another, smaller, pilot boat. Like two ants which stop suddenly when they meet and put their heads together, they lay now for a short time bow to bow, and then hurried up the channel towards us. As they arrived the smaller swung round to come alongside, while the larger continued on her way to her station. The new arrival, well protected by heavy rope fenders, came surging in with horrible momentum. A tall, uniformed pilot, with a narrow clipped moustache and flashing teeth, clambered out of the cockpit and stood at the rail. 'I'm coming on board now,' he hailed us in English. 'I'm sorry but it's the regulation. Don't check your speed.'

The bow of his boat still pointed at us amidships and I felt *Tzu Hang* falter like a horse about to refuse a jump and knew that Beryl at the helm was assailed by the thought of the dread stories that we had heard. I began to struggle with the lashings of the dinghy under which our own fenders were stowed. 'Keep on, keep on,' shouted the pilot. There was the clatter of a polished brass boathook on the rail, a mild creak from *Tzu Hang*'s side, and he stepped magnificently on board. He shook hands, seated himself beside Beryl in the cockpit and with an airy wave of his hand towards the harbour ordered 'Full speed, full speed.'

Our nerves, shaken by the dashing approach of the pilot boat and the jaunty pilot, had barely steadied before a new danger threatened. The pilot boat had taken station on the port quarter. Now, ranging up on our starboard side, with greater speed but less skill, came a glistening police launch as full of bodies as the South Kensington lift at rush-hour. In a moment, but this time with a groan from *Tzu Hang*, they were alongside and a flood of officials—police, customs, and immigration—burst upon us. I led the most thrusting down below, hearing as we disappeared into the doghouse the maniac chant of the pilot, 'More speed, more speed.'

Below, with much bowing and hand-shaking, they were finally seated according to rank and authority, which coincided with size, the larger in the cabin, the smaller in the galley and on the engine cover. All but a policeman, wearing a crown on his shoulder, who slid into the fore-cabin on a quick tour of investigation. He had pouched eyes and a long mobile moustache. The points preceded him and his weary, dissolute and suspicious expression, like antennae. He soon became our *bête noire*. I opened the drink locker and showed two half-empty bottles. The customs officer, who was sitting on a locker which contained a case of whisky, waved a deprecating hand and signalled to me to close the door. Our passports disappeared into one attaché case, our ship's papers into another, but with the assurance that they would be available to us again before we needed them. With the exception of the policeman they were jovial, efficient, and polite. With the engine humming at an unaccustomed speed, with the water talking along the planking and the sun sending bright shafts of sunlight into the cabin, with all these strangers on board who seemed to be enjoying their trip, there was a sense of urgency and excitement. Everything was going well, I thought, and led them up on deck. Even the cat and the dog had caused no comment.

Once on deck I found that we were accompanied by four launches, for a coastguard boat and a press launch on which a movie-camera was in action, had taken station astern.

'What on earth's going on?' I said to Beryl. 'We've never had a reception like this before.'

'They think that we are the stolen boat,' she replied.

'They can't do. We're twice the size.'

'But they do. The pilot has just told me.'

I turned towards him, but he was still chanting his cry of 'More speed, more speed.' We were approaching the bumboat area, and I left it alone. Beryl at the tiller was getting that set look that she assumes on a bicycle when she is going downhill and a corner looms below.

Even at slow speeds the entrance to Port Said can be alarming to a small newcomer. A ship was in the channel, bumboats speckled the water, and their owners paddled furiously towards us, setting up a yelping chorus like hounds in full cry, motorboats belonging to the more successful hummed backwards and forwards, ferries crossed and recrossed in front of us, and barges loaded with cotton moved in long strings behind their tugs.

'Faster,' said the pilot to Beryl, 'they must get out of our way.'

The most persistent of the bumboat men was Mr Moses. A banner stretched from stem to stern of his boat proclaimed that he was 'Mr Moses—Ship's Agent.' 'God help you,' he shouted as he swerved in towards us, making Beryl flinch at the tiller and the pilot call for still more speed, 'I very good man. I get you anything you want—God help you.'

Like a bull in a hen-run, but miraculously without touching anything, we scattered the bumboats and smashed our way into the Sherifa basin on the west side of the harbour, let go our anchor, and swung our stern in between two huge lighters, loading cotton from the quay. Almost as soon as we were made fast a small boat came up to the bow and there was a rush of our visitors, eager to avoid the dust and dirt of the wharf, to evacuate the ship. They left us, chattering like a flock of starlings, without a single paper of identification on the ship, and as the man carrying our passports stepped off, his attaché case caught on a rail stanchion, and passports and bag very nearly disappeared in the sea. One of our visitors had remained on board looking as if he wanted a drink. We took him down below. The lighters creaked on their hawsers and swung slowly in towards us like two huge nutcrackers. The wind whirled some straw off the wharf in a cloud of dust and dropped it on our deck. A bale of cotton swung dangling from a crane across our stern, just missing the topping lift on its way to the lighter. Something had to be done about changing our berth.

We had not been below very long, nor even discovered whom our guest represented, before there was a sound of a launch alongside and of someone stepping onto the deck.

'Quickly,' he said, 'hide the drinks!'

As Beryl and I stuffed them away a coastguard officer in a clean white uniform, well creased and bemedalled, appeared at the hatch and came below. The alarm whatever it was, turned out to be a false one, for he was prepared to have a drink, too. We soon tackled him about a change of berth.

'Of course you can't stay here,' he said. 'It is the police. They have mistaken you for the yacht that has been stolen in Cyprus. They don't know about yachts, but we have the description, too, and it is much smaller than you. I'll take you over to the yacht club on the other side of the harbour.' He passed his hand over his well-groomed brown hair. 'Anyway, it's next door to the Police Club,' he added. 'It will be better for them there too.' Whereupon we finished our drinks, squeezed out between the barges, and crossed over to the other side of the harbour and to a comfortable berth at the yacht club.

As soon as we were secured the coastguard disappeared for a short time and reappeared with a gift of dates and cheese. We sat down together to lunch and spoke of our mistaken identity. 'It is quite an adventure,' he said.

'When we were young,' Beryl said, 'I liked that sort of adventure, but now I think I'm too old for mistaken identities to be enjoyable.'

'But you are still young,' said the gallant young man, 'to do these things at all you are still young.'

'How old do you think she is,' I asked him.

'Not more than eighty-three, I think,' he replied, and then explained, after the laughter had subsided, that he had got it the wrong way round. He was very amusing, particularly about his time as a prisoner-of-war of the Israelis. He had been taken on the first day off the Egyptian destroyer that was captured, and thereafter had had the time of his life. He had been well-treated and he told us that in order to get any information that they could out of him he had been supplied with Arabic-speaking girl-friends who had been very kind to him. 'Of course I could tell them nothing,' he said, 'because I was only nineteen and really didn't know anything at all, so I got them for nothing.'

From then on we had a series of visitors. Most of them were Canal Company officials, interested in the yacht's measurements, the efficiency of our engine which had to see us through the canal, or the possibility of a job in Canada. Others were the police, still inclined to be dour and suspicious, and the agent to whom we had been recommended, Jim Cairo, once Jim England, who made no charge for his services and who provided us with landing permits. There was also the immigration official who refused us landing permits, because we wouldn't deal with the agent that he produced. As we already had visas the whole thing seemed rather silly, but in the end in the incomprehensible way things have always happened in Egypt we ended up with two sets of landing permits as well as our visas.

Our most determined visitor was the police major with the mobile moustache. Its ends reached forward when he believed that he was on a hot scent and drooped when it failed. At his first visit he brought a policeman, whom he said must remain on board. This policeman, to whom all yachts had so far been subjected, sat on the bridge-deck and sometimes hung his feet, in large black boots, down in the doghouse. He was unable to be quiet and sang for most of the time a sad little song, interrupted by heavy sighs and violent eructations. It was not so much what he did, but that he was there at all that annoyed, until we discovered after he had left that he'd taken the stainless steel bosun's knife from the pocket by the hatch entrance.

The major brought an engineer who seemed to be abnormally interested in our engine. It was some time before I realised that he was looking for the name Volvo Penta. I have never found the maker's name on my engine, and nor could he, so I gave him the manual in order that he might identify it. He left still unconvinced, and I knew that we would see him again.

'He does not understand,' said the coastguard. 'He says, "The ship is painted white, it has a pointed bow, it must be the stolen vessel." He is very suspicious. It is the Egyptian mentality.'

So far we had avoided, except with the coastguard, any suggestion that we were under any sort of suspicion. When the major next arrived, I said to him that it was ridiculous to suspect that we were a stolen yacht as I had my clearance from Famagusta, already checked by the customs, and which I still had on me. I showed him the green slip showing that we had left Famagusta 'in ballast' for Port Said. With a wooden look at such blunt speaking, he took the paper and his moustache began to droop, but almost immediately it quivered and rose again.

'Ah,' he said, 'you come from Ballastine.' To have come to Egypt from Palestine would have been far worse than to have arrived with a stolen yacht, and I had to explain what 'in ballast' meant. The moustaches fell.

The coastguard, bringing a friend with a small boy, came to tea. Half-way through there was a shout to the policeman on the deck. The coastguard jumped to his feet and started to smooth his tunic, 'The Chief of Police is coming,' he said. His friend looked wildly round the cabin. 'Hide me, hide us, please. Quickly.' We bustled him and his small boy into the forepeak where they crouched amongst ropes and sailbags. Beryl and I began to feel as if we were taking part in some illicit game—but we didn't know the rules. The coastguard reappeared in the cabin after shouting to the shore. 'It's all right. False alarm again. He's coming to see you tonight,' he explained.

The Chief of Police and the head of the C.I.D. arrived in the evening. They were both big men with an undeniable presence and seemed to fill the cabin. From the moment they arrived it was obvious that we were no longer under suspicion. Passports and papers came quickly home to roost, the prying major was discomfited, and at our special request the windy policeman was banished, taking our knife with him. We were free to go, but I had already arranged with the Canal Company to spend another day in Port Said.

As I crossed over by ferry next morning it seemed that very little had changed since I was there many years before. A cool wind blew freshly from the sea, the sun shone on sparkling waters, and the great ships came stalking silently across the flat landscape. On the ferry there was a dray of cement bags pulled by two mules who jibbed at the ramp when we arrived at the far side. The driver cracked his whip, the mules kicked, and every passenger or bystander loudly offered advice. Presently the driver began offloading his bags of cement on to the deck of the ferry in order to lighten the load. The captain of the ferry arrived and objected to the sacks being put on his deck. There followed one of those wordy turmoils as sudden and pointless as the dust-devils that whirl through the mud shacks on the outskirts of the town, and accompanied by such a wealth of gesture that it looked as if they had embarked on a round of fisticuffs. While this was going on the mules put their shoulders to their collars and trotted up the ramp and away. Nowhere else could there be so much noise over so little, nor anger turn so rapidly to laughter.

There were some obvious changes. There was no statue of De Lesseps to watch the ships go by. Instead there was a rusty anti-aircraft gun drooping on its mounting, left there by neglect or to remind the ships of the world of what the Egyptians call the 'aggression'. It seemed to draw attention also to the lack of any other damage to the town, which was otherwise exactly as I had known it. There were also more and larger ships passing through than when it was in the old Company's hands, as the folder that we were given was at pains to point out, but then there are infinitely more and larger ships at sea. Jim Cairo had lent me a guide and a bicycle to find the various offices which I had to visit to effect my passage. As we wobbled through the traffic he told me that he had once been a messenger at 'Navy House'. 'Those were good times,' he said. He wasn't by any means the only one who said it, but, of course, that is what one likes to hear—and they know it. Still I doubt if the Egyptian soldier fighting in the Yemen finds life any better. There seemed very little change either way. The people neither happier nor prouder, the town a little dirtier, but everyone seemed friendly.

Next day, with a canal seaman on board to see us through as far as Ismailia, we set off behind the morning convoy. We could hardly believe our good fortune. We knew of one yacht whose owner had been charged over sixty pounds by his agent, whereas ours had charged nothing. The Canal Company had waived all but the insurance fee and a few stamps, a total charge of just over two pounds. Including fuel and stores we spent only six pounds in Egypt.

We made six knots, timing ourselves by the kilometre posts, and the engine running a little faster than usual. As we slipped along the edge of the canal, the cars on the road, so used to seeing the big ships stalking majestically across the desert, stopped sometimes to see a yacht go by. The huge stern of the last ship in the convoy drew slowly ahead until it disappeared round a corner, but we could still see the long procession of masts and funnels ahead of us over the dunes. One by one the canal stations in their clumps of greenery appeared and disappeared behind us. The convoy ahead halted and tied to the bank. *Tzu Hang* went on. We passed the lot and then met the upcoming convoy from the Bitter Lakes. The big tankers seemed to fill the whole canal, so that it looked as if there would never be room for us to squeeze between them and the channel buoys, and just at this critical time I found that the fuel return pipe had fractured and was pumping fuel all over the place.

We made fast at a point where the bank had been newly revetted. As the next ship passed the water sank away from the bank about three feet and then came back in a succession of waves which made us plunge violently, until it looked as if we might either break away from our mooring lines or damage the hull against the revetment. We worked in a fever to get the joint repaired, prodded by the sight of the slow advance of the next ship and the look of despair on our seaman's face, who held himself responsible for our safety. My fingers were all thumbs, and every spanner fell into the bilge, while Beryl reported the ship's advance, and the seaman danced about on the bank, anxious to cast off as soon as the engine started. We got away in time and our seaman made an expressive gesture to show that his stomach had turned over.

The first boat that I had ever sailed in had belonged to the sailing club at Ismailia, so that I felt that we must at least anchor off the club now that we had a ship of our own, a circumstance that I had never dreamed of then. The difficulty was to recognize it, as it had grown enormously. The seaman pointed it out, and we anchored a cable away. I rowed him ashore and arranged at the Canal Office for our onward passage. By the time that I got back there was a horde of children swarming like a shoal of slippery fish all over *Tzu Hang* and talking in English, French or Arabic, which ever came first to their busy tongues. Below it looked as if a wave had broken over our stern and flooded the cabin. In the wake of these wet little guests came their parents who asked us to make use of the club, but in spite of our visas we could go no further afield, as the crews of ships in transit are not allowed out of the canal area. We spent another day at Ismailia, mostly in the water, and left early next morning with a Greek seaman of the Canal Company, before daylight and long before the down convoy. The seaman seated himself firmly at the tiller and Beryl and I had a holiday.

We passed one convoy in the Bitter Lakes and another in the canal, and we watched the Mig aircraft flying off Kabrit airfield, where there were a large number on the tarmac. The high banks slipped steadily past. A stout officer in khaki slacks and a tarboosh smoked a cigarette under a casuarina while his driver struggled with the engine of a broken-down jeep. In several places work was going on and the canal being widened. Early in the afternoon Suez was in sight. Everything had gone so smoothly that we determined not to try our luck any further. We told our seaman that we would drop him at the pilot station, and, since we were already cleared for Aden, would not go into the port. We dropped him at the pontoon and very soon afterwards got up sail.

'I vote we get out of the harbour limits and then anchor somewhere for the night,' said Beryl. Between leaving port and making a passage we always like to have that last anchorage, resting almost in suspense between leaving and setting off, when there is no more to do, and yet the real journey and its strenuous demands has not yet started.

The wind was very light as we slipped quietly along towards Newport Rock, intending—as soon as we were clear of the harbour limits and harbour police—to turn up to the Sinai shore and find a suitable place to anchor until either the moon rose or the breeze freshened. Before we reached Newport Rock we heard an insistent hooting on a Klaxon horn behind us. It was a police launch in hot pursuit. They signalled us to stop, and we turned into the wind until the headsail came aback and *Tzu Hang* slowed down on the other tack. This manœuvre caused a great deal of excitement on the police launch, who seemed to think that we were trying to elude them. It calmed as the mizzen came down and they laid alongside. A large police officer—they all seemed to be large—stepped on board.

'Are you John and Joan?' he asked solemnly.

Beryl and I burst out laughing and assured him that we were not.

'But I'm looking for John and Joan,' he said, scratching his head and looking puzzled. 'You must be very tired after your trip,' he said, 'we'd like you to come and spend the night in port.'

We reassured him about this and said that we'd had a marvellous rest in the canal and were going straight on for Aden. He continued to scratch his head and look puzzled, but after seeing our papers made up his mind, shook hands and wished us a good voyage. He stepped back on to his launch and as we started to sail again, his crew, who had looked so fierce a few minutes before, waved cheerfully.

That was the last that we saw of them. We sailed quietly along the Sinai shore, past an old wreck on the beach, until we found a good anchorage in sand at five fathoms. Ahead of us two lateen sails showed like pigeon's wings in the evening sunlight. From behind us came a dull distant throbbing, the pulse of the canal, as the down convoy burst out into the sea. Gradually as darkness fell their lights stretched out along the well-known sea road, hurrying to return again so that we should meet some of them on their way back before we reached Aden.

Tzu Hang swung quietly to her anchor. We lit the riding light and turned in. The last time that I had been in Suez roads had been at the beginning of another adventure and, on the next night, I remembered, the *Britannic* had been sunk by bombing. I wondered if we had sailed over her bones. A few hours later we woke up. A fresh northwest wind was blowing. We bent on the twin headsails, brought in the anchor, and were soon following in our own silent and leisurely way the urgent tankers. There was a full moon and the water whispered pleasantly along the hull. Of John and Joan, or of the man in the checked shirt and his lumpy girl, we heard no more, but we did hear at Aden that the missing yacht had been found abandoned on the beach at Beirut.

7 *Down the Red Sea*

THE moon was already behind us when we started off, casting the tracery of the rigging on the sails, turning the sea about us into a shimmering lake, and giving pale colour to the Sinai hills, which climbed steeply from the desert shore. Jupiter shone like a lantern in the crosstrees—a dim lantern for all the stars had withdrawn in honour of the moon. The chart table light was brilliant from the long charge coming through the canal, as I wrote the date in the log: 18 September.

'There are hundreds of ships behind us,' I heard Beryl say, and climbed up on deck to have a look.

We were rippling along at about two knots with the wind just stirring the sea and hardly any motion. Behind us a south-bound convoy had just burst from the canal, showing a perfect galaxy of navigation lights. Like a pack of hounds after a failing quarry they came panting after us, the palpitation of their engines throbbing in our hull and their bow-waves soughing through the still sea. We hurried out of their way as fast as the wind would permit and lit the masthead light as well as the stern light. When they were all past we set our own course parallel to, and two miles off, the shipping lane.

Our Red Sea journey was very different from any other passage that we had made in *Tzu Hang* because there was nearly always a ship in sight, and if there wasn't we began to wonder where we had got to. Owing to refraction our sights were not as accurate as usual, and owing to variable sets by the current it was difficult anyway to plot an exact position. But then the traffic route was clearly marked by the big ships, whom we assumed to have better facilities for accurate navigation than we had and knew exactly where they were. Although I took regular sights as always and carefully plotted our course, if we found that we were no longer seeing the traffic, we angled

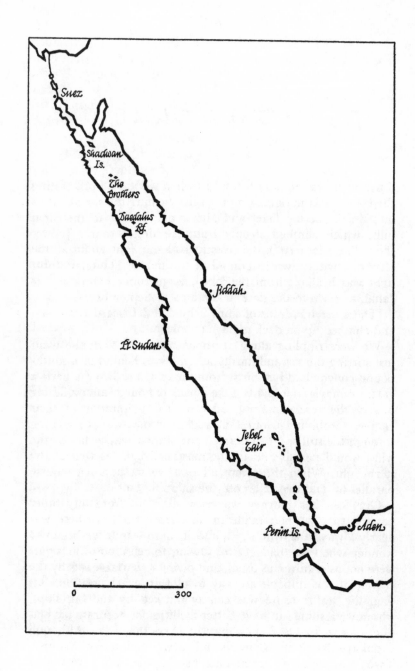

Suez

Shadwan Is.

The Brothers

Daedalus Rf.

Jiddah

Pt. Sudan

Jebel Tair

Perim Is.

Aden

0   300

slowly in towards where we had last seen it. The disadvantage
of having to be continuously on the alert was more than com-
pensated for by the interest that the ships provided. Even a
night watch passes quickly when ships' light appear, grow tall,
and finally slide smoothly by, and by day the glasses were
always in demand, to spot a ship's name or to take a look at an
officer waving from the wing of the bridge.

June to September is the hottest time of the year, but it is
also the time when a ship may carry a northerly wind right
down to the bottom of the Red Sea. We left it as late as we
dared in the hopes of finding it a little cooler, and we suffered
no discomfort until after we had passed Jebel Tair in the last
two hundred miles. To begin with nothing could have been
nicer. After crossing the shipping lane we kept about a mile
off the western shore of the Gulf of Suez, watching the dun
coast slip by, the dunes, the black burnt rocks, knowing from
afar, by past experience, their texture and how firm and cool
the sand would feel in the few dark patches of shade.

To seaward a huge Orient liner, beige and white, towered
elegantly over the loaded tankers, which pushed a mound of
sea ahead of them on the opposite course. Toward nightfall
we could see the oil flares at Wadi el Deir and Ras Abu Baka.
By five o'clock next evening we had Ashrafi lighthouse abeam,
heading for the Jubal Straits, and by eleven we were north of
Shadwan Island and had the Red Sea before us.

On our third afternoon out from Suez we passed close to
El Akhawein lighthouse, better known as the Brothers, after
the two islands that it lights, eighty-one miles beyond Shadwan
island, and that evening we were sailing square down the path
of the moon with the reddest of red skies still showing behind
us, painted in one great slash across the horizon, silhouetting a
sleek tanker at the head of a long line of ships, for the canal was
still sending its diurnal discharge hurrying after us, the fast
tankers leading the throng, high in the water, and elderly cargo
ships bringing up the rear. Occasionally there came one with a
tall thin funnel, low bridge, and inadequate accommodation,
her straight stem showing that she was probably years older
than *Tzu Hang*, and like her pursuing her slow and stately way,
regardless of the hurrying throng.

On 21 September, a brilliant day and Beryl's birthday,

having had as we supposed a four-mile set to the south, we passed black-banded Daedalus Reef lighthouse, a hundred miles beyond The Brothers. We had a strong wind now, and the twin staysails set as stiff as boards held out by the two big white spinnaker poles. These poles seemed to dominate our immediate surroundings rather than the sails, perhaps because they were newly painted and cleaner. They themselves seemed to provide the motive power, stretched like an albatross's wings, lifting, banking, and gliding, low over the restless waves.

Such movement and brilliance: the sunlit deck, the small white crests, everything leaping and dancing; then suddenly a ship, so solid and immobile that it reminded me of an old Roman fort that I had seen when driving across the Syrian desert, standing squarely amongst the sand dunes on the edge of the Euphrates, where a moment before there had been nothing but emptiness. A ship, not seen approaching, but suddenly there, so still amongst all the rush and welter of our own environment, that it looked like a model placed on a brilliantly painted cloth, and as if the cloth was then slid from under it, carrying us with it, dancing our merry dance, until the ship was left behind.

For the next few days watch followed watch with nothing of special interest. By day our watches are apt to be variable; by night we each keep one three-hour watch and one two. After supper from eight to eleven, from eleven until two, from two to four and from four to six when it is time to think about getting breakfast. The log is a long catalogue of ships passed. 'Tanker to port. Two cargo ships to starboard. Passed *Chelmwood Beacon*. Passed *Anthea* (French). Passed tanker, *Alan and Evelyn* (British).' 'Two porpoises to port,' the log goes on, 'and a small fork-tailed bird, looks like a bee-eater, trying to land in the rigging.' Then we had almost too much excitement.

It was my watch. We had had our evening drink. From the galley came the most delicious smell and the cat's loud voice proclaiming that she wanted her dinner before anyone else. Popa was sitting on the bridgedeck from where he could best watch every detail of the preparation of food. He swayed slowly in time with the ship and sometimes stood up, tucking in his belly to simulate a starved maltreated dog. The moon was not yet up, and I was lying back in the cockpit, watching the masthead draw its slow arc across the stars. I had had a good look round and saw no ships ahead and only one astern. Life seemed very good and dinner couldn't be ready too soon, when suddenly as the boat lifted, I thought that I saw a dark shadow ahead under the port spinnaker boom. I waited till *Tzu Hang* surged forward and lifted her bow again as the wave passed. There was something there. No doubt. Darker than the surrounding darkness and right ahead. It might have been a rock or a castle. I called to Beryl for the glasses and the sudden urgency in my voice made her hand them quickly up. Then I saw clearly that right ahead there was a tanker coming towards us and burning no navigation lights. She was as dark as the tomb and all too close.

Beryl started the engine to assist and I pulled the helm hard up. We swung out of her way with the engine racing and the port spinnaker boom bounding all over the place as the sail thrashed. There was little enough room to spare. On account of the traffic we had never lashed the sheets to the tiller for self-steering and so were able to take avoiding action as soon as I realized its necessity, and this was perhaps all that saved us. As she pounded past we saw that there was a blaze of light aft although none showed from ahead. The ship astern called her up with an angry flickering light to tell her that her lights were not burning.

On 23 September we picked up the radio beacons of Port Sudan and Jiddah, and saw a dhow making across the shipping lane. That night we rushed on over the corrugations of a tinfoil sea lit by a brilliant moon. The wind held fair for the next two days until we were ninety miles from Jebel Tair, when it began to fall light. We made slow progress that night. Two terns followed us calling to each other in the moonlight and trying to settle on the boom gallows, while the cat watched hungrily below. Eventually one settled on the furled mainsail and the portly Siamese cat caught it with an astounding spring from the deck. The other continued to follow us, calling for its dead and partially digested mate. It too settled on the main boom and I caught it and threw it away into the night. It returned and was killed and eaten in its turn by the cat—perhaps the best solution for this harrowing problem.

On 27 September, nine days and 1,010 miles from Newport

Rock we sighted Jebel Tair and from then on used the motor if the wind dropped. Not only did it drop but at times came light ahead. It was desperately hot on the following day. The cat lay panting on the deck with her mouth open and we poured cups of water on her stomach to keep her cool. The dog did not suffer so much as he was prepared to share the more robust relief of an upturned bucket. We hoped to stop between Coin and Pile Islands, but darkness just beat us to the anchorage, so we decided to hold on for Perim.

Beryl and I and the dog spent another blazing morning largely under buckets of salt water, but by 1430 we were at anchor off the quay at Perim, with a fresh breeze blowing to bring us relief. We had used the engine, running it quietly at half-throttle for just under thirty hours, or 120 miles, between Jebel Tair and Perim. If we had anchored and waited for it at Pile Island it would have brought us on only a hot day later.

Perim is a burnt-out place, a low lava-covered island, disfigured by the old roofless houses and empty wharves of the long extinct Perim Coal Company. On the north side there is a lighthouse, extensive sand dunes and an airstrip, on the south side a large horseshoe harbour, well sheltered and with numerous creeks and beaches. All drinking water is distilled at a salt-water distilling plant. The machine was then on its last legs, although new parts were expected, but it still managed to provide all the 286 inhabitants with drinking water. The water was distributed each day in four-gallon cans by camel, and cost the government two shillings a can, said Mr Shubailly. Mr Shubailly is the Government's round and hospitable representative—monarch of all he surveys in Perim.

Mr Shubailly twinkled under a special constable's cap which he wore in his capacity as Harbourmaster, Chief Justice, administrator and doctor, in fact as Her Majesty's only representative on this tiny island, except for two or three Arab policemen, who lived in a small police station on top of the hill above the harbour. He shone with good humour amongst the deserted buildings and barren rocks like the moon in the desert. He took us to his house to drink tea and introduced us to his lovely and slender little wife, relaxing purdah in honour of the occasion. She was overcome by my height and cried, 'Oh, oh, oh,' when she saw me, so that I felt as if I had eaten some of Alice's mushroom and was growing through the ceiling.

Mr Shubailly saw us back to the boat. A cool breeze was blowing. One can never think of Perim without remembering this blessed cool breeze, which, according to Mr Shubailly, always blows. He was going back to his house to discuss his visitors with his friends and to chew the green leaf, which is popular there and on which he told us he had worn out three pairs of Chinese teeth. 'It is not exactly intoxicating,' he told us, 'but it gives us great ideas, and we will talk too much.'

Next day we wandered again about the desolate scene. The houses that had been allowed to keep their roofs, for the timbers of some had been sold to contractors, were still in excellent condition, but it was a depressing place, an ideal location for an 'after-the-bomb' type of film. The resthouse was beautifully situated above the entrance point and still equipped in every detail—an exact replica of a good Indian guesthouse of thirty years ago. There were tin baths and commodes, string beds and crockery all dusted and kept in place by Said, the good servant, an old Arab who had been there for thirty-five years. From time to time there were visitors from Aden, but not often, and the place was dead.

'I see you have electric light,' said Beryl, looking at the carefully dusted electric light bulbs hanging on long twisted wires.

'Not for twenty-five years,' he said, and then with a gesture that took in the big room and conjured up life and gaiety and English voices, and an age of waiting for things that are gone, he said, 'We used to have dancing here.'

We bathed in an old swimming pool, protected by a lava wall from the visits of unwelcome fish, where the water by some trick of the tide or current was fantastically cool. By then the westerly wind was blowing again, fluttering the tattered Union Jack over the police station. Up anchor and quietly out of the horseshoe harbour and the black rocks at Pirie Point. Outside the breeze was not so fresh, and we made slow progress along the Arabian shore, a low hazy coastline, with the narrow sails of dhows, close offshore, standing like lighthouses at intervals along its length.

We decided to anchor for the night behind Ras el Ara, but

it was low and difficult to see. We groped our way in darkness, for the moon rose very late now, and there was not much left to light us when it did. I stood, as always when we approach an anchorage, in front of the starboard shrouds, swinging the lead and chanting the depths in the old-fashioned way. At five fathoms and a sandy bottom I called to Beryl to stop the engine and let the anchor go. *Tzu Hang* rode slowly on towards the shore until I judged that we had enough chain out. I stopped its run on the brake and dropped the pawl on the winch. *Tzu Hang* pulled her chain tight and turned to her anchor. Close behind us in the darkness we could hear men's voices and a dog barked. Popa climbed half over the stern in order to reply. We went below but before we had time to think of a drink or dinner or even the riding light, a fresh onshore breeze hit us. We felt too exposed to wait and see what it would turn into and hurriedly got under way. Up sail then again, and out on a long port tack to clear the reef, then about and parallel to the coast, inshore of the shipping. The breeze died away, and we made only fifteen miles during the night.

At eleven it freshened again from the west-southwest, and soon the steep cliff of Ras Imran was in sight, and in the afternoon, Little Aden. We anchored there after dark in Khor Gadir, lit by an oil flare from the refinery. Next morning we sailed between the ships anchored in the roads and into Aden harbour. I had been there years before in a troopship but could remember nothing of it and had no idea where to go. We hadn't got very far past the breakwater before we were picked up by a pilot boat. A large and masterful Scotsman, who knew exactly where he was going to put us, stepped on board. He turned us round and took us back to the Navy wharf, and we had just got our anchor down, when Commander Ken Alan-Williams, the R.N.O. came up in his launch and hailed us, '*Tzu Hang*,' he called, 'we are going to put you between those two minesweepers over there, one anchor out and stern to the wharf.'

Shortly afterwards he came on board. 'You'll stay with Freda and me?' he asked. 'We have a lunch party so I'll send a car for you at 12.15.'

When we entered Aden harbour that morning we had no idea that we knew anyone here, and had wondered how insupportable life on a yacht would be at this time of the year. In fact we had never met the Alan-Williamses, but someone had asked them to look out for us when we arrived, and this was their interpretation of their request. Freda Alan-Williams took the addition to her lunch party and the invasion of her house in her stride. 'But you are only two,' she said. 'You should see what he brings back sometimes, and anyway I don't have to do the cooking and washing up.' It was soon obvious that she did some very efficient organizing behind the scenes instead. It was all the nicer for being unexpected, and Beryl and I, leaving Popa and Pwe to experience the rigours of life afloat in Aden harbour, settled down to enjoy it.

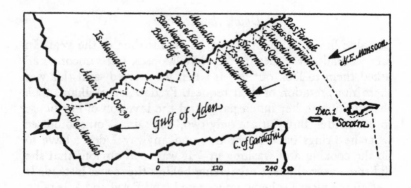

8 *The Hadramaut and the Arabian Coast*

ADEN was sweltering, waiting, as were we, for the 'Change,' when the Northeast Monsoon would bring cooler weather. When it arrived we would have a head wind until we cleared Cape Gardafui, then the monsoon would give us a fair wind down the East African coast. A head wind was better than no wind at all, and we proposed to get off as soon as it had arrived and before it was too firmly established.

Meanwhile we shopped for stores and whatever else we felt that we had to have at duty-free prices. Unlike the shopkeepers at Gibraltar, the Indians at Aden were quite unprepared to bargain or to lower their prices. In fact they did not seem to be particularly interested in whether we bought or not, and I suspect that a shrewd assessment had told them that there was not a great deal of money to be made out of us. Beryl managed to extort a small teak elephant with a broken trunk out of one Parsee for nothing and, as a result of this feat, she values it more than one for which she might, but never would, have paid a large sum.

Wherever we went in Aden it was impossible to escape the voice of Radio Cairo, an unpleasant voice and at a guess one that was talking about imperialists. It came from within the folds of every shuffling Arab's gown, all of whom seemed to be able to afford transistor radios.

The Chief Bosun's Mate came rolling up the quay to see us.

He was a round and glistening man with a pleasant South Country burr. 'I wouldn't mind doing this sort of thing meself,' he said, his weathered blue eye taking in the cabin, 'only the Missus wouldn't stand for it. We've got a nice flat you know, with a fridge and all that.' The sweat ran down his chest and soaked the waistband of his well filled shorts. 'I'd better be getting on with the job,' he said, as he eased himself round the cabin table. 'Proper hot, isn't it? I thought that I'd just see if there was anything the Navy could do for you. A pot of paint, maybe, or a couple of shackles?'

We couldn't think of anything that we wanted. *Tzu Hang*'s terylene ropes were still like new and we had just bought some shackles. We could have done with some spare rope to renew our mooring lines but did not ask for it. Before we left we found a coil on the deck. The Bosun's eye had spotted the necessity.

'Which way will you be going?' he asked.

'To Mukalla and then along the Arabian coast and across to Socotra.'

'You want to look out along that coast for pirates and such like. There was a German, a single-hander, went that way and claimed he was pirated. Lost his radio set and glasses and all. Packed it in after that and came back to Aden.' He mopped his face with some cotton waste and climbed neatly out of the cabin and up the steep ladder to the wharf. 'Let us know if you want anything,' he called down and disappeared towards his stores.

'I wonder if there really are pirates on the coast,' I said to Beryl.

'Oh no,' she said, her hands busy with something as usual. 'They only imagine it. I wonder if we should have taken him up on that offer of paint. There's so little room now.'

I made some enquiries about the German. 'He anchored on the Sultan's oyster-beds,' the R.N.O. told me, 'at Maqdaha and the Sultan's guards took him back to Balhaf. That really broke his heart after all the struggle up the coast against wind and current. He couldn't speak any Arabic and thought that he was being pirated. The Sultan's guards are the only people allowed to carry arms on that bit of the coast, and he was in no danger.'

We heard other tales of a yacht that had been stranded and

stripped within a few hours, but I believe that it had been temporarily abandoned. Even without tales like this to add a bit of spice to the adventure, it is an exciting coast to sail up. Few yachts have done it and then there are strong tides and currents and bad inshore sets. On top of this the *Pilot* is particularly lugubrious. 'A current sets northward into Ghubbat Sailan, at rates from two to four knots,' it says. 'All vessels should be on their guard against it. Several vessels in former times have been wrecked here and plundered by the natives.' Over the page it goes on in the same style: 'The coast between Wadi Mawatin and Wadi Maifa'a is inhabited by tribes of murderous and piratical habits. Care is therefore necessary in any dealings with them.'

Life would be miserably dull if one listened to every foreboding or took heed of every warning, and it is probable that the only danger to property would be if the yacht stranded. Still Beryl and I didn't propose to anchor on the way to Mukalla, unless we saw a particularly interesting place. We carry no arms, as they tend to lead to trouble, and the days of shooting it out are probably over. Anyway the best defence for a solitary couple in a yacht of *Tzu Hang*'s size is the mystery of the way they handle her, good manners and a cheerful face.

Before we left Aden we took *Tzu Hang* round to Ghul Mor bay, on the south side of the peninsula and well sheltered at this time of year. We anchored off the swimming club and swam ashore. We always try to climb the nearest mountain at any port of call and wanted to climb Sham Shan before we left Aden. Next morning we ran the dinghy up on the beach before daylight, just as the headlights of a car came curving to a halt above us. It was Ted Parke, one of Shell's most active representatives, fresh from a Norwegian holiday, with legs and wind in top fettle, come to chase us up the hill. We motored round to Crater and found that the first obstacle was a mound of blanket-wrapped Arabs still asleep on the steps that mark the beginning of the ascent.

There is no difficulty about the climb, although it is best to keep to the correct route, for the whole mountain is little more than a pile of heat-decayed rock rubble, steep enough in places to make a slip dangerous. Our guide shot up the hill. The sun climbed out of the sea and lit the summit and answering fires

seemed to burn within the ground that we trod, but he made
no concession to the heat, nor did he falter when we tried to
force a pause by admiring the view. It is said that if you wish
to return to Aden you must climb Sham Shan before leaving.
When from the top we were able to look down on *Tzu Hang*,
a little splinter lying in the still bay, the climb seemed worth
the risk of a return. On the way down, when our creaky knees
began to protest, we both might have had a change of opinion,
if it had not been for the thought of breakfast at the club when
we got down.

We sailed on 30 October against a light headwind and took a
long tack offshore all night. During the next few days our tacks
offshore were usually at about 130° and our tacks on shore at
10°. Next evening the wind suddenly freshened, and we had
no doubt that this was at last the monsoon. We were soon
plunging in poor visibility towards the shore northeast of Ras
Sailan.

We hadn't had much of this before there was a twang and
a severe jerk on the mast as the luff wire of the sail, commonly
known as 'the old jib', parted. While we were sorting out the
débris and setting the storm jib in its place, we saw what looked
like a motor-fishing-vessel with a small steadying sail boomed
out to starboard, reeling crazily towards us. The ship reeled
and yawed so violently in the following sea that it was impossible to say whether she intended to pass ahead, astern of us,
or straight through us. Soon I became convinced that it was
the last alternative, and began to imagine a wild hashish party
down below, while the ship ran on under her automatic pilot
or under no pilot at all. We were virtually stopped, pitching
slowly ahead into the steep sea under reefed main while we
changed the headsail. I could no longer bear the strain of the
approaching vessel's erratic course and jumped below to start
the engine. On the next yaw it looked as if she was going to
pass close astern of us and we made sure that she did so by
putting *Tzu Hang* ahead. As the small vessel passed us we saw
that the wheelhouse was full of grinning dark faces, and a branch
of waving hands grew suddenly from its entrance. She was
flying the blue ensign of the Aden Protectorate Fisheries
Department and had no idea of the fright that she had given
me as she wallowed and rolled away. I wished her at the bottom

and felt indignant and a little foolish as we turned again to the jib.

We were soon off on the other tack, and tacked regularly through the night, making the longer tacks offshore. Next morning the stiff wind found another weakness and the splice in a short wire pennant to the jib pulled out. We replaced it quickly with a length of chain. 'Tacked offshore. Tacked onshore,' the log reads for entry after entry, and then a note of doubt: 'Seem to have lost a lot of ground. Tacked offshore.' As we turned to close the shore again, we saw the great curve of a dhow's sail bearing down on us. It passed close astern, running at ten knots dead before the wind and its huge sail holding a bellyful, the *Nakhoda* standing high on the poop and the wild crew waving along the hissing rail. We were going to see many dhows, but never one quite like this one, going like wild Arab horses, manes and tails streaming, over the dunes.

Whenever we have been waiting expectantly for some regular wind it has arrived with a bang as if to dispel any doubt of its being really there, and has lasted in the first flush of its strength for three or four days. With the wind comes a balance debit of current like infantry and tanks behind the artillery barrage. It happened now. Here was the Northeast Monsoon at last, bringing cool days to Aden, a two-knot current sweeping down the coast, and a tough struggle for *Tzu Hang*. The wind blew straight down the coast and the current ran with it.

Assuming *Tzu Hang* sails five points off the wind in this sort of sea and sails at an average of five knots, to reach Mukalla 260 miles away she would have to sail, against a two-knot current, about thirteen hundred miles. The current didn't always run at two knots, and *Tzu Hang* did not always sail at five, but to reach Mukalla she sailed eleven hundred miles by log in eleven days. By day sailing close inshore, we usually made good progress, but we were watching our tacks and fighting every inch of the way. By night, particularly when standing on the offshore tacks, we left the helm and read below, with regular looks to see that there were no ships approaching. However much we would like to believe that *Tzu Hang* sails herself best unattended, she is never quite so close on the wind as with a hand at the helm, and so we often found, on closing the coast, that we had made no progress during the night. We could have found an easier current in mid-channel, but who would forfeit an exciting new shore when it is there to follow?

The worst of the struggle was to Balihaf, whose bay we entered one afternoon and again to our dismay on the following morning. Sikha Island also appeared in front of us on two successive days, white with guano, but once we passed it we made good progress, close inshore, partially protected from the current by Ras Maqdahar, and tacking between that Cape and Baraqa Island, close offshore. This was wonderful and exciting sailing. Great jagged cliffs, a weird variety of colour from black to red and the green of verdigris on copper; an indigo blue sea, for the rain and cloud had temporarily disappeared, and with fish leaping everywhere. These waters for the fisherman are like Africa for the big-game hunter fifty years ago—almost untouched.

We tacked close in to Ras el Kalb, always seeking but never finding a counter-current close inshore. As we approached the cape the water began to shoal quickly. 'Isn't it getting rather shallow?' asked Beryl, and at the same time I realized that we were being carried sideways towards the shore almost as fast as we were sailing. There was no need to sound. The water was so clear that we could see the bottom, and it was coming up fast. We went about without setting up the weather backstay, and for a moment *Tzu Hang* just held her own against the set. Then she began to draw clear.

'What a hell of a set!' I said to Beryl. 'Look at those bastards.'

The tide was swirling round the headland and rushing in towards the shore, and over the sand dunes came eager leaping black figures. To us, indoctrinated by the gloomy *Pilot*, they looked ready to draw their knives, eviscerate us, and loot *Tzu Hang*, should she have stranded, but probably they were just curious and would have offered us the traditional Bedouin hospitality. Whichever opportunity they regretted they were soon standing disconsolately on the wet sand while *Tzu Hang* made a rapid offing.

Once safely round Ras el Kalb, the current eased and the angle of the shore enabled us to make longer tacks. *Tzu Hang* seemed to leap forward and we advanced twenty miles in ten instead of twenty-four hours, our average for the past ten days. We were sailing now along a castellated coast lit by a moon

once more approaching full, so that its dark rocky ridges, with
white sand swept up from shore to shoulder lying between,
showed with pale colours over the glinting sea. *Tzu Hang* slid
close in under them and then turned away. She tacked for the
last time off Ras el Husa el Hamra, a name that seemed to echo
the hiss and hammer of the waves upon its black rocks. Daylight
next morning found us round Bundar Burun and off a great
sweep of level shore, misty with blown spray from its breakers,
which led to the white city of Mukalla, its houses standing
closely grouped and tall, and looking from the distance almost
as sophisticated as New York.

We sailed into the harbour and anchored amongst the dhows.
The town after all was not so sophisticated. The tall houses
were made of mud and only some of them whitewashed. They
huddled under the protection of watch towers on the ridge
behind. The streets were narrow and the few cars and lorries
hooted their way through death-defying small boys, old men,
shrouded women and numbers of donkeys and slow stepping
camels. Immediately in front of us at a rickety wharf two
dhows were unloading. Here all was bustle and excitement
within the walled enclosure of the customs area. The Arab
seamen bent their backs to lift and haul, singing an age-old
chanty as they swung the cargo by hand operated derrick and
tackle to the shore. Almost before we had our anchor down a
dugout canoe passed us, rowed by four tattered oarsmen. In the
stern sheets stood the *nakhoda* of one of the dhows at anchor,
bearded and erect, arms folded over white robes, while the
oarsmen chanted in answer to a single voice as they struck
together, 'God and the Prophet.'

Beryl and I felt like runners relaxing on the warm grass at
the finish of a race. It had been a much harder trip than the
Red Sea passage. We sat listening to the strange cries and
chanties all around us. There was not a steamer or a motor
ship in sight. The advance guard of an army of large and
sticky flies came winging in and the dog started snapping his
teeth at them.

I went ashore, threading my way through the piles of cargo
that had just been unloaded. Not, as I almost expected,
sandalwood and ivory or apes and peacocks, but fuel oil, flour,
corrugated iron sheets and case after case of tomato paste. At

the customs office I was hemmed in by a curious throng as I tried to explain what we were, when I heard an English voice behind me and turned round to see with relief a tall officer in the uniform of the Bedouin Legion. He was wearing a red checked headcloth and black agal, the camel hobble worn round it, swinging a short leather-covered stick and looking very elegant, English, and at home in these exotic surroundings.

'Hello,' he said. 'We've been expecting you for days. The Navy told us you were on your way. The Resident Adviser hopes that you will be able to come to dinner tonight.'

We dined that night in a huge white house under a high arched roof. Mr Watts, the Resident Adviser, drove down to the wharf where we found him waiting for us amongst a milling crowd, a very democratic and hospitable action for such a busy and important man. In spite of his portly designation, he was the most lively and entertaining host. The sort of host that inspires his guests to talk and to feel witty and amusing—and to think afterwards that they would have done better to talk less and to listen to him instead. We heard afterwards that he was one of the great Arabists, with an immense knowledge of the tribes of Southern Arabia.

During a pause in what was, because of our enjoyment, a rather noisy dinner, he asked Beryl if she knew what British characteristic the Arabs found most striking.

'The way they treat their women?' she guessed.

'No,' he replied. 'Eating with their mouths shut and their noisy and immoderate laughter.'

After dinner we went up on to the flat roof of the house and watched an old film of *South Pacific*. Behind us on the steep hill-side, beneath the watch-towers that had once protected them from Bedouin raiders, a large proportion of the inhabitants of Mukalla sat, white-spotting the stony slope, and marvelled at Mary Martin.

We spent two weeks at Mukalla so that we could both fly in turn up to the Hadramaut, where Jim Ellis, the Resident Officer found time to drive us in his Land-Rover to see something of the huge cliff-contained wadi and its perpendicular walled cities made of mud, with houses running up to ten stories or more, their walls stained by the 'long drop' latrines and streets like crevasses below. The walls were mud-coloured, a rich strong brown, but sometimes a Sultan's palace or a rich merchant's house was whitewashed all over, so that it looked like a huge wedding cake. The markets were bright with movement and colour, the streets dark-shadowed, barred by slashes of brilliant light, where the sun struck between buildings and illuminated momentarily the passing scenes from the life of the town. It shone on chattering women, shrouded in red or sky blue, black veiled and wearing a conical witches hat on their heads, a foot and a half high; it shone on a lithe young Arab, barefoot and arrogant, leading a camel whose load of forage brushed either wall; on a small boy with a brilliant grey speckled and red-combed cock under his arm and a troop of donkeys jostling and biting each other in front of a dusty hooting truck.

Beyond the walls of the town the great valley shimmered away into the distance between its purple cliffs. The dusty track which we followed cut across its curves, passing here and there a watch-tower or fort, here and there a patch of irrigated cultviation or a green row of casvarinas. Above the valley the desert's bony and creased back stretched unseen to the distance, northwards to the Empty Quarter and southwards to the sea, but as removed and distant from the valley-dwellers as the sea is from the land, marked here and there by an erratically etched yellow line among the dark stones where camel or wheel tracks followed some blistering and lonely road to the coast.

The Hadramaut comes within the Aden Protectorate, as did all the coast along which we sailed and is in administered territory, but beyond Musaina'a, roughly a hundred miles further up the coast—the Mahrar Sultanate which includes Socotra, is unadministered. Administered Territory means that somewhere within thousands of square miles there is a Resident British Officer, who guides or jockeys Sultan or Sheikh into the narrow paths that lead to law and order. Gradually blood feuds have been eradicated and the watch-towers and fortresses that used to cover the valley, so that cultivation might be carried out under their protection, are falling down. Diesel water-pumps have been brought in, and a new agriculture is growing, unhindered by the crack of a rifle bullet. All accomplished by these solitary Englishmen, sometimes at the cost of their lives, and backed by little more than a corporal's guard of Bedouin or Arab police.

The actual harbour at Mukalla is noisy and crowded, so we moved round to the bay east of the city, sheltered in this monsoon by Ras Mukalla. Everything was splendid here until the shark-fishing dhows arrived. They came fully loaded with putrescent shark which they offloaded to dry on the shore, where the flesh was later auctioned. Although the chief characteristic of the Aden Protectorate, not mentioned in the *Pilot*, is the variety and horror of its smells, from 'long drop' latrine to rotting sardine, the shark-boats lead them all. We could smell them a mile away and when they anchored to windward flies poured on board. Unfortunately they always anchored to windward as they went closer in to the protecting shore than we could do, but after the auction they left again on their forays, giving us once more by day the fresh monsoon and by night the clean desert air.

We left Mukalla with David Eals, the Bedouin Legion officer who had met us at the customs, in a combined operation. Two Land-Rovers of the Bedouin Legion drove along the coast, while their captain, towing a shark line, pursued a parallel course by sea. We were going to land him at various points so that he might make an official call on a local Sheikh or Headman or visit one of his posts. When we tried to leave we found that the chain was wrapped round a rock, but the water was so clear at four fathoms that we could see from the deck how to unravel it. With the genoa drawing we slipped away very quickly, passing close to the rocks on Ras Mukalla, to allow David's colonel to get some film of *Tzu Hang* under sail.

As soon as we were round the point we could see the two Land-Rovers speeding like beetles up the coast, a long strip of sand backed by low scrub-covered dunes, towards Ryan, the airport, twelve miles or so away. We had a perfect day with a light headwind, and beat slowly all day up the coast, heading for Esh Shihr, twenty-eight miles away, which used to be the capital of the Qaiti State still known as the State of Shihr and Mukalla. We could still see the Ryan lights astern at ten o'clock that night, and, as by now the wind had dropped completely, we motored in to the anchorage. The moon lit the white dunes, and we could see the outline of the hill behind the city and a flashing light which David assured us was his

men guiding us in to the anchorage. It turned out to be the
light on the stern of an anchored dhow, and that his soldiers,
as all good soldiers should do when their captain is at sea, had
already turned in. They came out next morning to take us
ashore in a large *houri*, or local fish-boat. In the bay many boats
were out laying nets round shoals of sardines. As soon as the
ends of the net were drawn together, one of the fishermen dived
in and drew tight the draw rope at the bottom of the net underwater, making a purse of it. The net was then hauled into the boat.

Ashore there were great masses of sardines, spread like a
carpet to dry in the sun. Pariah dogs, glutted with drying
fish, lounged about on the sand, and camels stalked past
superciliously, looking as if they would never deign to touch
such offal, although they were fed sardines in their forage. The
Arabs also pile their sardines to rot in the sun, so that the oil
from the decomposing fish runs down a little channel in the sand
into a small vessel, buried for its collection. This is another
source of the horrific stenches that are met with on this coast.

The coast continues low and sandy for several miles. We
sailed later that morning, beating slowly along the shore and
meeting many small shark-fishing dhows, laying or hauling
their short nets, which they leave inadequately buoyed so that
we had to be constantly on the look-out for them. Some of these
dhows we overtook as if they were standing still, for they are not
great goers to windward. We passed a ruined village and then
the enticing white village of Hami, set amongst date palms and
bananas, where there are reputed to be hot baths. Beyond Hami
the coast becomes high and cliffy. As we sailed I saw a huge
spotted shape beneath us, a whale shark, but I believe that
you could see almost any marine monster if you stayed long in
those waters. At anchor once a shoal of bonito came flying
round the boat, more in the air than in the water so that we
could sense their panic and hard on their tails, like the hounds
of heaven with relentless tread, came a school of porpoises. I do
not know for how long the porpoises had been in pursuit, but
they disappeared round the point behind which we were
sheltering running close together—a pocket handkerchief
would have covered them—and they were running to view.
David had a success on this day and landed a king-mackerel
as he called it, and thereafter retired from the fishing business.

We could see Ras Sherma before dark, a long headland with spits of sand running out to rocky outcrops and a pinnacled islet close off its point. There appeared to be a splendid anchorage in a small sandy bay, but it was dark long before we got there, so that we anchored far out, after homing once more on the flashing lights of the soldiers, and again finding that it was the light of a dhow at anchor some way off the beach. After Mukalla, Ras Sherma is the best anchorage along the coast in the Northeast Monsoon, but we did not have time to explore it.

Our next stop was at Ras Qusaiyir twenty-one miles further along the coast. We got off in good time, and were there by lunchtime. Qusaiyir is only partly protected by a reef, and we anchored close inside two big dhows in very uncomfortable water, but there was a sheltered beach for boats, where we could land and pull up the dinghy.

The dhows were unloading from a platform rigged on their sides on to slender dugout canoes who brought their toppling load to the same little beach, where it was quickly unloaded and stacked on the shore. The stores included, in this strictly Mohammedan setting, a case of beer. We drove up to the village in one of the Bedouin Legion trucks. There was a small bay on the east side of the point, protected by a reef, where the fishermen brought their boats. We watched one old man of the sea run his dugout under sail right up on the beach. He was very dark, his mouth full of a mass of yellow tusks. There were no fish in his canoe, and he was obviously in a very bad temper as he explained to David that he had lost the biggest fish ever known in that sea and that it had taken half his line too. In the village itself there were all kinds of strange sights to be seen through a fog of flies. Blue Bedouin, dyed blue from the indigo which stained their blankets, with huge silver-handled daggers stuck in the roll of cloth that they wore about their waists. An old man and a young one similarly dressed and dyed, walking hand in hand past the shops in the one street. We saw a small girl also, dressed in scarlet, her face stained with yellow ochre and her hair twisted into hundreds of tiny plaits.

The two-masted dhow near us had a glass-windowed cabin aft and a wooden snout sticking up at forty-five degrees from the stemhead, on which was a metal post to which a huge lantern was fixed. She looked like some old high-walled galleon

beside us. We spent an uncomfortable night, as we were anchored in rock and sand and the chain kept snatching and
grumbling all night. We rigged a spring of strong shock cord
to a bight in the chain and the jar from the snatching stopped
immediately.

We were off again at five-thirty, but not so early as one of the
shark-fishers who was already under sail. We gave the reef a
wide berth and went out on a good tack, but found when we
came back that we had just succeded in clearing the cape
while the shark-fisher was already two miles up the coast.
Learning from him and keeping well inshore, we soon overtook
him and then could see the fort at Musaina'a coming up over
the horizon like the white bridge of a ship. It stands on a small
hill on a point. The coast here is a low sloping plain backed by
a steep rock wall. A few miles behind the fort there is a rift in
the wall, and it looks as if a huge mass of molten lava once
burst through the wall and spread a fan of black rocks across
the plain. There are two or three small crater cones standing
on the plain.

We anchored in an open roadstead and were soon visited
by the local Rais and a gang of ruffianly-looking fellows in a
very small *houri*. We gave them tea on deck, fearing that they
might leave other visitors if they went below and summoned a
larger boat by firing a Very pistol, a pre-arranged signal with
the shore party, whose trucks we could now see below the square,
whitewashed fort.

We rowed in with the tape recorder on Beryl's lap, while our
oarsmen sang their chanties, but it was too wet to risk a record-
ing. At times during my life I have met some person so like
another, although colour, creed, and station may have been
quite different, that I have thought part of the same spirit
must have been reincarnated in both. Now I was suddenly
aware that Peter Pye of *Moonraker* was sitting in front of me.
As he heaved on his oar with such enthusiasm that he pulled
himself out of his seat, his eyes shone with the same delight, his
smile was as full of enjoyment as I have seen Peter's in similar
circumstances. The face and the figure were the same although
there was a discrepancy in colour and dress.

'The boat runs sweetly,' called the singer at the bow.

'God and the Prophet,' roared Peter.

'Through the white water,' sang the singer.

'God and the Prophet,' Peter bellowed, and I saw him singing with our American friends at the piano, on the island in Canada where *Moonraker* had come to visit us. He was undoubtedly here again.

The village at Musaina'a consists only of a few nondescript houses and the usual piles of drying sardines and bloated pariah dogs, but the fort is a delightful outpost, square, loop-holed and parapeted, looking across a dry wadi bed and over the austere plain. There was a platoon of the Bedouin Legion here, the main object of our visit.

The Bedouin soldiers were all small men, running here and there with great enthusiasm and activity. They were dressed in khaki frocks with red checked headcloths and black agal, crossed bandoliers stuffed full of ammunition, bare legs and bare feet. They wore their black crinkled hair bobbed. At sunset they 'stood to,' running eagerly to their appointed positions behind rock or wall, ready to repel an attack, just as the Indian soldiers used to do, morning and evening, on many a frontier post in India.

After the 'stand to' we all sat down on blankets outside the fort while the cooks started the preparations for a vast meal. Everyone was completely unselfconscious and delighted at the idea of a party. Beryl got out her tape recorder. There was some discussion as to how to begin and then two young soldiers started with the age-old dialogue between the stupid desert Arab and the smart town Arab when they meet on the road, but in which the desert Arab no doubt comes off best in the end. Their audience and they themselves rocked with laughter at the traditional sallies, but when we played it back they sat breathless, leaning forward, their dark eyes sparkling with excitement, a wonderful picture of men listening to the sound of their own voices. We went on to songs, to poetry, to a long chant punctuated by war cries, and back to dialogue. One of their songs was about the yacht that they had looted and of the Resident Adviser arriving to scold them. They sang this with much amusement. They would have gone on for ever if the cooks had not arrived with mounds of mutton and rice, served in flat baskets, which kept everyone silent until it was time to return to the ship. We were sorry to say goodbye to David, as he had now reached the end of the Administered Territory and proposed to return with his trucks.

It seemed that we had just got to sleep when we were awoken by a hissing rush of wind in the rigging and we felt *Tzu Hang*, who had been lying with a slack chain, turn and set off as if she was going to sea. Almost immediately she swung to her anchor again. We scrambled up on deck and let the chain go rattling out of the hawsehole until it seemed to be stretched almost parallel to the water. At the same time we saw that the *houri* that had brought us out was rowing out again to the dhow that was lying near us with the same intention. This time there was no singing. Both ships lay straining at their anchors, but the wind was offshore and the holding ground was good, and we turned in again, thinking gloomily of all the chain that would have to be recovered in the morning.

We were up early with the wind still blowing freshly offshore and set to work at the solemn task of getting our anchor in. With frequent pauses to 'see how she's lying,' to hoist the topping lift, to get up the main, to give the winch a bit of oil, and any other excuse that we could think of, we finally broke the anchor out. The shaking main set suddenly smooth and stiff and *Tzu Hang* forged ahead while I brought up the last few fathoms. I hooked the boathook into the 65 lb C.Q.R. and hauled it in board, then jumped for the jib while Beryl tackled the mizzen. In a very short time we were all set and secured and on our way. *Tzu Hang* heeled, and the first splash of water hit the foredeck while we looked back at the square fort.

A solitary figure stood on the beach, a matchstick against the vast empty background of sand, black rock and hill, waving his Arab headcloth. It may be that he, seeing us go, would have liked to have voyaged further, and I, seeing a young soldier standing in those desert surroundings with a good job to do, wished that I was still young and still a soldier in his place. We waved back, and then leaving him to his desert, turned back to our sea. We were bound for Socotra.

'Being exposed to both monsoons, and having no harbours in which vessels can at all times anchor, coupled with the unfavourable character that the natives have hitherto borne, it is but little visited.' That is what the *Pilot* said in its pretentious Admiralty prose.

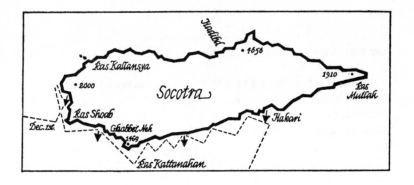

9 *Socotra*

I t is hard to find places that are seldom visited these days and Socotra is certainly one of them, but unfortunately it is not so seldom visited as we would like to imply. During the war I believe that there was a small anti-submarine Coastal Command R.A.F. Station there, and it is now occasionally visited by Service or Government Officers with the aid of a Royal Navy minesweeper and a prayer for a calm day so that a boat landing can be effected. There also has been a University expedition there in recent years although I do not know what they were studying. There are no Europeans on the island, but there was a small radio station at Hadibo manned by Arab operators. We were lucky to meet the Wazir at Mukalla, just arrived by dhow from Hadibo and he gave us a letter to the Sultan, so we were well-armed. *Tzu Hang* was probably the first yacht to visit the island and it is still one of the most isolated places, between fifty north and fifty south, to be found from the sea. The difficulty is, as the *Pilot* says, that it is exposed to both monsoons and landing is more often than not impracticable.

The strong offshore wind, called the 'Delat' which blew us out of the anchorage at Musaina'a, behaved exactly as described in the *Pilot* and died at midday. Our hopes for a great sail in calm water died with it. Back came the first light breaths of the Northeast Monsoon, and we started to tack slowly out across

the shipping lane. By dark we were becalmed but well clear of
the two great traffic streams that head for the Persian Gulf and
the Indian Ocean.

We beat slowly on and off shore all next day. On 28 October,
off Ras Shurwain, we found a better wind and laid a course for
Socotra, but found also a strong west-going current and made
little progress in that direction. At last on the following day,
the monsoon came back in all its blustering strength, sending
us close-hauled and well reefed down leaping like a porpoise
into the short grey seas.

Popa, looking over the cockpit coaming, judged that the trip
to the foremast was altogether too wet and dangerous and
decided to wait for better weather until he attempted it. As he
turned away he had the resigned look of a man who finds the
lavatory occupied after a long trip down the swaying railway
corridor. I turned *Tzu Hang* down wind and told Popa to get
on with it. He jumped carefully over the cockpit coaming, took
a quick look to weather, and ran forward keeping as close inboard as possible, till he reached the mainmast, where he
balanced himself on three legs, an urgent anxious look on his
intelligent face.

'What are you doing?' called Beryl from below, as she felt
the change in motion.

'Running off for Popa,' I replied, and then,' Come on Popa,
for heaven's sake, man, it'll take us hours to win this back.'
Popa looked as if he was trying to tell me that he was doing his
best and soon came scuttling back, relieved and apologetic, to
ask if he might go below. In his old age he didn't like to tackle
the ladder when it was rough.

On 1 December, under storm-jib, reefed main, and mizzen,
with low clouds dragging their ragged hems in the sea, *Tzu
Hang* was throwing the water away from her bow as she approached Socotra. Visibility was down to a mile or so, and I
was at the chart-table trying to figure out our most likely
position from dead reckoning and thinking that this was more
like the weather that I should have expected with the Southwest Monsoon, when Beryl at the tiller called to me that the
sky was clearing, and we might soon get a sight. A moment
later a fleeting and watery sun appeared. I passed her up her
sextant, took the time for her and worked out the sight.

'According to this,' I said, climbing the ladder to look forward, 'we ought to be just about running into Juzirat Sulanya.' And there indeed was Juzirat Sulanya a mile ahead and just showing through the greyness, dark rocks capped with guano, over the white-capped sea and backed by the grey sky with its sullen weeping clouds. There was no sign of Socotra only a few miles beyond.

From the position of the rocks that we were now passing it looked as if we could weather Ras Shoab, the most easterly point, and sail into Ghubbet Shoab where we could wait until the weather moderated and gave us a chance to sail round to Kallansiya to deliver the note for the Sultan. It was obvious that we would not be able to sail to Hadibo, or rather to land there, as the beach was fully exposed to the Northeast Monsoon.

On such a grey day as this I have often looked across the sea, knowing quite well that there, only a few miles away but as yet invisible, is land. Often as I have looked, I have seen for a moment just the faintest variation in colour or texture, showing as a hairline crack in the dull porcelain bowl of the sky. I have looked away and looked back again to find it gone, only to discover that it was the ship that had swung, and to see once more the same shaped crack a little more amidships or a little nearer the bow, until doubt is turned to certainty and the crack revealed as the edge of an island, cliff or hill.

It was the same today. We sat in our yellow oilskins, for it was cool enough to wear them in this weather, and watched the hard edge of a dark rain cloud take on more definite shape until we could see that it was Ras Shoab. The dead greyness began to give way to colour and soon we could see, like a row of white fangs, the breakers on the rocks at its foot, and beyond the rocks a single curving brush stroke of white sand, disappearing once more but marking the southern shore of Ghabbet Shoab. There, plucked out of what had been half an hour before only the restless and close bounded sea, was our anchorage.

Although the sun did not appear again that day, at least the sky became brighter, so that we could see something of the country that we were approaching. Ras Shoab was now close on the starboard bow and, although we were pointing high enough to make our anchorage well up the bay, a strong current was setting us towards it, and we soon had to tack to keep clear. Ras Shoab was the bluff termination of a long ridge of jagged grey rock, identifiable if we had been in doubt by two tall stones like asses' ears that sprouted from the ridge a mile inland. Between this ridge and the great cliffs and hinterland of Ras Baduwa to the north, there was a wide valley containing one or two small hills, which sloped down to the curving white beach of Ghabbet Shoab.

The whole country behind looked wild and barren, the mountainsides brown and red, with sparse scrub scattered about the rocks, the ridges grey and jagged, a waste of desolate stone. Only at one point behind the beach, where there was a mangrove swamp, was there any sign of green. Nowhere was there a habitation, or cultivation, or any trace of a domestic animal to be seen. Nothing could have been more satisfying for those who like to seek out deserted places. Only the sea was full of life, and great stout porpoises came rolling out to greet us, too indolent to do more than just break the surface of the water as they breathed. Popa pattered from one side of the deck to the other, barking furiously, and his voice came echoing faintly from the cliffs in reply.

In order to try and find as much shelter as possible from the northeast wind, we went far up the bay, anchoring about a mile from the northern end of the beach, and close in shore. We let out many fathoms of chain and took *Tzu Hang* hard astern to pull the anchor home. A big swell was swinging in from round Ras Baduwa, and furious blasts from the high cliffs south of it came volleying down at us, sending *Tzu Hang* reeling and staggering at the end of her chain. We rigged the shock cord spring on the chain to ease her and fortunately the holding ground was good. That evening thousands of cormorants came flying low over the sea so numerous that they looked like a vast black net being dragged across its surface. They were making for the cliffs of Ras Baduwa where row after serried row perched on shelf after shelf for the night.

Next morning the wind and swell were as bad as ever and there was no chance of getting a boat ashore. We were quite happy to remain in these wild surroundings and contented to spend a day doing nothing catching up on sleep. Soon after daylight the shelves of cormorants exploded from the face of the cliff, like shell bursts in a bombardment, as they left for their fishing grounds. After their going the whole great sweep of the beach and the hills behind were as empty as when we arrived, until at the farthest end of the beach a small black figure appeared, one of the natives of 'unfavourable character' making his way towards us. If we had landed on Mars and this had been our first sight of a Martian, we could not have been more interested. He grew slowly from pinpoint to match-head size, plodding wearily along the beach, until we could make out that he was a man wearing only a blanket. Presently he lay down.

By the time that we had finished breakfast he was on his feet again, dragging wearily down the beach until he was opposite the ship, where he lay down once more and rested, first on one elbow and then on the other, but without showing any sign of interest in the yacht just opposite him. After half an hour he got up again and walked on until he finally disappeared in the vicinity of the mangrove swamp. This was the only sign of human habitation that we saw during our three days in Ghabbet Shoab, while we waited for the weather to abate.

Soon after his disappearance the cormorants began to come in from the sea. They appeared swimming behind the breakers as they ran up on the beach, struggling against the backwash until they got a foothold, when they waddled quickly out of range of the waves. They formed up in regiments and brigades along the beach, standing in ranks, facing the wind, with their wings held out to dry. As the gusts hit them a quiver ran through the black-coated army and they took four or five steps backwards, gradually withdrawing along the shore before the onslaught of the wind. As they withdrew they passed a party of indignant black-backed gulls, standing on the wet sand at the edge of the ripples. From time to time by sections and platoons, without taking wing, the cormorants dived once more into the breakers, until after an hour or two only the gulls with their wind-ruffled feathers were left standing at the water's edge.

The following day we thought that the wind was down a little and decided to sail round Ras Baduwa to the north. We were beating again, and, once round the cape, we found that the wind had freshened considerably and the sea was so rough that there was little chance of finding an anchorage. We could see the hills beyond Kallansiya sticking out into the sea like a row of stacks and haycocks, but not far enough out to give any shelter in this wind, so we turned and sped back to Ras Shoab. Waves were breaking over underwater rocks some distance off the point, and we gave it a good berth, finding as we cleared the cape that the wind was blowing down this side of the island, too, but that the sea was calm. We tacked inshore.

Round Ras Shoab the hills deeply trenched by gullies ran down to low eroded cliffs. A small encampment was there. A few 45-gallon drums, some tarpaulins covering what we supposed were stores, a few ramshackle shelters and two or three men moving about. They looked like shipwrecked mariners, and we could not imagine what else they were in such a place, but they made no signal as we stood in towards them. We were making for Ghabbet Neh further up the coast and carried our investigation no further. At Ghabbet Neh the Southwest Monsoon had piled the sand in dunes along the shore and at one point into a high sandhill running up the mountain slopes, which can be seen from some distance away. Between the dunes and the foot of the mountains, before reaching the big sandhill, there is a narrow strip of salt marsh and mangrove swamp.

We could see some *houris* drawn up on the beach as we came to anchor. We soon had the dinghy in and rowed towards them, while some raggedy men appeared from behind the dunes and came down to meet us. Popa was standing like Captain Cook in the bow and as it was soon obvious that we were likely to take a spill in the surf, Beryl and I went overboard in our clothes outside the breakers and guided the dinghy in swimming on each side. As we scrambled to our feet they came into the water and helped us run the dinghy out of reach of the waves. Popa jumped ashore dryfoot, leaving the men in some doubt as to who was the master and who were the servants, a question that we sometimes ask ourselves.

The men were not of Socotra but from Zanzibar. They had come up from Zanzibar on the Southwest Monsoon and had been marooned on the coast with their *houris* for the fishing. This explained the other encampment that we had seen. Just behind their camp, under the shelter of the dunes, the fishermen were mending their nets and drying their catch—mostly shark and a species of tunny and a longer thinner fish whose name I did not know.

We took the delighted Popa for a run on the dunes where he scuttled about and buried his head in the sand. In the fisherman's camp he behaved in an irresponsible and extrovert manner to our embarrassment and their distress. They were friendly people of varied colour and race, but apart from 'Zanzibar' we had hardly a word in common.

Next day we set off again, beating slowly in a light wind up the south coast. We rounded Ras Kattanahan, which drops sheer to the sea, fourteen thousand feet of cliff as stark and impressive as Foula. From then on the high wall of the limestone plateau recedes, leaving a coastal plain between it and the sea. Here the sea is edged by low cliffs about twenty feet high, made of brown weathered rock, loopholed and spiked. We anchored less than a cable from the shore where some camels were grazing.

The existing chart of Sokotra, as it was spelt in the days when it was made in 1835, was drawn by Lieutenants Haines and Wellstead of the Indian Navy and has not been amended since. The path of their traverse and all their survey points are marked on the chart, together with notes as to the nature of the country. 'Date trees here with a stream of very fine water' in one place, and in another, 'No water attainable here other than in the hollows of the rocks.' It reads like some old treasure chart out of the past. Opposite the coast where we were now anchored they had written, 'Scattered villagers, some living in huts and others in excavations in the mountains.' We could see nothing of the scattered villagers, and only the heads of their camels, as we were close inshore and they did not come to the edge of the cliff. There was no landing place. The chain grumbled and growled all night amongst rocks and coral and we were glad, when it came up without a hitch in the morning.

We set off early and soon had a fresh wind, reasonably calm water, and a brilliant day. It was our last day to windward. The great limestone wall now ran parallel to the shore and about two miles back. Between it and the sea the stony plain was covered with the sort of scrub bushes that camels seem to love, chomping on dusty thorns as if they were plums. Amongst them occasional large boulders that had fallen and rolled from the cliff face stood like houses or ruins. Here and there the

light-coloured trunk of a palm tree looked like an artificial
beacon against the drab background. We could see one or two
rifts in the limestone wall, where passes led through to the north
coast, through which we could have walked to Hadibo if we
had had a third hand to leave with the ship. Further up the
coast we could make out the green of one or two plantations
of date palms, the only green in the whole landscape and
beyond them the pinnacle of Ras Mutlah, the western end of
the island.

To seaward we could see the single curved sail of a dhow,
and anchored within Hakari Bay, a shallow kidney-shaped bay
towards which we were now making, the black hull and forward
raking mast of another dhow. We tacked right in alongside,
and, as we went about, they broke out their anchor and got up
their sail as if to make a race of it. They too were going to
windward but could not point as high as *Tzu Hang*, and we left
them far behind. If it had been downwind it would have been
another story, for we could never touch a dhow downwind.

We went on and into the eastern half of the bay, anchoring
close offshore. Half a mile away we could see Hakari village,
a small group of conical huts on the edge of one of the date
plantations. Two figures appeared on the beach, each with a
blanket over their shoulders and little else, and their legs looked
long and skinny beneath it. They beckoned to us with the
overhand signal of the East, but it was too late to go in and I
summoned a word of Arabic out of my past and shouted
'*Bokra*,' at which they redoubled their signals and waved their
blankets. When darkness fell they were still sitting huddled
together on the beach with their blankets over their heads.

When I looked out next morning they were there again,
almost as if they had never left. Again we swam through the
surf with Popa in the bow of the dinghy between us, and a
packet of tea and the Wazir's letter to the Sultan in a plastic
bag on the seat. The watchers turned out to be two Arab boys
of about fifteen, with a yellowish tint to their brown skin, thin
cheeks and the tired eyes that mark chronic malaria. They came
forward, knees bent and stooping shyly to shake our hands. We
made them understand that we would like to go to the village,
and we set off immediately across low swampy ground that
buzzed with mosquitoes, towards the huts on the ridge behind.

The huts of the village, conical in shape, were roofed with the leaves of date palms. The top of the hut was about fourteen feet high, the roof coming down to low walls. On the top of each hut sat an Egyptian Vulture, white, yellow-headed and black-tailed, an excessively untidy bird. There were several huts in the village, the majority in disrepair like the weathercock vultures. Our arrival was expected or even feared, for all the inhabitants were huddled in one hut, and it was obvious that we too had an 'unfavourable' reputation. This hut, like all the others, had a low circular wall of about three feet, and in the top foot, under the eve of the roof, was a lattice-work all-round window. Through this window a number of round brown eyes, set in whiskered or wrinkled faces, stared at us, so that I felt as if I was looking into a beehive. We said '*Salaam Aleikum*,' and there was a relieved buzz from within as the faces nodded and moved in the dark behind the lattice.

One of the boys, who in spite of his malaria behaved as if he was a leader, strode into the hut with the assurance of one who had already faced the monsters and come to no harm, and shortly afterwards an old consumptive man came out and spread a mat on which we sat down. One by one the others came out, two men and three women. We nodded and smiled and reached some sort of an understanding. The three women were dressed in tattered black. They were dirty and weather-beaten, but had fine courageous faces and a masterful manner. It looked as if they might have wielded the stick to such a tune that the able-bodied men had fled, leaving only the sick to their administrations and ultimately to that of the attendant vultures. The old man was continously afflicted by his cough, the youngest could hardly see because of the thick discharge from his eyes, and the third was lame and malarial, complaining that he had been left here seven years before by a dhow from Hami, and had never been able to get back again for the lack of a dhow returning.

The young man with the discharging eyes was sent off and returned with a mess of dates in an enamel pot, into which we all dipped our fingers, I with reluctance, but Beryl with an enthusiasm only equalled by that of the two boys. As soon as the dates were finished we presented our packet of tea. At first it seemed as if they did not know what it was, but perhaps the

oldest crone had heard of it for she opened the packet, took a
pinch, and smelled it. 'Do you boil it,' she asked, and Beryl who
somehow understood her nodded vigorously.

'Come with me,' said the Bedouin woman. Beryl got up,
stooped under the low roof, and disappeared into the dark hut,
followed by the other women like crows behind the shining
plough. For Beryl this was the very spice of travel, and the
aura of her enthusiasm spread to the fusty women like a dose of
Benzedrine, but I am no such traveller. By the time that they
returned, bringing a strange brew that I knew I should have to
drink as if I liked it, I was beginning to suffer from an incipient
trachoma, the first twinges of dysentery, and I was being
bothered, like Popa, by camel-flies.

We wondered what we could do for them in return for taking
the Wazir's letter to Hadibo. We had decided to leave from
here for Lamu on the East African coast and since we couldn't
leave the boat for long enough to take it ourselves, we had
arranged with the boy to deliver it for ten shillings. Although
frail by our standards and malarial, he obviously thought
nothing of the twenty-mile trip through the stark mountains.
There remained the sick, but our own medical box was almost
as sparsely equipped as the Bedouin's hut. We had various small
unlabelled bottles which might well have contained worm pills
for the dog, something for poison inside and something for
poison outside, and rolls of elastoplast. We also had a large
box of aspirin, or something like it, in cellophane sheets, each
pill in a little pocket. This seemed to be about the most harmless
thing to give them for their coughs and malaria.

We had also noticed that the biggest hit of our visit had not
been the packet of tea but a page of *Life* magazine in which it
had been wrapped, bright with an advertisement of many
coloured jellies. This they had passed round and round and
twisted in admiration in all directions. On board we had a large
glossy book of coloured photographs that we had been given
by the tourist office at Bizerta, designed to persuade tycoons to
invest in Tunisia and called *Tunisia at work*. This would do for
the spiritual side. It was very well produced and full of pictures
of camels, date plantations, dancing girls, donkeys, and the
brilliant Tunisian seashore, all of which we hoped that they
would understand.

We walked down to the beach accompanied by one of the men and the two boys. I rowed back to the boat and brought out ten shillings, the box of aspirins, and *Tunisia at work*. Beryl explained how to tear off a tablet and to take one or two when they had fever, but their interest was already in the book, and, as we rowed back to the ship, we could see them sitting in the sand, their three heads close together, as they reverently turned the pages.

Up sail and up anchor—twelve hundred miles to go, and a fair wind at last. On the sand dune the heads were still bowed over the book as we slid off to the south. Suddenly the man sprang to his feet and started shouting and beckoning. Did he want to join us and seek out the lovely land of the pictures? Did he want us to take him back to Hami? Or was it a question about the aspirin? 'I never explained,' said Beryl, 'that they had to take the tablets out of the cellophane cachet before eating them.' But whatever he wanted there was no chance of our knowing now.

We had a fresh wind on the quarter and set the genoa and the mizzen as *Tzu Hang* in calm water can be persuaded to sail herself like this for long periods. As soon as we were out of the shelter of the islands we realised that this was not going to be one of these days. It was another grey wet day with rain squalls marching like a procession of black-robed monks solemnly across the sea. We struck the mizzen at night but held on to the genoa, knowing as the squalls struck, or as the big sail sometimes emptied and filled again with a crack and a jar, that it was not the right sail. Nothing gave way, and at daylight we changed to the twins.

December 9 was another wet and squally day with rain drifting in through the open after-hatch, soaking the chart on the table and making everything wet and unpleasant, but from that afternoon the weather improved, the decks dried, and we were able to sail with no one at the helm, parallel to the coast, and getting some help from the East African current. The East African coast provides one of the great ocean currents of the world. It comes across the Indian Ocean, driven by the South-east Trades as the Equatorial Current, and turns north and south off the coast of Madagascar. The northgoing current driven by the Southwest Monsoon has been known to run at

up to 168 miles in the day, an Olympic record amongst the
ocean currents. During the period of the Northeast Monsoon it
runs down the East African coast, after shedding the branch
that we had already struggled with in the Gulf of Aden. At this
time it cannons into its normal origin, the Equatorial Current,
off Lamu, and sets off to sea again—eastward—as the Equatorial Counter Current, which we were later to find a very
elusive stream. Even along the East African coast it is not a
great current, and we only averaged a lift of fourteen miles a
day. On one day we had a contrary current and on one day
a lift of fifty miles. I have come to expect this sort of variation,
particularly after a change in the monsoon.

Never have we seen so many flying fish. By night and by day
they scattered in shoals across our path. We saw them in
hundreds at a time, as if the sea was putting its wealth on display and emptying whole sacks of shining dollars across our
bows. We had a constant escort of brilliant turquoise dolphins
who preyed on them, called '*lucies*' on the East African coast,
after the Arabic word for money, '*filoos*', because of the brilliant
gold and silver of their bodies out of the water. I saw one of
thirty pounds or more flashing just under the surface of the
water, one eye cocked on a flying fish above it, that was trying
to prolong its glide at just under stalling speed. At night the
phosphorescent trails of the dolphins radiated like rockets from
the ship, as they shot off in fishy exuberance or perhaps—if they
hunt at night—in pursuit of a quarry.

It was the flying fish that made this trip quite different from
any other that we had made under twins. Whoever was on
watch, slept or dozed on deck. In theory they slept, but in fact
sleep was impossible because of the constant peregrinations of
the cat in search of flying fish, and her return with a fluttering
victim. She carried them as high as possible, like a spaniel with
a cock pheasant, to avoid tripping over them. Her head shook
violently as they struggled and once inside the cockpit coaming
knowing that they could now no longer escape over the rail, she
would let them go, usually close to the head or the feet of the
person stretched out on this arduous watch. When their tan-
trums had died away she would begin to eat the still living
flesh, making a loud crunching and tearing sound. Sleep was
impossible. She ate sixteen in one night. When sated she would

lie on her side and dab them with a paw until they fluttered again. Popa, unable to bear the sight of Pwe being fed by the sea, ate three and was then violently sick in the cabin.

One night when I was fast asleep in the berth below, I was awoken by a violent cold fluttering between my legs and found that I had a flying fish lodged there. It had come in through the skylight. 'Haai, yah, ow, oh!' I yelled, scrambling out of the hammock berth and shouting as if I was being held down by a horde of murdering blackguards who were cutting my throat.

'What on earth's the matter?' I heard Beryl's startled voice calling from the cockpit.

'A bloody great flying fish in my fork,' I shouted back.

'How ridiculous,' I heard her say.

Next night it was my watch on deck. The twin staysails set dark against the starry sky as *Tzu Hang* rolled herself down the coast, a hundred miles offshore, and the swollen cat, no longer able to keep a proper equilibrium, rolled with her. The little wave crests sometimes broke near the quarter and hissed along the side, and small flashes of phosphorescence showed all round. We had not seen a ship since we had left the gulf of Aden. I was lying on an air mattress rocking gently with the ship's roll and half asleep when suddenly I heard a shrill and quavering cry from below, expressing every degree of fear and horror. 'Oh-h, ah, ugh!' it whinnied. But there was no need to ask what was the matter. 'There's a flying fish in my bunk. Come and do something about it,' cried my usually stalwart mate.

The wind fell away as we began to close the shore, and on the nineteenth we had a Cabbage White and a Red Admiral on board in corroboration of my supposed position. In the afternoon the wind freshened again, but we held on in anticipation of the evening calm. This night the wind kept on blowing, and by midnight it was obvious that we were going to overrun our harbour. I had no intention of approaching the shore by night. The coast was low and unlit except for the feeble Shella light, and we might be up or down it or much closer in than we expected. We took down the staysails and lay drifting under bare poles for the night.

At daylight we set the main, and with what excitement we stood in towards the shore. This was to be for both of us our first visit to Africa. Lamu, we had been told in Aden, was an

Arab town, little changed for the last few hundred years, and only dhows went there. Almost immediately we saw on the horizon the curve of a dhow's sail, and then another. Soon we could make out that they were small dhows, probably standing out for fishing, which meant that the coast was near; and long before the sun was high enough for us to get a sight it had appeared. We stood down the coast as I had made a liberal allowance to ensure that I was north of the entrance, and very soon the small white square of Shella light showed up.

We turned towards it and sailed well past Ras Kitao until we were able to tack on to our leading marks. A dhow sailed in ahead of us up the twisting channel with the tide swirling against sandbanks. To port a large sandhill, on which stand the lighthouse and in which the pottery from Chinese junks, visitors of hundreds of years ago is still found. To starboard a low man-grove- and bush-covered island, although it looked as if we were sailing into a river mouth, and as yet, except for the lighthouse, there was no building to be seen. We carried on under sail, glad to follow the dhow until it turned suddenly to port, shaving a rock as it entered the port-hand channel as another island appeared, of mudflats and mangroves, which split the reach in which we found ourselves. The dhow had ignored two markers which were not shown in my chart and which filled me with doubt. We were coming in fast on the tide, and as we now saw a buoy far up the starboard channel we took this one instead, sailing up between the mangrove-clad banks of the two islands. It was just what I had expected an African river to look like, Conrad's river of the two storekeepers, although in fact it was a passage between islands.

Presently across the mudflats we could make out the mirage-disturbed houses of Lamu, as tall and set as close together as those of Mukulla. We could see dhows anchored off the water-front. If Vasco da Gama had sent one of his ships' boats in here they might have seen just what we saw now. The green heat-ridden swamps, the sluggish stream, some white egrets on the trees and great clouds piling over the land behind. No sooner had we anchored to consider our next move than there was an ugly clamour from round the bend ahead, and a helicopter, tilted forward as if to look at its own reflection in the water, came swinging over the channel.

It crossed over towards Lamu and alighted in a dusty whirl close to the beach, where there were some tents and stores. No sooner was it settled than the clamour sounded again and its mate arrived and was soon sitting beside it. With the glasses we could pick out another buoy and a launch at a mooring. We got out the lead, sounded across the shallows, and anchored below the helicopters. Soon a blue launch arrived with gleaming brass-work and a smartly uniformed African crew. The coxwain handed me a note from John Simpson, the District Commissioner, asking us to dinner and offering us a mooring opposite his house. With the help of the splendid African crew we got up the anchor again and transferred to the mooring where *Tzu Hang* could swing to the tide just inside the traffic in the channel.

As we made fast a dhow sailed past us, gaily decorated with flags and streamers, the crew dancing on the deck, singing, clashing cymbals and blowing conch shells. They went about and sailed past us again, parading along the waterfront and the anchored dhows. We heard that it was to celebrate their safe arrival after a voyage, and it may have been the same dhow that we had followed in.

John Simpson's was an old two-storeyed Arab house with wonderful doors, studded with brass elephant spikes. From the upstairs verandah we could look through a network of branches of parkinsonias, that shaded the house, on to the bright fairway, seeing always movement, a dhow gliding past under sail, or slipping swiftly and silently up on the tide alone, guided by the crew with poles along the edge of the channel. The house had originally been built round a small courtyard. In order to achieve its present status the courtyard had been roofed over and a floor put down on the level of the upper storey to provide a large dining-room for the Commissioner.

The helicopters were from H.M.S. *Centaur* and had been sent to Lamu on famine relief. A long drought had ruined the crops, and distribution of relief had then been stopped by torrential rains. The inhabitants had not only lost their crops, but they had lost their opportunity for planting, too. It was interesting to see how this little white community, the District Commissioner, the Veterinary Officer, the Prison Officer, and the owners of a small tourist hotel, cut off by road, were all working together in the distribution of relief. The three officers and fourteen ratings had been divided between them, and they were giving whatever assistance they could, acting as guides to the pilots in locating remote little villages and ensuring the relief got to the right people. In fact they were all enjoying themselves and their visitors. The Navy as usual had tackled the job with tremendous zest and hundreds of tons of grain had been distributed and the helicopters kept flying day after day. The responsibility for the distribution over the two thousand square miles of his district rested, as did all other points of law and administration with John Simpson. Early every morning he walked down to his office in the town, greeting here someone in Arabic and there in Swahili, dressed in white stockings, white shorts, white shirt, a panama hat, and a black umbrella. Even to Beryl and me, once accustomed to formalities of dress, he looked like a cartoon of a British officer in Africa and we almost expected to see a large lion or a string of cannibals following him. He started at sunrise and there were no halts at midday. He returned long after we had had our tea. He thought never of himself, nor of his pay, nor of his pension, nor of his future, but only of 'his people' and how he could best look after them. Yet it wasn't all work and no play for he obviously enjoyed his work, and if ever there was a right man in a right place it was he, for he was mad on boats, and much of his work was done in his launch. It was he who was responsible for the new markers that had frightened me in the channel.

Once, to his acute embarrassment, I asked him, 'Where will they find a disinterested, incorruptible, gentleman to look after them when you have gone?'

'Oh I don't know,' he said, noncommitally, 'actually I shall stay on if possible. I like Africa.'

He told us of an old Arab, a friend of his, who had come to see him. They were talking about the coming changes. 'I want to die now,' the old man said suddenly, the tears running down his cheeks, 'it is all finished. They say such terrible things. None of them true. None of them true. It is finished and I want to die.'

In East Africa we met and stayed with several of the District Commissioners. In a country where isolation and responsibility develops character, they were all as different as could be, but they all had the same high principle of service to the people that they were in charge of. Something that is forfeited for freedom. We have lost something too in the disappearance of the opportunity for this sort of life, although it did not bring any great financial reward. It gave young men great responsibility in an adventurous outdoor life—a job which they did so outstandingly well because they enjoyed it so much.

A day or two later we went down to Shella, where we spent the night on a mooring put down by the survey ship *Owen* for one of her launches that was working with a detachment here. There were two moorings and one launch, so that *Tzu Hang* did not feel that she was intruding. Two of *Owen's* ratings had come on board at Lamu and—since one was an engineer and one an electrician—they had offered to fix the water-pump and the electric light circuit both of which had a leak. They piloted us down and put us on the mooring. When we met them in the town on our way to a last dinner with John Simpson they told us that they were in trouble with their officer over the mooring. We rowed ashore next morning and found the officer, a bearded and insignificant man, and thanked him for his kindness and the help that his crew had given us, but I doubt if it helped our friends.

We sailed with a fine following wind, keeping about four miles offshore and raised Malindi light soon after dark. There is no suitable anchorage there so we kept on and the wind soon dropped. It was Christmas Eve. Once before Beryl and I had spent it alone on *Tzu Hang* at sea. That was running south off the coast of Chile with a falling glass and a big gale menacing. We had no such anxiety here, but we had no celebrations either. Christmas Day was sunny with a light wind, and we continued about four miles off a low green coast. Soon we could see the three hills which mark Mombasa and the Mombasa Gap. The sun was westering as we approached the harbour. We could see the reef along the coast and dhows sailing faster than we were, using a counter current either within or close outside it. Owing to the sun being in our eyes it was not easy at first to pick out the marks, and the lighthouse might also have been a factory chimney. Presently we saw the turning buoy and from then on had no difficulty. To starboard was the entrance to the old port of Mombasa, used only by dhows now, with Fort Jesus glowering over the entrance, and to port the channel curved between hot green banks into Kilindini harbour. We followed this channel until we had found the yacht club. *Omoo* was moored there, whom we had last seen in Panama, but the shallow water where the small yachts were dropped so quickly into the deep channel that we went on in search of a better place. We found it round the next point where there were some more yachts moored, and it was to be *Tzu Hang*'s home for the next few months. An Englishman was rowing away from his yacht and pointed out a mooring for us to make fast to. Soon afterwards a rather chunky yacht came in under power and moored to a neighbouring buoy. A big man, pink from the sun, with a large and dilapidated straw bonnet on his head looked across at us. 'Hello there. Where are you from?' he roared at us, and his lusty English voice might have come from any southern English yacht yard. 'From Aden? Well you'll be all right there. We'll be over in a minute. Would you like some shrimps?'

'We haven't passed quarantine yet.'

'Ah they won't bother you—it's Christmas.'

Beryl and I had forgotten—perhaps it wasn't only the sun that coloured that fine homely English face. He was Arthur King, the owner of the yard on whose mooring we were now lying.

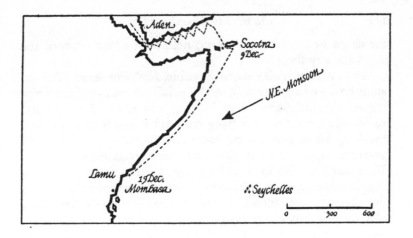

10 *Interlude in Africa*

WE should really have been in the Seychelles, waiting for the
Southwest Monsoon to take us to India and Singapore, but we
heard that there was quarantine for animals in the Seychelles
and that the cat and the dog would not be allowed ashore. This,
the invitation to the Okovango, and the feeling that we should
not miss seeing something of Africa, now at the end of an era,
had brought us to Mombasa. We decided therefore to spend
six months in Africa, then to take the South East Trades up to
the Southwest Monsoon and so by way of the Seychelles and
the Maldives to Ceylon and Singapore. We arranged to leave
Tzu Hang under Arthur King's eye, to buy a car, and for Clio
and Ann to join us.

The little bay in which we were anchored was well sheltered.
We put *Tzu Hang* on the beach, propped up on legs, and painted
her bottom in two awful sweltering days. Clio and Ann arrived
and we took them first for a sail to Zanzibar and Pemba,
where the smell of cloves reached us off shore, and where they
spent hours diving on the reef and filling *Tzu Hang* with evil
smelling shells. Back in Mombasa we left *Tzu Hang* on a mooring, between her two anchors, with the chain stretched so that

she could lie to either monsoon, neither of which reached the
bay with any force.

We bought a Volkswagen Kombie, and wondered after we
got it how we had ever managed the daily shopping trip, tramp-
ing up the hill past the yacht club and down the Kilindini
Road, while the heat rose from the tarmac as if from a fire, and
the long black centipedes, known as Mombasa trains, crept
uncomfortably across to the rank green grass on either side.
We loaded it with food and cooking utensils from *Tzu Hang*,
sleeping bags, and an old sail to use as a shelter, or a floor under
the stars, and then set off in a cloud of red dust on the beginning
of a journey that was to take us all over Kenya and down as far
as the Okovango swamps in Bechuanaland. We set off in the
evening and drove all through the night as we were to do many
times in the days to come, two sleeping and two driving, as if
we were keeping night watches on *Tzu Hang*.

Of all the miles that we drove in East Africa and further
south, it was the night driving that I enjoyed the most, when
the headlights lit the dusty lane ahead and the mysterious
night clung close on either side, and when a young companion
leant eagerly forward to identify bright eyes that shone ahead,
or to judge whether droppings on the road suggested a meeting
with elephant round the next corner.

After a few days in and around Nairobi, revelling in the cool
air, we started south. We drove again at night over the upland
country, with Wildebeeste and Zebra crossing the road in the
headlights and leaving their path as reluctantly as cattle. At
the border between Kenya and Tanganyika there was a gate
and a sentry box with a book to be signed. The wind blew coldly
off the mountain behind and there was something about the
feel of this open country that made me think that I was driving
in Scotland.

The next day in a green and hilly country we had trouble
with the fuel pump and while I was trying to repair it a truck
with three Americans, bound on some project, came past.
Beryl thumbed a lift with them to Kondoa, fifty miles away, in
search of a spare part, but being unsuccessful went on to
Dodoma, where she spent the night. Meanwhile Clio, Ann and
I had managed to repair the pump and, since we found no trace
of Beryl in Kondoa, camped at the side of the road, fearing that

otherwise we might pass her returning in the back of some dusty lorry. No sooner had we camped than a huge lorry drew up beside us and an African held out a crumpled piece of paper from the cab, a note from Beryl to say she'd be back next morning.

Beryl changes her skin like a chameleon in whichever country she may arrive, and since Africans walk incredible distances without thought or provision, she started off next day on foot up the dusty road to join us a hundred and twenty miles away. She was first given a lift by an African on the back of his pedal bicycle, and as they wobbled the six miles to the threshold of his hut, her only regret was that her family could not see her. Then she was picked up by some Indians in a truck. The time of the East African Safari was approaching, and every driver Indian or African pictured himself as taking part, so that we could see the signs of their approach and hear the noise of their arrival for miles before they stopped beside us, and Beryl arose from her dust bath in the back.

While we were waiting for her some Masai passed us, singing a song, bass and falsetto, to their cattle, sleek from fresh grass and recent rains. They strode past as if nothing could tire them, wonderfully free in these wild hills, and yet imprisoned by a pride that would permit no change from their old way of life. Once as we passed a group in argument I saw one fling his spear point downwards in the ground, so that the haft stood quivering between them. Whatever was its import, it was a lovely wild gesture, one of those kaleidoscopic pictures that have stayed in my mind and colour the memories of our drive.

Presently we came by way of Mpika, because a bridge on the Iringa route was down, up eight thousand feet above Mbeya, and were able to look down to the great Rift Valley, cleaving its way to the south, before we descended to the leveller going of Northern Rhodesia, and to the miles and miles of endless unpopulated bush, stretching hot and interminable in every direction, with bark beehives like milestones, high in the branches above the road. At night we camped under the stars and threw a log on to the camp fire from time to time, because we felt that it was the thing to do. Sometimes we heard a panther sawing, or a jackal or hyena cry. Sometimes we heard an animal moving not far away, but neither man nor beast disturbed our camps. The dog we kept at night in the car for fear of leopard but the cat was out hunting most of the night, except when there were hyena about, and fed herself all the time she was ashore in Africa.

We drove to see the sweep of the Kariba dam, where the Zambezi bellowed at its curb, and the growing lake disappeared into the shimmering haze behind. Then on, over good tarmac roads, through Salisbury in the moonlight, towards Marendellas, the Kombie flying as it had never done before as it approached Sam Whitfield's farm. Suddenly there was a notice at the side of the road which read 'Deadly Hazard' and brought us up as effectively as if it had smashed the windscreen. It turned out to be only a narrow bridge and a little further on we saw the lights of the farm. As we drove in there was another notice beside the road which would have identified Sam's place to me anywhere, 'Beware Puppy Dogs.' There he was, standing in the light of the headlights, his hair as dark as ever, his legs rather more bowed, wearing khaki cords that I felt sure I had seen him wearing twenty years before in India, a couple of border terriers yapping round him, while from somewhere in the darkness behind came the comfortable wicker of a horse. How good it is to travel so far and meet old friends at the end of the journey.

We spent a couple of weeks there, riding every day, and marvelling at all that had been accomplished in so short a time, in the making of a tobacco farm and a cattle ranch, understanding a little of the risk and the courage required to make it a success, a little of the bitterness that must come with the fear that it has been wasted. While I was there Sam took me to a farmers' meeting. Amongst the thirty farmers there, there were few who had not fought in one war for England, some in two. They were loyal men of fine calibre, the aristocracy of the country, and as they stood up and talked about this and that, for which they were variously responsible, I wondered why its future could not safely be left in their hands.

From Marandellas we set off for Francistown on the north eastern border of Bechuanaland. The Okovango river rises in the highlands of Angola, and runs like the Zambezi to the southeast, but it does not turn eastward and find an outlet to the sea, it turns south into five thousand square miles of swamp-land, known as the Okovango Swamps. Once a year its thousand fingers reach out, seeping, swelling, growing with the annual pulse towards the Kalahari, through Mopani and thorn, through reed and papyrus until its ultimate traces wither and dry in little muddy cakes on the desert edge. It was still one of the great untouched reserves of wild game in Africa and round the edge of the swamps and on the shores of Lake Ngami grazed 120,000 head of cattle, belonging to the Batwana who yearly drive their cattle to the Rhodesian market, 300 miles and more away to the north, through lion and elephant country.

Francistown is a hot and dreary little shanty town with a few houses of government officials standing bleakly alone amongst scattered thorn trees. We spent a dusty day on the edge of a dry river bed and found absolutely nothing to recommend it at all. We left in the evening to drive the three hundred odd miles to Maun, on the edge of the Okovango. The big Chevrolet trucks, which most people drive in Bechuanaland made nothing of the roads, but our little Kombie, which had a narrower axle, so that one leg was always in the air, could only compete successfully at night when the cold and a little dew gave the sand a better consistency. It had one advantage in that it had not the strength to dig in and when we stuck we could always push it out again. We pushed it for miles, or rather we plodded for miles behind it, while Beryl churned her way out of sight afraid to stop to pick us up again. On this night, just when we felt that we could push no further, a big lorry overtook us and since it couldn't pass us its crew helped to push us until the road improved. They padded merrily along with Clio, Ann, and I, their laughter exploding into the night with a flash of white teeth, which was all of them that we could see.

On arrival at Maun we found the Kays' tents deserted as they were out in the swamps with a broken down lorry, but there was a message to make use of their camp until transport could be arranged. It was some miles away from Maun on the bank of a river amongst trees. On the first morning, sleeping on a low camp bed, under a skin karess, I was awoken by a measured tramp along my back and turned slowly, and in some fear, to find a hen arranging herself like an old lady in a deck chair. There she laid an egg and conveniently continued to do so every morning that we were in camp.

Eventually we got out to the Kays' camp in the swamps, and they spent the next few weeks showing us round the country in which they spent so much of their time, where the blue reed-enclosed waters stretched for long miles between the trees, and open brown grassland or green hollows, from which the water had recently receded, made sudden contrasts with the bush. There was plenty of wild game to be seen, but we saw no elephant and no lions other than the two that the Kays had in captivity. We were a day too late, for the female—now in the Jersey zoo—had only just come off heat and the camp, together with its sleepless occupants was only newly released from regular nocturnal siege by her suitors.

The Kays were embattled in Bechuanaland, endeavouring to make a living as guides in the country where they had made themselves expert. A life of dusty tracks, of sunlit camps, of carrion smell and broken down vehicles, a life of elephant and crocodile adventures and of heroic tales told with a background of shadows from the camp fire, dancing on the boles of trees. Through it all the diminutive June, as neat as a humming bird, wrestled her diesel lorry through thorn and sand, and somehow managed to step down from the cab as if she had just got out of her Jaguar.

One day, shortly before we started north again, a telegram arrived at the camp at Maun. It told us that poor little Popa whom we had left with Sam because of the lions, had died suddenly of pneumonia. He was twelve years old and had had a very varied life, but the highlight of his career was undoubtedly his winter in Paris. A cruising boat is no place for a dog, but he was ours, with his lovable and unpleasant habits, and we never felt justified in saddling anyone else with him—except great friends like Sam—nor did we think that he would prefer a life ashore to forfeiting the companionship of his own people.

The annual drive of the Batwana cattle is one of the great romantic cattle drives that remain and we were lucky to be able to drive up the route to the Zambezi. Erick Krog, a most sophisticated and cultured Dane, a very unusual type to find in Bechuanaland, who was the government veterinary officer, asked us if we would like to drive with him. He was on his way to check the bore holes that he had arranged to be put in so that the cattle could follow a route free from Tsetse fly without extending themselves between water points. Provided they are not stampeded by lion or by an angry elephant they put on condition during their leisurely trek to the north. The road north of Maun was sandy and deserted and we were glad to know that there was another car keeping a look out for us, and glad to arrive in camp and find the most delicious meals already prepared. We came on the cattle only a day from the Zambezi, drifting through the bush on each side of the track, their many-coloured coats glowing in the sun, their long horns thrusting the bush aside. Ahead of them rode a cowboy, rifle at his saddle and shells polished in his bandolier, but his little pony was not quite up to the romance of the journey. Its legs sprouted from a narrow chest and the rider's heels seemed to knock together under the girth. At the Zambezi the cattle were swum across fourteen at a time, attached by their horns to a motor-boat. When they arrived at the other side and were set free to scramble up the bank I felt that after so great a journey it was freedom that they should have attained, and not the holding ground for the abattoir.

We left them steaming in the sun and set off up the right bank to try and find elephant, and as if to make up for all that we hadn't seen we found them standing on the road. A few days later we set off north again, by way of Tete in Portuguese East Africa, first settled in the sixteenth century, and through Nyasaland, and Tanganyika by way of Iringa, so that much of the road was new.

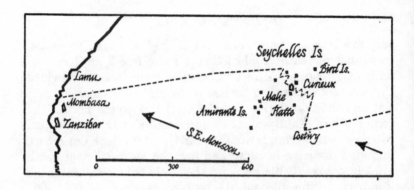

11 *To the Seychelles and Coetivy*

AT the beginning of August we spent our last night ashore in
Tsavo Game Park. As we were leaving next morning, a few miles
out of the gates (which are over the road only, to check cars,
for there are no fences defining the park) we passed a large
elephant, smeared with red mud, standing like a watch-tower
beside the road. He spread his ears, and then as if impatient
at our photography, shook his head and shambled towards us.
'Get off back to your boat,' he seemed to say. 'Oh wait, wait.
Please wait,' called Clio, her head out of the window of the car,
busy as usual taking photographs, but I felt that it was time to
be going, too, and let the clutch in before he got any nearer.

We drove all night, anxious to see *Tzu Hang* again, and to
find out how she had fared without us. We arrived at daybreak
and hurried through the still silent yard with the eagerness and
heart-searchings that all boat-owners must know, in order to
get our first sight of her after our long absence. There she was,
lying placidly at anchor in the still water as yet untouched by
the morning wind, the early sunlight just catching her white
masts and looking as if we had only left her yesterday.

In spite of the southerly monsoon that was then blowing, she
was in good shape. The yard had kept an eye on her, run her
engine, and pumped her out from time to time. She felt clean
and dry, and nothing had been stolen. Only her bottom was
foul with a prodigious growth of weed. The East African Navy,

closing down like so many other things in Kenya, lent us their unwanted slip, and we were able to haul *Tzu Hang* out on a hand-operated winch, with the aid of the spring tides which gave us four days on the slip and a few inches to spare.

After she was painted we made another short trip to Funzi Bay and down the Wasin Channel, for the East African coast south of Mombasa is a splendid cruising area with sheltered anchorages within a day's sailing and good fishing and goggling. Then it was time for Clio and Ann to return to London. They left still well smeared with anti-fouling paint, weighed down by evil-smelling sea-shells, skin karosses, and African carvings, but protected from charges for overweight baggage and from the queries of customs officials by their disarming smiles.

It had been our intention to take the Southeast Monsoon across to India and Singapore, but for various reasons (chiefly because, having seen so much of Africa, we wanted to see some more) we decided to make a circuitous trip by way of the Seychelles, Rodriguez and Mauritius, to Durban. Norah arrived to join us from Paris, after doing some touring in Abyssinia on the way and, in spite of this, looking cool and elegant and unperturbed at the news that she was going to be dumped in Durban rather than Cochin. Beryl and I were looking forward to the luxury of a third watchkeeper on a long passage, especially such a good companion as we knew Norah to be.

We set off on 29 August, tacking quickly down the long harbour. A signal was flying from the yacht club mast, and we had to take it as a signal of good wishes for the voyage, because we had no flag code book on board. The monsoon had relaxed, so that the sun was shining, the genoa set, the sea blue and small waves sparkling on the reef as we turned for the outer buoy. With friends who would give their unsaleable farms to be able to do the same thing, we felt guilty at leaving in such perfect weather, unfettered by any responsibility ashore.

'Stand to the eastward,' says *Ocean Passages of the World*, 'regardless of crossing the equator in doing so, until eastward of the Chagos Group, when southing should be made into the trade wind, until a direct course can be steered for Mauritius.' It sounds so easy to follow, but it entails almost two thousand miles hard on one tack and a thousand on the other, and as for recrossing the Equator, we wanted to visit the Seychelles between latitudes four and five south and 900 miles east of Mombasa.

The voyage began well as the light southerly wind enabled us to lay a course that offset the current sweeping up the coast, and we were fortunate in a quiet sea, so that I was soon able to forget any regrets that I had at leaving, and even to be bold enough to smoke a cheroot in the cockpit while the lights of Mombasa still glowed in the night sky.

Such pleasant beginnings seem often to be the harbingers of uncomfortable days ahead, and I regard too easy a start with distrust. The following day the wind was backing, and we were plunging with hatches fastened down and shortened sail into real monsoon weather—poor visibility, low cloud, and sweeping wet squalls. On the evening of the ninth day out from Mombasa we were approaching Bird Island, the most northerly of the Seychelles group. Only on the first and on this day had we been able to carry all sail and had continually worn oilskins on deck. We had been lucky with a fix early in the morning, but there had been no chance of another sight, and with the variable currents that sweep through the islands at thirty miles a day, we wanted to make a landfall before dark, so that we would know exactly rather than approximately where we were.

With an unlit low island somewhere in the offing we would soon be faced with a choice of one of three alternatives. To hold on and hope that we would not come upon it in one of those black squalls with which the night was burdened, to tack, in which case if we had already passed it we might bring it ahead again, or to heave to and lose ground in current and perhaps a day ashore as well.

Everything was grey and heavy with impending nightfall, with here and there a crest breaking listlessly as the wind eased. Even the water about us and its endless voices seemed as undetermined as my own mind. In my imagination the six islands and a hundred rocks and islets of the Seychelles grouped themselves in unseen and ominous array on the outskirts of the night. Then suddenly an outpost showed on the very limits of our visibility, a patch of white and something dark beside it. I looked away, not saying anything, and then let my eye run once more, almost casually, along the darkening horizon. I saw again the same patch of white, the same dark shadow, still on the same bearing, so little different except in its immobility from a breaking crest and the dark hump of a wave, but soon unmistakeably a patch of sand with casuarina trees growing behind: Bird Island—and just in time for a celebration. Without anxiety, or at least with a minimum of anxiety, we could now tack into the hag-black night.

We tacked several times during the night, seeing nothing and hearing nothing except the grating cry of a night-wandering tern and the sudden murmur of tide-rips over the noise of the sea. Next morning Bird Island was still in sight, but to port instead of to starboard, and we saw that we had only made about fifteen miles in the right direction against the current during the night. That day also we were bewitched by constant squalls and wind changes, so that we found that we were more often than not losing ground rather than making it, especially during a long bout of sail repairs, for two yards of stitching went in the main.

The last day made up for all the labour and the wetness of the voyage. As on the first day the sun shone again, showing with its early rays the twin-peaked outline of Silhouette Island, and soon the green and blue mountains of Mahé beyond. We could see that we would have our anchor down that night, if not at Port Victoria, then in North West Bay, or even in the little anchorage behind the point of North Island. We sailed in the afternoon between Silhouette and North Island, seeing coconut plantations below the steep bush-covered hills, a solitary shed at the head of a sandy beach, and patches of cultivation on the slopes. Ahead on Mahé the coconut trees curved in a dark line behind a long beach. The wind dropped and night fell. We went on with the aid of the motor and saw a light flashing as if signalling from the shore and the lights of cars driving on the road behind the beach. We went in slowly, until the shore and the coconuts seemed very close, and anchored in five fathoms. As soon as the rattle of the chain had stopped there was only the sound of the wavelets rustling on the beach until a dog barked close by: alas, there was no Popa to reply. We would see it all in the morning, but the thing of the moment was to have arrived, to relax, to enjoy the stillness and the safety, and the thought that there was no watch to keep. Next morning the beach looked much further away than I had thought, but that is usual when anchoring at night, and we intended to go on to Port Victoria that morning, so it was of no matter.

In the time of the southeast wind the sail up the west coast to the north point of the island is hard to beat. The wind came over Signal Hill and over the tree-tops by the sea, filling the sails yet hardly riffling the still water, clear blue water backed by rock and sandy cove and an everchanging pattern of greenery ashore. Once round the rocky islet off North Point we were banging into the Southeast Monsoon again, but not for long. Away to port we could see the low outline of Praslin, where the huge double coconuts come from, the *cocos-de-mer*, which are made into hideous polished ornaments, and, as we rounded into the long fairway between Mahé to starboard and St Anne and Cerf to port, we could soon pick out the buoys and markers, helped by a large white B.I. ship anchored in the roads. *Tzu Hang* followed as usual the battleship course, but, with the clear water and the breakers showing clearly on the reef, we could have easily taken a shorter inshore route.

From the roads where the liner was anchored a channel marked by a lighthouse leads through the coastal reef to a small basin about half a mile from the shore, and from the shore an embankment has been built out across the reef to a jetty on the basin's edge. It is here that the small traders and schooners come, mooring stern to the quay and pitching into the short slop that washes over the reef. Here also there are warehouses, the harbour office, the customs house and a turtle pond.

When the schooners are in there can be few places that present such an old-fashioned sight. A forest of masts and cord-age, a throng of many-coloured dresses and many-coloured people on the shore, and a frieze of dark figures as the stevedores pad up and down the stern planks under sacks of copra, vanilla and yams. The turtles in which there is a considerable trade are dragged along the deck and slid on their backs down a chute to the quay. Here they are loaded on to hand-carts and trundled along the quay to the turtle-pond, their great eyes weeping and their mouths drawn down in long-suffering disap-proval of such indignity.

There is no place for a yacht to lie, but a narrow boat channel leads past the south end of the jetty, available for yachts of *Tzu Hang*'s size if they can find someone to show them in, brushing two stone beacons that mark the channel and mooring anchor out astern across the channel and on to the reef and bow to a small jetty. There is hardly room to turn here, but it is an absolutely safe and steady anchorage once you are in.

Having got in we were very soon contemplating getting out again, because there is little except a feeling of security to keep a yachtsman lying at Port Victoria. The town itself is a dull and dilapidated little place, the houses occasionally brightened by a splash of colour, of poinsettia or bougainvillaea, at their fronts. We were glad to be in for a day or two for the wind piped up, and, while we were walking down the embankment on the way to the town, blew a boy on his bicycle off a low bridge in front of us into the sea. The water was shallow and both were recovered without anything worse than a wetting. It didn't stop the fishermen from going to sea, and in the morning they came racing in under sail to the mole behind the main jetty. As soon as they were moored up the fishermen jumped ashore and, with their catch in two baskets slung on a pole across their shoulders, ran in to the market in the centre of the town. At this time the market hummed like a hive of bees as the women crowded round the stalls, but very soon the last fish had gone and the crowd thinned, leaving only a few hagglers round the vegetables. It is a common story of increasing population and decreasing fish, or perhaps of decreasing fishermen, for the best of the young men, natural sailors and often good carpenters and mechanics, go to find their living at sea or in Africa. In the evening at school-leaving time, the streets are suddenly filled with children in school uniform, still looking brushed and neat, and predominantly girls. One wonders how so many will ever find themselves husbands, or even employment. While we were in Port Victoria there was a breathless hush over the town as the female population polished their fingernails and combed their glossy black hair. Never were the arrows of enchantment so assiduously sharpened, for a British frigate was due to arrive, and in the prevailing excitement the courtesy visit of an Ethiopian destroyer, except for its Norwegian officers, went almost unnoticed. The huntresses were out for fairer game.

Soon after we arrived we went on board one of the schooners

to discover what information we could about the other islands that might lie on our route to Mauritius. They periodically visited Coetivy and Agalega, and even went so far afield as Chagos and Mauritius. The captain was helpful, but he looked a tired and disillusioned man. His ship was called the *Revenant*, and had once been wrecked on one of the island reefs during a hurricane, but had later been salvaged and brought back to service. That was why she had been renamed the *Revenant* we were told—but it was also the name of Robert Surcouf's ship—the great corsair who was based in the Seychelles. If she had come back to this world she only looked as if she had a precarious hold on it now. She had a musty smell, a combination of damp, fish, sweat and the rancid odour of copra. He pulled open the drawer of the chart-table in the cramped little after deckhouse, and there was a scurry of enormous cockroaches across the yellowing charts. He showed us where to anchor at Agalega and explained that from there, going to Mauritius, the schooners went two hundred and fifty miles to the westward before turning south. This was their normal route, and the three-masted schooner the *Iles de Farquhar*, had just returned from beyond Agalega, having broken her forestay on the way to Mauritius.

This is not the route recommended in *Ocean Passages of the World*, but these schooners are nearly always under their engines even when under sail. *Tzu Hang*, although she has an engine, has to rely on the wind, and we decided on a compromise; to beat down to Coetivy, half-way to Agalega, and then to make our easting as far as the Chagos Archipelago. Coetivy is a small coconut island privately owned by Monsieur Delhomme, the French Consul at Mahé. We had to get his permission to visit it, so we turned this responsibility over to Norah, who soon charmed him into an invitation to go there, an honour rarely given. 'But you will have to work for it,' he said, 'you will have to take them some newspapers and some carottes of tobacco.'

On the way back from the wharf, full of new plans, we ran into a nautical figure in white shoes and stockings, a white shirt, voluminous white shorts, and an old Navy cap, propped up by two enormous eyebrows standing like the last two windblown haycocks in a hilly field. In any dress he would have been unmistakeable as a Royal Navy or ex-Royal Navy officer. 'Ex' it was, and now he had left his retirement for another spell at sea, working for an East African firm, and had brought a small coastal tanker loaded with fuel for Mahé. He had also brought a note for us, and, after we had been hailed and identified, Beryl asked him what sort of trip he'd had.

'Nine days of purgatory,' he replied. Nine days. *Tzu Hang* had not done so badly then.

We walked back with him to have tea on board. The tanker was moored stern to the fuel wharf. 'Goodness,' said Beryl, when she saw the deck almost awash in the chop, 'she looks as if she's sinking.'

'Sinking,' he roared. 'She's coming up. We're discharging.'

We went up to his cabin just abaft the bridge. 'What I object to,' he said, 'is the bridge being the fo'c's'le.' In fact the ship was so short that it looked as if every sea that came over the bow would take the bridge too. It must have been a wet place pounding into the southeast swell.

'I've got an Arab mate, and the crew are all Seychellois,' said the captain. 'Poor bastards. I'm going to give them a day off. They've deserved it. They gave me a cake and a couple of handkerchiefs yesterday, for my birthday. Rather nice I thought.' In the corner of the bridge was a damp chair. 'I spend most of my time sitting there,' he said, 'the helmsmen are not very experienced you know, and one wants to be there in case something turns up.' I thought of how much comfort the young helmsman must draw from the knowledge that the old man was in his damp chair, when the black night wrapped the ship, the spray slashed the bridge windows, and the compass needle went haywire against the turn of the wheel.

Back on *Tzu Hang* we found another visitor, a dapper military figure of bounding enthusiasms, Gerry Legrand, who owned the hotel at Beau Vallon Bay. It was he who had tried to signal us as we came in on the evening that we arrived, and had come over to persuade us to move back to his beach. His coxswain, an old seaman in charge of the hotel launch, could restitch our mainsail, he said, and he promised us a room to change in when we came ashore. He was the self-constituted and unofficial host of the island, not because he wanted to attract people to his excellent hotel, with its separate guesthouses scattered amongst the palms by the beach, but just because he wanted people who came to Mahé to enjoy themselves—or so it seemed to us. The islands are in need of more people like him. Behind their lovely façade there is a feeling of stagnation and decay, almost the last and apparently the least wanted of England's colonial possessions, the Isles of Disenchantment. It is hard to see what can be done for them. The Japanese find it profitable to fish in those waters. Perhaps there is a future there with a canning plant ashore. Since the people are good carpenters and seamen something might be done in yacht building. Or perhaps fortune's wheel will bring a nice large base for the Armed Forces there, and that seems to be the only real answer.

We extricated ourselves from the little harbour with Gerry Legrand's help and sailed back to Beau Vallon with the wind gusting so strongly over the hill that *Tzu Hang* fairly hissed through the calm water on the western side while catspaws rushed out at her from the beaches. Next morning she was invaded by a number of the crew of the British frigate that was in Port Victoria, whom Gerry had invited over, and who swam out to us until *Tzu Hang* was loaded with wet and happy sailors.

A short way from where we were anchored a treasure-hunting operation was in progress and had been in progress for about fourteen years. We had met several people in Kenya who had invested in it and who asked us to have a look and see how it was going along. As a conversational subject it ran about level with *Uhuru* and had about the same chance of a successful outcome, and was gunpowder if treated too lightly with the wrong person. I had already had an explosive reaction from a bank manager with whom it seemed a very sore topic.

We walked up the beach to a point of rocks where the operations were going on. There were various neat markings on the rocks in yellow paint, dates, tide limits, and bearings, and we found two Seychellois repairing a diesel pump, which was being used to empty a tide-filled cavern. While we were looking round a big man burst breathlessly round the rocks and asked us what we wanted. At first he seemed to regard us with suspicion. Eventually, mollified, he launched into a story without a beginning and without an end, a spate of words that sounded like a barker outside a 'Tent of Mysteries' at a fair. The clues included the collar-bones of King Solomon, the head of Medusa, buried scimitars that pointed from one clue to another, a complexity of the signs of the zodiac, the measurements of the sarcophagus of Cheops, and had eventually led to the present cavern. The ingenuity with which the trail had been unravelled was as surprising as the erudition of the corsair who had laid it. A female sage, we were told, in Greece, had confirmed by telegram that the hunt was approaching the climax, but as the tide filled the cavern and the diesel pump had broken down, it looked as if the hunters might be in business and the shareholders in eager anticipation for some time to come. I never heard what they discovered when the pumps finally emptied the cavern, but wild horses could not have persuaded me to invest in the venture.

On 21 September, a crowded year since we had passed Daedalus Lighthouse, we left Beau Vallon and sailed down to Port Launy, another sheltered sandy bay, and the following day we set sail for Coetivy, passing close inshore round Capucin Point, the southern point of the island, while to seaward the big swell spouted whitely over Capucin Rock, as if lovely, slatternly Mahé was waving her handkerchief in good-bye.

Coetivy sounds like the name of some mouse-like little animal, and it is a little mouse of an island a couple of miles long and a mile wide, hiding in the hollows of the Trade Wind swell 150 miles south-southeast of Mahé. It took us a little under four days and over 300 miles of sailing to get there. At one time, in the vicinity of Zoroaster Shoal, but not in its exact location, we found that we were sailing over shallow water with the bottom clearly visible. With the lead stowed away we did not have time to sound, but I should guess that it was between eight and ten fathoms below us, which looks very shallow when there is no land in sight.

We got a good star fix on the morning of 26 September and I noted in the log that we should see the tops of the coconut trees at ten. The next entry is at ten and says, 'Tops of coconut trees visible ahead.' This is so smug that it must have been a bit of showing off to Norah, who always seemed to take it for granted that I knew where I was, and never expressed the admiration and wonder that I should have liked when we found our objective. I long for someone to say 'What a good bit of navigation,' and, since no one does so, I have to say so myself.

The island, end on, appeared almost as a bush growing out of the sea, but it grew and lengthened until we could see the shallow bay opposite the settlement and the swell breaking on the reef at the southern end of the island. We felt our way in slowly until the brown of coral heads and detached reefs began to appear in patches round us, and we anchored, making sure that the anchor went down in a small stretch of pale blue water, showing that there was coral sand beneath. We were still some way from the shore, from where a boat was putting out, but well sheltered from the trade wind.

The boat, a long, narrow, whaler type, driven by several paddlers, came out through a channel in the reef, marked by sticks. A stockily built Seychellois, Clemont Potter, the manager of this island domain, was sitting on the centre thwart. They circled us, hostile and silent, while we stood grinning foolishly at the shrouds, feeling even at this distance and to our surprise, that we weren't wanted. 'I have a letter for you from Monsieur Delhomme,' I shouted in French across the water. A broadside of huge smiles flashed out in reply, and they paddled to the side of the boat laughing and joking.

We handed over our letter and had soon offloaded the carottes of tobacco and the newspapers. The carottes or plugs were shaped like large carrots, made from local leaf and weighed about six pounds each. 'Like gold, here,' said Clemont Potter as we handed them over. 'No one is allowed ashore here except by invitation of Monsieur Delhomme,' he explained, 'that is why we have to be so careful and did not welcome you at once. He says in his letter that we are to make his house available to you so that you may live ashore, and to stock you up with all the fresh food that you may require.' He also told us that a schooner only called three or four times in the year and that there had been great excitement when our sail was first sighted. 'Sail ho,' had been the time honoured call from some-one working at the north end of the island who had seen us first. 'Sail ho,' had been taken up by the men picking and husking in the trees, and the cry had been passed on through the settlement and out to the east coast, where Clemont was supervising the building of a copra shed at the landing used during the Northwest Monsoon. He had jumped into his Land-Rover and had just been in time to get out in the boat to meet us.

Coetivy is a most self-sufficient little island. It has no radio communication and has to reply entirely on its own resources during the long gaps between schooner visits. Clemont was not only the manager, but he was every other sort of authority for the three hundred persons who lived and worked temporarily on the island. He was doctor, engineer, storekeeper, builder, shipwright, policeman, magistrate and priest as well, and he bore all these responsibilities with great unconcern on his young and broad shoulders, well supported by his pretty, fair-haired, wife. They, and a regularly increasing family, lived in the main house of the settlement, a large whitewashed house built of coral blocks and cement, set a little back from the sea. A large fig-tree gave shade to the front of the house, and under the fig-tree for most of the day lay a troop of woolly, pale-eyed dogs, who as might be expected, all looked very like each other.

In the settlement there were also the storehouses, the copra barns, curing sheds, a school, and a small white church, together with one or two better houses provided for the schoolmaster, the sectional overseers, and other specialists, for apart from the labour force there were also fishermen, masons, and boatbuilders, all imported from Mahé. A short step from these houses were the labour lines, small rectangular houses built of bamboo and plaited palm leaves, in neatly brushed yards. They were being replaced by degrees by more permanent, although less attractive and hotter houses of coral and cement. There were one or two good-looking and none too bashful coloured girls about.

'Don't the women get bored,' I asked Clemont, 'stuck away on a little island like this?'

'Oh no,' he replied, 'they are very popular.'

That evening we were sitting on the veranda of the house that we had been lent, whose steps led down beneath a line of casuarinas to the beach. Just in front was an upturned fishing boat which an old man had been caulking all day. Beyond the reef, as darkness fell, another boat was coming in from the sea. As it came to the passage through the reef the breeze died. It dropped its sail and the men took to their oars. One of the crew stood up in the stern and blew two long blasts on a conch shell—a most romantic and far carrying noise.

'How lovely,' Beryl said to Clemont, 'do they always do that? Is it to let you know that they are back?'

'Well, not me, exactly,' he replied, 'although I tell them that that is the reason. With so many men and so few women I make it a very strict rule. It gives the women warning in the lines that the husbands are back, so that they can make some adjustments if necessary.'

Except for these buildings and another small labour camp near the north end of the island, everywhere else was coconut trees. In places they were well spaced and planted, in others twisted and leaning in a tangle of grey trunks, but everywhere thick enough to transform the brilliance of the sunshine, which outside on the coral sand hit you like a hammer blow between the eyes, into a shaded green. Here the Trade Wind rustled between the trunks and stirred the latticed shadows, and without there sounded always the murmur of the sea. Under these trees there ran a large herd of donkeys, ponies and mules as fat and as fit as one could hope to see. There were cows, pigs and chickens round the huts, and all looked fat and well, although usually animals seen under coconut trees are inclined to be skinny. The pigs were bred centrally, and the piglets, like foxhound puppies, were sent out to walk. They and the chickens in the compounds boasted immaculate little bamboo houses to which they retired separately at night.

There was no money in Coetivy. The labourers received a staple food ration and above this could buy on tick in the store, but their wages were credited to them in Mahé, and they were paid only on their return there. The owner thereby saw some of his money come home again and the men had something to show for their work, which they would otherwise have gambled away or spent on home-made brew—a hard life for some of these people who still bear the names of the pirates who infested these islands before the French occupied them, but they seem to come back for more. They are required to complete one task a day, be it digging a large pit for planting a new tree or picking and husking 500 coconuts. This seems a fantastic labour, but Clemont said that a task was usually finished in four hours, and they could do another if they wished and earn good money, but that they were almost invariably content with one.

One of the major tasks undertaken by Clemont on this island was to build an eighty-foot schooner for which all the timber and all the material had to be imported. It was being built by two carpenters—they could hardly be called shipwrights—on the beach on which she sat on her broad bottom, although she showed a lean bow and stern. The only drawings were done by Clemont, and she was already planked up and the deck partially laid. She towered above the beach, her bowsprit in the coconut trees.

'How on earth are you going to launch her?' I asked Clemont.

'That's easy,' he replied. 'Just dig a trench under her.'

The materials were strong enough. Huge wooden knees were fitted or partially fitted to every angle, and reinforced by great bolts and angle-irons. She bore every evidence of the amateur designer and amateur carpenter and there wasn't a flush-joint in the whole ship. We wondered how she'd stand up to a gale. Yet what a heroic task! One cannot expect too high a standard of carpentry with two men building with hand tools on the beach, and she will probably be as able as many an island schooner before her, which has held together with the help of red lead, pitch, and a great deal of oakum.

We would like to have stayed for days in this entrancing spot, but *Tzu Hang* was lying beyond the reef prodding us to be gone, and, after a couple of nights ashore, we felt that it was time to go. We walked over after breakfast to say goodbye to Clemont. He was away in the Land-Rover, as someone had fallen out of a coconut tree—all in the day's work for Clemont. He was back soon, calm and confident, and said that he believed the man was not seriously hurt. He had only fallen thirty feet—and it would be hard to fall further on that island—but had landed on a stump. Clemont took us out in the motor-boat, towing our dinghy, and loaded with such a profusion of coconuts, yams, bananas, and even eggs, as would feed a platoon for a week.

Soon the anchor was aweigh, and we were off to the eastward on the long haul to Mauritius. In half an hour Coetivy, most confident and self-sufficient of small islands, had slipped behind the long blue swell.

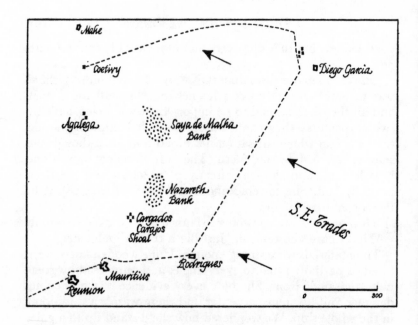

12 *Rodriguez, Mauritius and Réunion*

IN 1810 Lord Minto, the Governor-General of India, wrote to his wife in England, discussing the proposed attack on Mauritius, then known as the Ile de France. 'If the troops do not rendezvous off the island in time to attack by the middle of November,' he wrote, 'it is not entirely prudent to attempt it later, for the violent hurricanes that seem to live in those islands and to come out, like swallows, at certain seasons, sometimes are experienced in the course of November, though seldom before the middle of December.'

The South Indian Ocean has on an average six severe tropical storms in a year westward of Longitude 80° East and south of 10° South, and to be entirely prudent we hoped to be west of the southern tip of Madagascar and on our way to Durban by the end of November.

Now it was 28 September. Twenty miles on the log, as night fell, and the little island of Coetivy long out of sight, when the rain squalls, hanging around, persuaded us to change the genoa for the jib and to hand the mizzen for the night. About two thousand six hundred miles to go before we were clear of Madagascar and two months to do it in, but so much to see as well: the Chagos Archipelago, Rodriguez, Mauritius, Réunion, and Fort Dauphin in Madagascar were all on our way. *Tzu Hang*, like a horse on the galloping track, plucked at her bit and settled down into her stride, and we with greater reluctance settled down to our night watches, ducking plaintively to an occasional douche of salt water, as we smacked into the south-east swell.

From Coetivy to Chagos is now a very deserted part of the ocean as no regular steamship routes cross it, and if any vessel is seen it is most likely to be a Japanese fishing vessel. Even in the days of sail it was on no regular route. Before the occupation of the Seychelles by the French in 1743 the islands were occupied by pirates who preyed on the East Indies trade. During the Napoleonic wars the islands, including Mauritius and Réunion provided shelter for the corsairs and French warships that continued to exact a heavy toll on the trade from India, until the expedition that Lord Minto referred to was undertaken. Our route therefore was the pirate road, and we could imagine pirate ships, or the corsairs, beating out, as we were doing, like hungry birds of prey, to watch the great trade route, or thundering back to their eyrie loaded with plunder.

For the next few days we made good time, with very much the same sort of weather as we had had on our way to the Seychelles. On one day we found the elusive Equatorial Counter-Current and had a lift of thirty-six miles in the right direction, but for the most part the current was still against us, and the nights as black and wet—though fortunately warm—as ever I remember them at sea. At times we could not see the doghouse from the cockpit, and the rain came down as if we were under fire-hoses.

All the time the wind was well in the east, and we were losing ground to the north until we were up to approximately 3° South—'approximately' as the sun was always hidden at midday and we were lucky if we got one hazy shot during the morning. Our course had varied between 90° and 70° until on 5 October we were in a position Longitude 68° East, Latitude

3° South. The wind then changed to the south, and we were able to make our way southeast until on 8 October, when we had our first calm day since leaving Mombasa. With occasional lapses to fresh southeast winds we were able to continue in this direction until on 10 October the wind came surprisingly and fairly from the west. We had left a visit to Diego Garcia, the blue lagoon of the Chagos Archipelago, as a possibility rather than a probability, depending on what sort of course the wind would force upon us. Now it began to look as if we might sneak past to westward of the scattered islands, and I began to think of getting on to Rodriguez, helped by the knowledge that I had let the battery run down and now couldn't start the engine, so that we might have some difficulty in entering the lagoon.

It was an exciting night as we approached Danger Island, the most westerly of the group, wondering whether our sights were really as right as they seemed, and whether the current would help us to keep an offing, or some counter-current would set us toward the shore. On watch I walked up to the bow and stood looking ahead with my hand on the forestay, the moon just bright enough to cast a faint shadow on the deck although it was shining through cloud. *Tzu Hang* sailed steadily on. Presently we could make out a shadow on the port bow which turned to palm trees and a white beach on which the surf murmured as we slid quietly past. We should have gone in and anchored, for the next day we were becalmed on Pitt Bank, forty-five miles to the south, and we stayed there for most of the following day.

On Pitt Bank we could see the bottom quite clearly a few fathoms below us. We bathed while *Tzu Hang* rolled above us, showing one or two goose barnacles on her otherwise clean underwater paint, and during the hot afternoon a big marlin came and lay close under our stern, resting, while the sunlight on the wavelets dappled his flank. Away to the eastward the clouds sometimes reflected the pale blue of the Diego Garcia lagoon. The barometer dropped from 1,010 to 1,005 millibars, a big swell came rolling up from the south, and the wind had died in the west leaving a strangely troubled sky.

It wasn't the season for hurricanes, so obviously there couldn't have been one, but it looked as if something nasty had passed away to the south and we were glad to be well north of its track. If we'd followed the schooner captain's advice and gone down to Agalega we might have run right into it.

On 13 October the Trade Wind was back. The shadow of *Tzu Hang*'s hull slipped off the bank below her, and for the next 750 miles she steered herself, heading as if on an automatic pilot, straight for Rodriguez, which we made at four in the morning six days later. It was boisterous sailing, usually well reefed down and much appreciated by the porpoises. The wind was fresh enough one night to make us heave to for a few hours under our reefed main, but there was little other incident except that one day I saw a splash in the sea about two miles away, as if a fifteen-inch shell had landed. A moment later a huge shape leapt twisting out of the water and came down with a similar splash. I thought at first that it was a whale, but later that perhaps it was a manta ray and engaged—from the general distant commotion—in some titanic drama.

The dark shadow of land, at first only guessed at, which had gradually grown into Rodriguez, had first appeared well on the starboard bow, as I had allowed too much for the current setting us towards the west—all to the good as long as we could see the island, for we were now well to windward, and as soon as we were sure that it was land and not a low cloud or rain, we freed the sheets and ran quickly down towards it. Norah came on watch and took over with her back to the island without having noticed it.

'By the way,' I said to her, 'if you look behind you you'll see Rodriguez.'

'Oh yes—so it is,' she said, but nothing more. I stayed up with her waiting eagerly for the daylight to give us a better view as we skirted its northern edge. Gradually the shadow took substance in dun rocks, a bareboned hard island it seemed from the sea.

I had no chart of Rodriguez, but had made one from the sailing directions, drawing it several times on a large scale until Point Venus, Booby Island, Diamond Island, the flagstaff at the Commissioner's residence, the Cable and Wireless Company's buildings, the reefs and passes, sailing marks and beacons, fell into their appointed places. When we eventually came to enter Port Maturin I felt as if I had been there before. One thing was missing. The forward sailing mark for the passage through the reef. We tacked off to check our bearings again, and came in on a bearing on the rear marker. As we entered the passage a small white launch, flying a huge blue ensign, came out to meet us, and relieved us of any further anxiety by motoring ahead of us tack for tack, until it had shown us to the anchorage. Even without its help we would have managed all right, as the sailing directions were very detailed and the reefs were visible. It is almost impossible for a far cruising yacht to carry all the charts that it is going to need. I have often managed to take a tracing of a chart from a merchant ship in port, if it has not been otherwise available, and failing that have made one on a plotting chart from the sailing directions, and gained much post-arrival pleasure by its use.

The worst of the anchorage at Port Maturin is that it is so far from the shore. A long narrow channel leads through the shore reef to a boat harbour, but it is much to shallow for a ship of *Tzu Hang*'s size. In order to give her room to swing we had to anchor a mile offshore, in water, although still protected by the outer reef, rough enough to cause the complete collapse of a young police inspector, one of the lesser dignitaries from the white launch who now came on board. 'My God, *je deviens malade*!' he exclaimed, and all formalities of entry were waived immediately.

The Commissioner himself, who was also on board, a magistrate from Mauritius of great charm and hospitality, asked us to lunch. As the passage to the shore was obviously too long and too rough for our dinghy, he put his launch at our disposal for the time of our stay. They left, the minor officials following the Commissioner, like polyglot ducklings after a white duck over the side, and they were soon quacking and cheeping their way to the shore. From the anchorage the island appeared as barren hills running up to the peaks of Le Piton and Molinser, a few terraces, a few casuarinas, here and there some small white houses on stony ridges, the barracks of the Cable and Wireless Station, the mast at the Meteorological Office, and the low red roofs of the flat little village, crowded in between the foothills and the sea.

The boat was soon back and we set off to see more, leaving the Siamese cat and *Tzu Hang* rolling heavily almost hull down on the horizon. Ashore to the luxury of hot baths, to a meal for gourmands of underdone steak and good wine, to the luxury of a walled garden, and stretched out legs in a chair firmly planted on a solid floor.

After lunch we drove up to the Meteorological Office and there found a man passionately addicted to the winds and the weather. He blew out of his office like one of the gusts that he loved so much and seized me by the hand. 'What sort of weather did you have?' he asked. 'Did you meet Amy?' We found out that the swell that had been pushed up to us on Pitt Bank had been caused by Hurricane Amy, who had passed between us and Rodriguez. Not a serious, but a very early storm, and important enough to have earned a name.

'Now we will go and see what the winds have been,' he said taking me in to see the filed daily wind sheets, which showed by an ink line the strength of each gust that had blown. 'See here,' he said, 'forty miles an hour—phew, and here forty-six— pheew, and here again, forty-seven—pheeew.' His happy season was approaching when the gusts and the phews would come thick and fast.

From the Meteorological Station we took the road up the mountain to a point where we could look round most of the circumference of the island. On the southern and western side the reef extends four miles or more from the shore, and the pale blues and greens of the huge area enclosed are surrounded by a wide border of breakers. This is the island's most striking characteristic. Wherever you look is the brilliance of the shallows, white spotted by the sails of fishing boats gliding in still water, while outside the surge of the trade wind sea grumbles forever on the coral edge. Yet this brilliance and the rumbling reef, usually framing rustling palm trees, white sands and tropical greenery, here sets off sparsely clad brown hills standing brusquely out of the sea.

We drove on to St Gabrielle, where there is a wooden barn of a cathedral, and found about thirty Creole girls playing rounders in front of its steps. The Creoles of Rodriguez are of all shades of colour, tending to the very dark. They look a cheerful people, and we were always struck by the cleanliness of their clothes and the muscularity of their legs. The colours of the girls' dresses, all washed and bright, the brilliance of the all

surrounding shallows, a splash of colour from bourgainvillaea
or flamboyant, a darting cardinal or a quarreling mynah, all
gain value in contrast to the universal drabness of the land—a
clean wind-washed, sun-scoured drabness of stone and rock,
and not the drabness of street and slum.

After the lush and tired Seychelles—apart from Coetivy—
Rodriguez is an exciting place, for everywhere there are signs
of successful attack on the boulder-ridden land—an attack
spear-headed by an agricultural officer from Yorkshire, obstin-
ate like most of his countrymen, and with a superabundance of
good humour and tact. He has walked every inch of the island
again and again, pushing, pulling, and prodding the conserva-
tive Creole farmers into better ways. Almost the whole of the
farmland was now being terraced under his direction, whole
hillsides had been reafforested, irrigation ditches had been dug,
and in one place rice was being planted.

There were six breeding stations on the island, where Large
White sows and Black Australian boars were founding a new
Creole pig, where Black Spanish and White Sussex are probably
doing the same thing for the hens, and where an Indian and an
African humped bull regarded each other with the same
suspicion that the Indians and the Africans do in Africa, as they
father a milk herd and make their progeny available to the
Creoles. Only the ducks seem to require no improvement. Never
have I seen such stout ducks. Perhaps the hills exercise has the
same effect on them as it does on Creole legs.

Round the island runs a tract of free grazing, known as the
cattle walk, where the thin herds wander on the cliff edge, in
sight of the golden fish-nets stretched on racks to dry along the
sea-shore and above the brilliant water. The grass is coarse and
sparse, beggared by erosion from the hills above, an erosion that
the Agricultural Officer spends most of his time in trying to
check. Beryl and I walked round to Grand Baie on the cattle
walk and down to its wide sandy head where children were
running races in the sand. Rodriguez has a great runner called
Le Race and the island is full of stories of his prowess, a rival to
Abebe if he could be 'discovered.'

We couldn't leave Rodriguez without seeing the 'Cavernes'
on the south side of the island. These limestone caves stretch for
five hundred yards underground, with many side entrances

waiting for enthusiastic spelunkers to explore—a succession of halls and passages, filled with stalagmites and stalactites, peopled by the strange shapes of leaping shadows, thrown from the blazing branches that we used as torches to light us through.

It is 330 miles from Rodriguez to Mauritius, and it took us just under three days easy sailing. For some time after we had left the island we could see the waves humping up to port and the smoke of their spray drifting over the long extension of the reef. We set the twins and rolled comfortably on our way to the well-remembered downwind noises, the clink of a cup, the gentle surge of water along the hull. It was a pleasant change after so many miles to windward.

One hundred and fifty-two years before, the expedition that Lord Minto had referred to in his letter was just getting under way from the same place. It had been mooted and very nearly put into effect ten years before, when Lord Wellesley was Viceroy and his brother Sir Arthur was Commander-in-Chief in India, but owing to trouble with Admiral Rainier, the Naval C.-in-C. in India, the invasion never took place.

Before its postponement Lord Wellesley wrote to the Admiral in charge of the Cape Squadron asking for the intensification of the blockade of the French islands in preparation for the attempt. In order to deny the islands to the privateers a partial blockade had been instituted, but the ships were withdrawn during the winter to the Cape. The Admiral replied that his ships enjoyed such good relations with the inhabitants that any intensification of the blockade would arouse their suspicion. The Wellesleys didn't have a great deal of luck in their relations with the Navy.

Nothing more was done about the occupation of the islands until 1809, when a small force was sent from India, of British and Indian soldiers under the command of Lieut.-Colonel Keating, to occupy Rodriguez. This they did without opposition, as there were only two French families on the island, and they were not on speaking terms with each other. After organizing a base and landing stores Lieut.-Colonel Keating and Captain Willoughby, of the sloop *Otter*, went on to try out the defences of the Ile de Bourbon (Réunion), where they carried out some exciting and successful combined operations and created a fine moral ascendancy before they withdrew.

The Navy used to use Flat Island, one of the four islands just off the north coast of the Ile de France (Mauritius), for exercise and Willoughby here had a gun explode, breaking his jaw and exposing his windpipe. He recovered from this, being now promoted to command of the frigate *Nereide*, in time to take part in the final occupation of Bourbon, with a mixed force that had arrived from India and was again under command of Lieut.-Colonel Keating. No landing party ever seemed to go ashore without Willoughby at its head, and the presence of this terrible sailor seemed to overawe the enemy, for he complained that when it came to running they made better time than the sailors.

He was in at the occupation of the Ile de France too. As a preliminary it was decided to capture the Grand Port in the southeast of the island, a large area within the reef, studded with coral and gained through a narrow channel, which was guarded by the Ile de Passe a small island on the edge of the pass. Willoughby carried this by a night assault by boats and was then left in command of the island, with the *Nereide* anchored close by. Soon a French squadron of three ships and two captured Indiamen arrived. The French flag was flying from the fort and a ship anchored close by, so they stood in through the pass, glad to do so because the fort on the Ile de Passe sent them a perfidious signal to say that the English were cruising in superior strength off the north coast.

As they entered the pass the Union Jack was run up on fort and ship, and fire was opened. All except one of the Indiamen, who turned aside and was later captured, withstood the fire and managed to make Grand Port, where they set about re-equiping and repairing the damage as quickly as possible. Captain Pym, the Navy commander, hearing of the engagement, left the blockade of the French ships in Port Louis and hurried round. He decided with Willoughby to enter Grand Port, destroy the enemy ships, and then return to deal with the four that he had been blockading.

The *Iphigenia*, *Nereide*, *Sirius* and *Magicienne* all stood in, but *Sirius and Nereide* grounded, and, although the French were all put ashore, the British were in no better state, and those who remained found themselves shut up in their turn by the French ships from Port Louis.

The *Nereide* was a wreck with no single man left unwounded, amongst them Captain Willoughby who had lost an eye. *Magicienne* and *Sirius* were set on fire in order to prevent them falling into enemy hands, and *Iphigenia*, who had also been aground but had been got off again, with the Ile de Passe, was surrendered. It was a resounding set back after a very hot fight, of which I had never read, but with what confidence the British had sailed in to destroy an equivalent force, under the cover of shore guns, satisfied that to be English gave them sufficient superiority!

This left the French temporarily in superior strength, but not for long as other British sail were on their way, and what remained of the French squadron was soon locked up again in Port Louis, and surrendered on the capture of the island. When the invading force arrived the landing was made just north of Cape Malheureux, and the surrender followed only a day or two later. One might say that sufficient resistance was put up to satisfy honour, but there was no life and death struggle. It may have been that the previous good relations between the blockaders and blockaded helped. By the terms of peace the islanders kept their language and their laws and until today have been happy to be British.

We sighted Round Island early on the morning of 25 October, and then sailed between Flat Island and Gunner's Quoin, and on past where the ships had anchored to put their troops ashore. The island seen from here could not have altered much since those days, for there was hardly a house to be seen, only the green canefields and the mountains behind with a great boulder balanced on top of Pieter Both. It required no great feat of imagination to picture the three-masters at anchor and the lines of boats filled with redcoats rowing in to the shore. We sailed on in calm water keeping half a mile off the reef, as bay after bay, all with attractive names, appeared. As we approached the channel through the reefs into Port Louis, a Japanese trawler, a little more confused in its history than we were, hoisted the French flag as it turned to enter the passage. A pilot boat came up to us and called to us that it would show us to a mooring. We followed it up a long double row of shipping, moored fore-and-aft along the edge of the reef up both sides of the channel, to a buoy at the head of the harbour. Here we would lie comfortably, as the wind, they said, would always come offshore, and where we need have no anxiety about leaving her.

Our first visitor that same afternoon was a very enthusiastic and energetic young Muslim who was building himself a 'Tidewater' design sailing yacht in which he and his attractive wife Rasoul intended one day to sail to England. He was running a stevedoring company, had a furniture factory and a sugar plantation as well. He delighted in business, and we knew that much of his pleasure in building a boat would be in using the very best materials which somehow or other would be obtained at bargain prices. He and Rasoul drove us round the island on the following day and from one Indian picnic to another until we ended up at their house for dinner. With them we met Dr Mansour a Muslim, and his wife, an Austrian and also a doctor, who was in charge of the Family Planning Clinic. She told us that she had some difficulty in persuading people not to have too many children when she herself had had four in under four years.

All Ismail's activities were insufficient for his energy, and he showed us some plastic buttons that he was starting to make. He said that the trouble with plastic goods was the cost of the machines and that it varied in direct proportion to the size of the article. A button machine was the cheapest. 'Now that is something that you could do in Canada,' he told us, 'the two of you could manage very well.'

'But if I made buttons I should then have to dispose of them.'

'Of course you'd have to have a van, or a station-wagon would do. And a good slogan on the side, "Smeeton's stay-on buttons," or something like that. You'd load it up with buttons and drive round selling them. You'd make all kinds of money. People are always in need of buttons. Especially in the backwoods. They simply fly off in the woods.'

Somehow I could not really picture myself as a button salesman, even if I succeeded in making them. Neither could Beryl, but she was enjoying the idea so much that she continued to egg him on to expand his theory, until I really began to fear that she'd have me making buttons before long.

Roughly three-quarters of the population of 667,000 are Indian, of which a third are Muslim. A nineteenth are Chinese and the remainder are the descendants of the old French families or of their slaves, and the few English and people of other nationality who are lumped together as 'general population.' When the island was first taken over by the British and the slaves were freed, it was found that they would not work as free men on the plantations. Indian labour was imported for short periods, but later, at the request of the planters who wanted to retain experienced men, allowed to stay, with the result that the government of the island by democratic vote is now in the hands of the Hindus. That it should be entirely in the hands of the Hindus with the coming of independence, was viewed by Ismail, the proud Muslim, with concern. 'Independence without economic independence is plain nonsense,' he declared—good words to hear from someone about to emerge (although unwillingly) from the yoke of colonialism. But independence might make sense for Mauritius if the price of sugar holds up and the hurricanes stay away. The majority of their population are an industrious people, prepared to work in order to get on.

Unfortunately the hurricanes have not stayed away for the last few years, and rows of close-grouped and appalling little houses of concrete or asbestos, slums before they were occupied, have been built to house the cane workers who had lost their homes in the storms. They were built with English money by South African contractors and it would be hard to imagine anything less imaginative, or why the contracts were not given to a local contractor and local architect, who would surely not deface his country as these have done. 'This is the 2,000th house built by so-and-so,' said a notice beside the road, but it would have been better if they had kept quiet about it.

While we were in the harbour two American oceanography ships working for the Scripps Howard foundation were in. The skipper of one of them hailed me across the street to drink a beer with him. Soon he was telling me some of his history. 'I was a wrassler at first,' he said.

'A wrassler?' I repeated, quite at loss and then, remembering my Western lore. 'You mean you broke horses?'

'No, no. All in,' he said and tapped the table with the palm of his hand in the wrestler's signal of surrender.

An hour or two later on his way out of the harbour he was

'wrassling' with the reef. For some reason he took his staunch ocean tug across the channel and down outside the line of moored ships.

'Quick!' I shouted to Beryl below. 'He's going aground.'

Everyone who could see the scarlet-shirted captain on the bridge, waving goodbye tried to tell him by voice, whistle or signal what he was going to do, but he took it all as a popular response to his farewell.

The captain of the Messageries Maritimes ship outside which he was passing ran to the wing of his bridge and shouted down to him, '*Non, non. C'est impossible par là,*' at the same time waving both hands across his face in a negative signal.

'Goodbye, Captain, goodbye!' roared the American, and he continued to wave merrily as the tug rose slowly out of the water and came to a halt. Gradually the wave died and his big hands fell to his side. He was hard and fast for twelve hours, and only got off with every available tug pulling at the very top of a spring tide. It was his last chance for a month.

When Matthew Flinders was returning from his exploration of the Australian coast he called at Mauritius, and was made prisoner by the French, who held him for seven years until he was released by the British when they captured the island. Of the inhabitants he wrote: 'Many of them are of the ancient noblesse families ... a great deal of cordiality and mutual and unaffected kindness exists in their society . . . the number of elegant females is surprising; they are remarkably handsome, have a great deal of wit and vivacity, and are very engaging in their manners.'

One hundred and fifty years later they are still the same. In their lovely homes they still manage to live a wonderfully gracious life, under the shadow of an uncertain future. A particularly dark shadow, I felt, for those who had fought so bravely for England in the last war, but then the whole world is changing, and who shall bear the blame, if blame there is, for something good and gracious that is passing?

At length, after climbing both La Puce and Pieter Both and looking down at the green apron of sugar spread below and the emerald ring about the island's coast, we released the wind from its responsibility with the buoy and allowed it to waft us down the double row of shipping. We had a volunteer crew on board and the Harbour Master at the helm, and needless to say they consisted of some of those elegant females who had so impressed both Matthew Flinders and me. As we passed each moored ship, Norah and they were greeted by successive broadsides of wolf-whistles and invitations to desert sail for steam.

We went up the coast in two brisk tacks to Grande Baie, which is entered just south of Canonnier's Point, south of Cape Malheureux, using the Butte aux Papayes as a leading mark—but all the sailing directions round Mauritius abound with romantic names. In a couple of hours we brought the wind abeam and slid in with little to spare under the keel and the coral clearly visible, but without a care in the world since the Harbour Master was still at the helm. A three-cornered match was being sailed between Mauritius, Madagascar, and Rèunion, and the bay was bright with coloured sails hunting eagerly round the fluttering markers. We anchored off the yacht club. The bay was surrounded by a low green shore, the lovely green hills behind, the water pale blue and the trade wind kept us cool and sent the small yachts hissing through the water. Next day we sailed down to Black Bay on the other side of Port Louis, another deep indented sheltered anchorage, over-shadowed by the hills. From there we had to make up our mind to leave, but it was on no great journey, for the Ile de Rèunion, our next objective, was only seventy miles away, and Port des Galets on the northwest corner, thirty miles further. I think that there is no place that I have enjoyed more nor left with greater regret than Mauritius in all our travelling.

We left in the afternoon. The sea was calm, the Trade Wind cut off by the mountains, and it was some time before it could greet us again. Then up went the twins once more, and next morning we could see the great mass of Rèunion, standing like Teneriffe, high in the sky. We idled across with only a light wind, watching the afternoon clouds gather in a dark mass, and the lightning flicker and dart about the mountaintops as we closed the shore. Presently the lights of St Denis in the north had joined the show and started winking away to port as we approached the northern end of the island. We picked up Pointe des Galets light and hove to for the night off the entrance to the port.

Owing to the way that the mountains of Rèunion plunge

down to the sea there are only two harbours, both artificial, where it would be safe to leave a yacht. The rest are open road-steads and ships are advised to quit them at the first sign of a storm. Of the two harbours St Pierre is so ill spoken of by the *Pilot*, that most yachtsmen would content themselves with the Port des Galets. We visited St Pierre—but by car—and found that it did not look as bad as it sounded. The harbour is in disuse owing to its silting up, but a yacht could probably get in. Port des Galets is also waging a battle against silt in its entrance, but it is quite safe although less attractive.

We went in under power between two jetties, up a channel which is only half a cable's length wide at its narrowest point, and then, after squeezing round a dredger, we turned sharp to port and then to starboard. Then we sucked in our sides and crept up a narrow alley between the dark perpendicular sides of two merchant ships, either of which we could have touched with a short boathook. On arrival at the far end, and after disentangling our masts from their mooring lines, we tied up to a platform surrounded by the sort of rubbish that always seems to fill dead-ends in harbours. It included, as on every beach in the Indian Ocean and amongst every collection of flotsam, a Japanese plastic sandal.

The arrival in Port des Galets is the only unattractive aspect of Réunion. Ashore it was obvious that we had arrived once more in a *département* of France. Here again were the debonair and friendly police, the nonchalant customs official, and the missing Harbour Master, enjoying no doubt his aperitif. Here were the well-known posters, but no well-stocked bistros, and no bread to be carried like spears down the road. In fact most of the edible and potable things that make landing in France such an exciting affair seemed to be missing. These were all in St Denis, and also our letters, lost in the bowels of as maddening a post office as ever one could find in France.

The local yachtsmen carried us away to the yacht club. Not only was the Commodore a doctor, but all the members seemed to us to be doctors too. There was bathing in a sucking current that swirled along the coast, a barbecue and 'Le Twist.' The doctors were indefatigable, and so were their wives. They were ardent dinghy racers, and two of them were having a cruising yacht built in France. They were pilots who flew small aircraft round the steep edges of their island, all of them seemed to have one of the latest types of sports car.

'I've never been in a Porsche,' I said unwisely.

'Never been in a Porsche! That must be remedied immediately.'

I soon began to wish that I was back at sea. The mountain road wound steep-sided in cascading hairpins high above the breakers, and it began to look as if I soon would be. If the tyres were not screeching as we drifted sideways into the corners, dogs and chickens were doing so in the straight.

'That is where Madame Pelte spent the night in her car,' said my driver waving his hand to a treetop below the road edge. I didn't have to ask how she got there but how she got down.

'With ladders,' he replied as if it was the normal thing to park your car on the top of a tree.

Next morning Madame Pelte herself drove us faultlessly down the west coast, down the rich sugar-growing coastal plain, and over a bridge that crossed a deep and narrow gorge, where a mountain torrent had cut its way to the sea, and at the bottom of which, as might be expected, was the remains of a touring car. We drove with gorgeous views of blue sea and white-footed brown rocks, and then high up through narrow green-hung gorges to a mist-shrouded village below the Piton des Neiges. As we climbed higher the hill peasants grew paler, the *Pattesjaunes*, until we wondered if there was any mixture of Creole blood at all.

At midday on 13 November we set off again, bound for Fort Dauphin at the southern tip of Madagascar and 500 miles away. Although the official hurricane season had started, we felt no sense of urgency, as they are not expected before mid-December. Once we were away from the lee of the huge mass of mountains we were able to set the twins, and we made good progress until we anchored under the shelter of Pointe Itaperina, four days later.

As we ran down towards Pointe Itaperina, wondering if the furthest hill-top that we could see on the horizon was actually the cape, the wind freshened steadily until we were fairly slicing along. Over Pic St Louis the clouds swelled and towered, until all was lost in darkness and the one point that I thought I had identified had disappeared. We wanted that hill to give us a bearing, so that we could clear Itaperina rock, four cables south of the point, which we now seemed to be approaching at unprecedented speed.

'What course are we supposed to be on?' asked Beryl.

'The course that's set. 230 isn't it.'

'Well we're steering 200 and if I steer 230 we are not going to clear the cape.'

Curtains of rain began to drop across the hills and little whitecaps to flicker all around us. *Tzu Hang* was racing with the wind almost alee, for the twins had come down that morning, and now the wind had shifted back to dead astern. Anxiety began to flutter in my heart, and I hopped up and down hoping to find a breadknife or a spanner near the compass that might explain the sudden discrepancy between where I thought I was and where the compass told me I was.

'Isn't there something about a compass anomaly in the book?' Beryl asked. I looked and found that there was—experienced sometimes up to twenty miles offshore, northeast of Itaperina point. With a squall whipping us along, Itaperina rock still unidentified, the compass unreliable and a warning from the *Pilot* that the anchorage at Fort Dauphin was untenable in a northeast squall, and with only a roughly-drawn chart to go by, small wonder that the only entry in the log for this day is, 'At 0630 handed twins and set the main. At 1730 at anchor due west of Evatara lighthouse in a small bay.'

Yet there was really nothing to be worried about. Just as I was wondering whether we would not have to jibe to give the cape a wider berth, Itaperina Rock spouted hugely like some great whale, throwing a mist of spray to show that we would clear it nicely. We swung round and under main alone forged steadily up to anchor under the shelter of the cape. Across the bay veiled in rain a white box showed, the bridge of a ship at anchor off Fort Dauphin, although we could not see the port. That could wait until the morning. I wasn't going there to see if my anchor would hold in this wind. We closed the reefs under Evatara lighthouse in short tacks until we were just outside the Anse Itapere. Down came the main, away rattled the anchor, *Tzu Hang* paid off and then swung to a taut chain and rode up towards it. We picked up some convenient marks to see that she did not drag and went below for a late tea, and soon the wind died.

The following morning being fine and calm we sailed across to Fort Dauphin and anchored among the ships loading and discharging at the harbour entrance. As soon as we were satisfied that the anchor was well in, we took the dinghy into the little harbour, riding the long swell that rolls in between the cliff and the mole that forms its entrance. If there had been room for *Tzu Hang* to anchor between it and the boats moored at the jetty, which were as restless as a picket-line of mules at feed-time, she would still have been in danger from the lighters which reeled behind tugs in and out of the harbour, like drunks being led off to jail by small policemen. We decided that we were better outside, where the *Norefiord* was anchored, whom we had already met at Mauritius and Réunion.

Fort Dauphin is on the route for ships sailing from Mauritius to Durban, and it is a pity that so many yachts sailing this way should miss it. They are hurrying to put the Cape of Storms behind them, or to enjoy the sophistication of Durban, but in spite of the *Pilot*'s gloomy description, it is well worth a stop; a foothold on the edge of the jungle with a wild and lovely coastline, better seen from ashore than from close offshore, where winds, currents and partial surveys give the yachtsman an inhospitable reception.

Both in Réunion and Fort Dauphin we had to speak French and were so glad to have Norah with us to help us out when in difficulties, and she bore our appalling English accents without sign of shame or suffering. Now she collected a Mr Boitsche, a Swiss businessman and a miner of mica, who took us all for a drive in his car along the new road that was being put in by the Common Market. He also drove us through numerous and devious dirt roads, through green naves of jungle, past little houses built and thatched with traveller's palm, which looked so much cooler than the concrete blocks in Mauritius. Wherever we stopped he was surrounded by a clamorous horde of brown children, who knew that he had a large tin of toffee in the back of the car. Their mothers, sitting at their vegetable stalls, or on wooden benches at their house doors, were slicing mica with deft strokes of a knife into paper-thin slices. These were rejected pieces from the mines, unsuitable for machine cutting,

but once they were so sliced they were of marketable value
again. Mr Boitsche had his manual labour scattered in little
villages all over the district, and wherever he went 'Mr Toffee'
was greeted by shouts of delight from the children and by wide
smiles and a merry roving eye from their stout Mamas, for he
was an upstanding man. These people looked very happy. No
one had interfered particularly with their way of life, and yet
they had the opportunity of working to make a little more
money. Their advance was slow but they seemed to be none
the worse off for it.

At one village he took us to see a sick man who was having
the sickness danced out of him. At the back of his hut his friends
had gathered, women and children sitting on the ground and
beating time with sticks and drums, while man after man danced
a spear dance with the invalid. Although he looked weak and
ill, his skin dry with fever, it was obviously a big day, and he
was enjoying it. Between dances he tottered and looked as if he
would fall, but he wasn't allowed much respite, and soon another friend would come and incite him to dance again to the
admiration and encouragement of his neighbours and, if only
the sweat would break out, to the benefit of his health. 'And
if they don't cure him,' said Mr Boitsche, 'they'll throw him in
the river and see if the shock doesn't fix him.' One way or
another it looked as if it was going to be the end of his moping
about and feeling miserable.

Next day we left for Durban, and as we left the anchorage
the ships and tugs blew their whistles and sirens for us in
goodbye—the only time we have had such nice attention.
We had a grand wind to send us on our way and were soon
under main and jib, then under twins, then under jib alone,
spinning along. Before dark the Norwegian freighter the *Nore-
fjord* came throbbing past us, giving us another salute as she
passed.

The following morning was grey and windy, and even allowing for the coast to be further south than is shown on the chart
—mentioned in a note on the chart—we still found that we had
a big set towards it. *Omoo* had the same set when she made
this passage. By the evening after making a good seven knots
since we had left Fort Dauphin, Madagascar was out of sight.
From then on until we sighted the South African coast a week

later, we had light winds, misty weather, heavy dews and a high glass.

We sighted Cape St Lucia at 0500 hours on 27 November, and to welcome us the wind freshened strongly, so that we came bursting in to the shore, to red cliffs topped by green grass, somewhere between Port Durnford and Cape St Lucia. We stood out again and tacked back picking up Port Durnford light on our quarter soon after dark. By midnight we were becalmed with the same heavy dew dripping off the sails and soaking the deck. A stream of shipping passed up and down the coast, their lights hazy, ringed in the dank mist. Daylight showed nothing but fog, its edges forming a close circle round the ship. We motored in for the shore, and just as it seemed that the swell was beginning to change its form, the coast appeared close to us as if lightly etched on grey paper.

Gradually colour came: green fields, red earth, river-mouths and woods. A pale green aircraft, translucent and immensely high, droned its way over the lovely prosperous land. And with the sun a fresh wind, a perfect day, and the end of another cruise, another passage.

13 *Durban and a Southerly Buster*

EVER since I had read *Jock of the Bushveld* as a small boy I had wanted to go to South Africa, but the nearest that I had got to it was to fight beside the South Africans in the desert. Now, when I see in the press some article about apartheid or the imposition of sanctions, I put my paper down, and my memory flicks back to dust and sand, to camel scrub soughing in the wind, and the shimmering haze on distant dunes, to a South African pilot falling dead as he stumbled away from his burning aircraft, shot down beside us on the escarpment. I remember the relief with which we watched the recce flights from the South African and Rhodesian squadrons come winging home low over the stony ridges, the laconic reports from their armoured cars, and the joy with which I once, myself a fugitive, saw and recognized their patrols. I think of the engineers moving off in the darkness to clear the gaps in the minefield, and of the anti-tank gunners crouched behind their thin shields amongst the smoke of the shell bursts as they tackled the enemy armour. We were glad enough to have them with us in the dark days.

Cape Natal, or the Bluff as it is also called, marks the entrance to Durban harbour and stands out unmistakably, topped with trees. As we approached it I wondered if I'ld meet some of those soldiers that I had known in the desert; I knew I'ld meet other soldiers, friends from Indian Army days, who had settled in Natal after the war. Just within its northern side are two break-waters guarding a narrow passage that leads into the wide open spaces of the harbour, with its deep channels and wharfage, its shallows and mudbanks, and on week-ends its hundred small yachts racing round. Northward the town stretches east and west with good buildings rising from the long Esplanade to the Berea hills. Our first impression as we approached the harbour entrance from the north, was of the roomy spacing of the houses on the hills. Before we had cleared the passage through the breakwaters, a pilot boat had picked us up and a pilot came on board and took us across the harbour towards the north shore.

There, west of the long pier where the Union Castle ships go was a low breakwater behind which a double row of yachts were moored, while a hundred more stood in rows on the yacht club hards, a variegated fleet of fit and unfit boats with names that varied from lovely Zulu words to something as solidly ordinary as *Mabel*. There are few places in the world where travelling yachtsmen will find a better welcome, or better facilities than in Durban. While still in the hands of the pilot we were boarded by Arthur Jones, the kindest of yacht club secretaries, from the Royal Natal Yacht Club, who showed us to a mooring, and before we were moored up we were hailed from a passing yacht and told to make use of the Point Yacht Club whenever we wished. With the ship secured, with a free boat service to the shore, with baths and a club, and a good slip available when we wanted it, we couldn't have been better off, and if we wanted a night or nights ashore an invitation was never lacking. There is nothing superficial about this hospitality. It is something deep and genuine, growing from the richness of the land itself.

Durban is pre-eminently an English town, and Natal itself pre-eminently English. When we were there the Union Jack still flew over the town hall in Pietermaritzburg. Most of the people we met were British or of British extraction. I would have liked to have met more Afrikaners and if we had, I am sure that we would have found equal kindness. We found our old Indian Army friends quite unchanged. Age had not wearied them nor the years decayed. They had worked hard and successfully, and in their spare time still hurled themselves over showjumps on their horses with undiminished youthful enthusiasm, and only now and then an arm in a sling to show that bones were more brittle. Mine certainly were. My arm was soon in a sling from a too vigorous attempt to run out Arthur Jones at cricket.

Perhaps the oldest continent—unchanging—affects those who come to live there, and they too remain thereafter unchanged. Perhaps that is the whole trouble in Africa and explains the lack of effect that two thousand years of contact

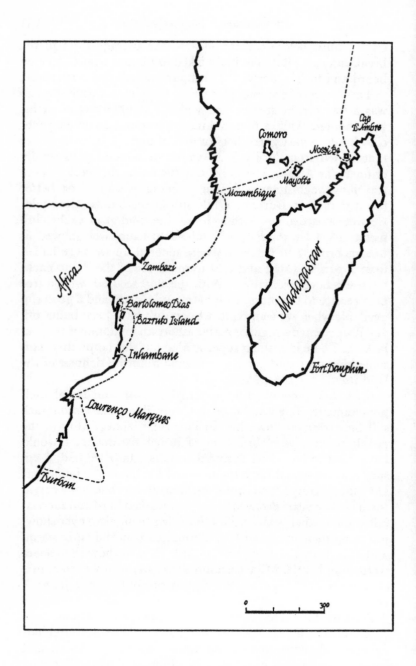

Africa

Comoro

Cap
D'Ambre

Nossi Bé

Mayotte

Mozambique

Madagascar

Zambezi

Bartolomeo Dias

Bazruto Island

Inhambane

Lourenço Marques

Fort Dauphin

Durban

0   300

with different civilisations has had on the people of Africa. Perhaps that is the reason for apartheid and that whereas everywhere else in the world now, man insists on the equality of races, the Afrikaner still insists on his superiority over the coloured peoples. Considering what they and the British have achieved in the short period of their occupation and what the coloured peoples achieved in the two thousand years in which they have been in touch with civilisation, it is an understandable mistake.

The existence of apartheid in Durban was not particularly obvious. The stone benches on the grass that ran along the side of the Esplanade were marked in large letters for Whites or Blacks, and looked very silly and pompous, but most people who wished to sit there sat on the grass under the shade, and the grass was free from racial discrimination. I, being absent-minded, often found myself in the coloured queue at the Post Office, and was ordered to my right place with just as much severity as a coloured man would have been ordered out of the white queue. This sort of differentiation is objectionable to most of the people of Durban, but the rules are imposed by a government of great authority whose power falls equally on black or white who may oppose it. We had friends whose houses had been searched and friends who had been warned that if they continued too ardently on the political course that they were pursuing, they would be subjected to house arrest. 'You may wonder why I don't go into politics,' said a man we met, young and able and brave too, I have no doubt, 'but I have a wife and children that I have to think of.'

As we were visitors and guests we avoided talking even with our best friends about the emotional subjects of apartheid and the secession from the Commonwealth. They feel too deeply about these things; and one avoids the subject as one would avoid talking about a young wife who had gone off her head to an anguished husband, or about a moronic child; a tragedy that exists but isn't mentioned. Whoever they were, farmers, business or professional men, their relations with their labour were exactly as we would have expected or hoped that they might be—in the factory or the field the relations of an officer to his men, in the home one of affection and trust, and compared to other parts of Africa the wages were extremely high.

Behind this of course there is the harsh discipline of an extremely efficient police force and a rigid and bigoted government, convinced that they are on the right path and that only they know. Most of the people of British extraction and a great many Afrikaners are much more liberal-minded, but they are being forced over to the narrower Afrikaner view by continuous criticism and the threats and appeals for the imposition of sanctions that abound in the United Nations. British people too, who return to England, who may have spent a lifetime working for Africans, for the improvement of their health and their social conditions, are shocked by ignorant and almost hysterical accusations and have come back no longer opponents of the present government. The feeling that all the world is against a country leads to a war psychology that draws all parties together. Whatever we may feel about apartheid and the dictatorial ways of the South African government, although we may regard them both with horror, by threats and continuous criticism we do the cause of Justice nothing but harm. What after all is freedom anyway? There are not many places in the world where it exists, and the lack of it in South Africa, for most coloured people, is nothing more than an inconvenience to set off against good pay, good food, and employment. How else does one explain the hordes of recruits that come down from neighbouring African countries for labour. What freedom exists in Ghana or Malawi?

If one believes in the ultimate good in man it must be that the racial question in South Africa will eventually be solved and not necessarily by our ideas of democracy, any more than our ideas remain applicable in the other African countries enjoying freedom. There are proportionately just as many noble and generous men in South Africa as anywhere else in the world, and the future will lie in their hands, with help, not with enmity, from outside. Anything else, attack from within or without, they are strong enough, rich enough, and hard enough, to withstand. And should it come to that, there will be both a racial and a religious war with all its ruthlessness, for which we outside will be partially to blame for denying the right of those to govern who are best qualified to govern, for what amounts to denying the South Africans a right to their country.

When other nations in Africa have proved over a period of

years that it is possible for white and black to live together peacefully and equitably under a democratic black government, then is the time for further action. In spite of the idealistic western outlook which we can so comfortably afford, the common man, most people, in Africa and Asia, do not want freedom if it brings hunger, poverty, and anarchy in its wake.

Tzu Hang rested for four months in Durban, peering over the breakwater wall at the channels and shallows of the main harbour, and at the flamingoes on the mud flats at low tide.

By an extraordinary chance she was lying next to a great green painted Colin Archer, the *Sandefjord*, once Erling Tambs's ship, that had also pitchpoled and survived, although with the loss of one of her crew, in the Atlantic. Her huge bluff bows, great beam, and short stubby masts, made *Tzu Hang* look unusually slim and elegant. Seeing them side by side like this, made us think that no matter what the design or who the designer, there are waves, particularly in the higher latitude, that can make a nonsense of all our plans. I know that I do not want to meet one again.

Norah had had to leave us soon after we arrived. She was off to the East with a date to keep to motor back to England from India. She was going to be missed. Even in the early days when she must have been miserable with seasickness, she never showed it, nor missed a moment of her watches. I shall always remember her, her dark hair escaping from the hood of her oilskin, bent over the compass with so much intentness that she did not notice the rain pouring down as if she was under a fire hose and finding its way through the joint between the hood and the collar and trickling down her back.

It was now the end of February and time for us to be on our way again. *Tzu Hang* had been slipped and painted, and as she watched the week-end races, the Dutchmen, Finns and Sprogs, tearing and planing in a many-coloured exuberant horde down the windy channels, she seemed to stir with a vague excitement as if she too was eager to be off.

Early in March a southerly buster arrived, screaming white-faced across the bay and hurling itself at the thin line of yachts entrenched behind the breakwater It was the sort of wind that makes the heart of the most bearded and salt-encrusted yachtsmen think twice about going to sea. We laid out an anchor,

hooking it behind a rock at the foot of the breakwater while
Tzu Hang strained back at her mooring.

For once it was too tough for the little yachts, so used to
strong winds, and they piped their protest on the yacht club
hard. In spite of this a blue sloop was making ready for the sea.
I walked down to the steps where it was tied, thinking of a very
experienced Canadian sailor who once said to me, 'At least I
know enough to know when not to go to sea.' I wondered if this
owner knew enough. They were already in oilskins and too far
advanced in their preparations before a watching crowd for any
change in plan, and shortly afterwards went scudding out under
a headsail, fading quickly into the gathering darkness and looking very brave against the big ships looming through the rain
at the wharves. Outside they found conditions much worse than
they had expected and managed to put about, but it took them
all night to get home again, chastened and glad to be safely in.

This was the wind that we needed if we were brave enough
to use it, to rush us up past Cape St Lucia against the swift
flowing Mozambique current, bound for Lourenço Marques,
then up the coast of Portuguese East Africa to Mozambique,
across to the Comoro Islands and Madagascar, and then to
windward across the Indian Ocean, into the Southeast Trades,
until we could pick up the Southwest Monsoon to take us to
Ceylon and Singapore. Without a southerly wind the current
can still be beaten by keeping close inshore, but I felt that we
needed a full moon, a depth-sounder and a fisherman's knowledge of the coast to do that sort of thing. It is a job for power
and not for sail. The other alternative is to go right out to the
centre of the channel, two hundred miles offshore, but this
makes a long journey of the 340-mile passage to Lourenço
Marques.

While we were in Durban we had had a letter from Chris
Rosslee, an airlines pilot, asking if he could sign on as crew for
a passage, as he intended to build himself a big trimaran and
take to a cruising life when he retired from the airline in a few
years' time. It was such a nice letter that I went to see him when
I was in Johannesburg. He had a lovely house which he had
built himself with a couple of African helpers, high up on a
ridge, so that he could look down on a street below him as if it
was a strip on which he was about to land. He was an enthusiast

for anything, but particularly for flying, and I'm sure that every time he looked out of the window he thought with satisfaction that he was well lined up and on a good angle of descent. We were convinced that he was so keen on a trimaran in order that he might still have wings on each side of him. His offer came at a very good time as the sailing doctors had refused to let me go off with a loose shoulder and had just cut it open and done a splendid repair job on it. With a reef and some stainless steel screws it is now as good as ever, but we were glad then to have a third hand. Since it was Durban they had refused also to charge for the operation.

Unfortunately another southerly had just blown itself out on the day that Chris arrived, but since he only had a limited leave, we left anyway. It was on the lightest of the northeast winds, but with an ugly oily swell left by the southerly in which we wallowed about outside the harbour.

We had not gone far before I saw something floating in the water. We made our way towards it and I saw that it was a piece of carved wood. By lying on my stomach on the deck I was able to pull it out of the water. It was a carven image about two feet high of a bearded man sitting on a stool with his hands placed inwards on his thighs. He was wearing something round his neck that might have been a cross. He had a black face, and his robes had been coloured. Somehow I did not like him. He had an unpleasant aura. But Beryl was delighted. We tied him to the mizzen-mast below deck, so that he surveyed the length of the ship. Almost at once the wind strengthened and we were able to lay the course, close hauled along the coast. A rolling rich coast, cut by river after river, with tall gums standing by white farms, and soon the sugar growing close and stretching far as prairie wheat.

By nightfall we were off the Tugela river, the land showing indistinctly through rain and low cloud. We checked the current by keeping the bow on a clump of gums and watching to see if the bearing changed, but found no set either way. This was the coast that had extracted such a toll from the great Portuguese carracks four hundred years ago, homeward bound and overloaded from Goa. Here their survivors had struggled up the coast beset by tribesmen and enduring the most appalling conditions of thirst, starvation and sickness, hoping to reach

Delagoa Bay and some ship trading in ivory and amber from Mozambique.

The comfortable settled land has long forgotten these tragedies, but the sea and its currents, the winds and the rocky shore are as harsh and untamed as they have ever been. We decided to give the coast a wide berth for the night. The wind strengthened as we heeled on the port tack, and the small lights from farm and village that had begun to prick the darkness quickly faded—course east and a set to the south.

We spent the next day and the one after that virtually hove-to under the mainsail on the port tack, knowing what little benefit is obtained from a thrash to windward against a strong current, and hoping to edge out of its main drift. None of us were feeling too strong after a long spell ashore. It was the sort of time when we wonder what on earth started us on this uncomfortable and nomad life, when the restless night stretches interminably ahead, full of crashes and buffetings, and the morning brings no great cheer either. It is fortunate that everything passes, that the sun and fair winds will soon come again, and that folly is easily forgotten. But I didn't like the image, glowering at the foot of the mizzen-mast, any better.

By the end of this we were once more in the latitude of Durban and 150 miles offshore. Jerry Troubridge, the bearded South African who sailed round the world in his ketch *White Seal*, told us that in similar circumstances he had found himself away south of Durban until picked up by a southerly and deposited at Lourenço Marques.

The same thing now happened to us. On the afternoon of the third day the wind died altogether and early next morning came from the south. But there was to be no moderation in its treatment. For six hours we had splendid sailing with the main reefed and the jib boomed out on the other side. Suddenly the seas seemed to be mounting very high and looking dangerous, probably as a result of the current against the wind, and we brought down the main. Once a retreat starts it can soon become a rout, and no sooner had we one sail down than we began to wonder why we were carrying any sail at all. Down came the jib, and we ran on under bare poles. A suitable moment arrived, and we swung into the wind and held *Tzu Hang* there under the engine while Beryl and Chris set a very small trysail. As Chris was a beginner at this sort of thing and I was one-armed, Beryl was the only really able seaman that we had on board. It was blowing 38 to 40 knots on the ventimeter, a corrected Force 9, and it continued to blow Force 8 all next day. We had the most uncomfortable night as the trysail turned out to be too small to keep *Tzu Hang* pointing high enough to avoid some nasty thumps.

We set off again under our tiny trysail next afternoon, running twenty miles in three hours but hove-to again for the night as we were unable to see the run of this irregular and uncomfortable sea. Next morning the gale had blown itself out, the sea was down, and we were on our way again. At nightfall there was a glow in the sky that I confidently announced to be the lights of Lourenço Marques. They turned out to be those of a Japanese fishing vessel, working under brilliant arc lights, the first of several that we were to meet all across the Indian Ocean.

On 26 March, a week after leaving Durban on this 340-mile passage, we were still at sea. It was a perfect day under all sail, and in the afternoon with the genoa set, the bow rippled through dark blue water. In spite of the rough weather and the long passage there was no dent in Chris Rosslee's enthusiasm. A question about flying was better than any seasick pill when the weather turned bad on us, and he charmed away all our doubts including his own, about the stability of our stomachs. He was the pilot who some years ago landed a big Boeing jet at Nairobi airport in the dark in thick weather with his landing gear and most of his controls out of action, and as he told the story we lived every second breathlessly as he brought the great aircraft down for a belly landing through low cloud and without the help of any ground landing control system.

That night we really could see the lights of Lourenço Marques in the sky. We closed Cabo Inhaca early in the morning, the cliff standing black and high beneath its lighthouse, and lay off for an hour till the coming day brought first greyness and then colour to our surroundings. We found our way in through the well-marked shoals that guard the entrance to the bay, passing a black pilot boat in the channel. A long spring tide was ebbing, and the wind blew right out of the head of the bay, twelve miles away.

'When will we get in?' asked Chris, eager now to get back to his flying or perhaps to his family to tell them of his sailing.

'Some time this afternoon,' I replied.

'Good God,' he said, 'if I was in my aircraft now I'd just be reaching for my cap.'

Lourenço Marques grew slowly out of the haze; the curved waterfront took shape, and the grey-painted dredgers, working in different channels, hurried off to the dumping grounds and back to work again, as we slowly stemmed the tide, ate our lunch, and drank our wine—the locker being freshly filled from Durban.

The wind freshened as we passed the buoy at the turn of the waterfront, and we found ourselves sailing faster, down a line of ships moored at the edge of the channel, just when we wanted to go slower. After a turn back we picked out the narrow entrance to the boat and ferry harbour, a pocket in the long line of wharves, half closed by the stern of the off-duty dredger. Through this narrow opening ferries kept popping, as cluttered with a flock of dark figures as a bush of roosting starlings. We went in crabwise against wind and tide. Inside we felt like a large bird pushed into a small cage filled with nestlings. On every side, from every ledge and corner, wide mouths were opening in incomprehensible advice. Then, above the multitude we saw a tall Englishman, removed, alert and cool, standing at the top of the steps. It was Charles Spence, an old friend who had already smoothed our passage with the authorities, and he now stepped on board and offered to pilot us across the river to Katembe, where he said we'd be able to anchor in peace.

We anchored there in good mud, a cable off a Goanese fishing village which stretched along the shore, with boats pulled up in front of the wooden huts, and nets stretched along the beach to dry. Charles Spence and Chris rowed themselves ashore in the dinghy through an ugly chop that had been whipped up by the afternoon wind. They were loaded with baggage and cameras, and looked about as safe as if they were afloat in a dish of *Tzu Hang*'s Cornish kitchenware, but they made the shore without a wetting and promised to send a boat so that we could recover the dinghy.

Next morning a Fokker Friendship climbed and circled above the estuary before leaving for Johannesburg. We guessed that Chris would be looking down to see the white pencil of *Tzu Hang*'s hull in the river and wondered what impressions he would be taking away with him. He was one of the pilots that did the longest over-ocean passage in the world, from Johannesburg to Cocos Keeling and Perth. The possibility of ditching and how to do it was consequently often in his mind. 'I never realised before that gale,' he said, 'how hard the sea is.' Another time he said, 'You know that from the moment I take off until I am down again my mind is always occupied with details of time, distance, ground speed and fuel consumption. I know that I have only a limited time in the air. You take off and the one thing that doesn't seem to worry you is time. I suppose that I shall just have to get used to that. It's just as well that it doesn't matter to you, or you would be round the bend by now.'

Beryl and I sometimes think that is exactly where we are.

'And will you still build a trimaran?'

He wasn't sure.

14 *To Inhambane—and More Wind*

LOURENÇO MARQUES, which curves round the shoulder of a hill and overlooks the wide estuary of the Espirito Santo river and across Delagoa Bay to the blue-green Inhaca peninsula, has no great historical background and few fine buildings, but it has a lovely sea front road that runs the whole length of the shore below the hill, lined with trees and bright with flowers and bougainvillaea, with ships passing close through the sparkling waters of the bay. In the old days it was a small trading post to which the Portuguese ships came for ivory from Mozambique. The bay is said to have been first discovered by the captain of one of Vasco da Gama's ships, on his return from India, who went in in search of supplies and water, and named it the Baia da Lagoa. The original trading post was on the other side of the estuary, and the fort and settlement that have since become the great port of Lourenço Marques, named after the navigator who explored the bay in 1544, were only established in 1871. It is as different from Durban as Calais is from Dover.

The shopping centre extends for a few streets behind the wharves on the river bank and is crowded with a humming throng of Africans of all colours, of Goanese and Europeans— such a mixture of races that when a large spaniel trotted past me on the pavement, sniffed at a lamp-post and went on, entirely preoccupied in his own affairs, wearing horn-rimmed glasses and carrying a pipe correctly in his mouth, it only struck me as remarkable after he had passed. I looked round, thinking that my imagination had been playing tricks, and saw Beryl rooted to the pavement in astonishment. It is lucky that she saw him too, otherwise by now I should have said that the dog had a paper under his arm.

There is no segregation of races, and if there was any under-

current of unrest, there was no sign of it. The Africans seemed
as happy and as at home, and as assured, as anyone else and it
felt just as much their town as a Portuguese town. They jostled
on the ferry more efficiently than we, a good humoured throng,
and they drank strange coloured drinks in the public park in
the centre of the town, sitting on whatever bench they fancied.
There was a holiday atmosphere about, perhaps increased by
the holidaying South Africans who filled the town. At least they
seemed to fill the town, so starkly large and luminous did they
appear amongst the dusky small-statured throng. Tall fair and
fecund, they looked as if they were newly arrived from another
world. The hoteliers and the shopkeepers call them the 'Banana
Tourists' because they are heading for the beaches, and with
large American cars and trailers, stuffed with camp beds and
good South African provisions, bananas are all that they are
said to buy. Not all their time was spent on the beaches, for the
tourist launch that made a trip round the harbour was loaded
with them and *Tzu Hang* was brought into the sight-seeing
itinerary. One morning we heard the guide explaining on the
loud speaker: 'That is a special kind of boat, owned by wealthy
Portuguese.'

We went to a bull fight, where in the Portuguese fashion the
bulls were not killed. They were recently imported from
Portugal and were game enough, particularly one who made
himself virtually master of the arena and was most reluctant
to leave. The best spectacle was when twelve tough Portuguese,
local townsmen, tackled the bull barehanded and on foot, the
object being to bring him down. The bull's horns were padded
but were still formidable weapons, and the leader of the team
went in between them, and grappled the horns, while the rest
of his team pushed and pulled and tailed the bull in an effort
to bring him down. That seemed to be the idea, but the bull had
ideas of his own, and he bowled them over right and left and
scattered them as a Springbok forward might scatter a pack of
small boys.

Charles Spence lent us an outboard engine, and on fine days
we used it on the dinghy to cross the estuary to go shopping or
visiting. This led to one or two return passages in the dark,
when a fresh wind had got up and small waves were running,
and we were very glad to get a hand once more on *Tzu Hang*'s

rail. As an alternative we left the dinghy on the beach by the Goanese village and took the Katembe ferry across to the other side. One night we returned by the midnight ferry, dressed in our best clothes. We found that an extra high tide, combined with a fresh wind, had washed the dinghy well up on the beach. It was now full of sand and water and weighed a ton. We undressed, put our clothes in a plastic bag that Beryl was providentially carrying, and half naked on the beach set about emptying the dinghy and launching it through the surf. There was a feeling that all this had happened before and was exceedingly likely to happen again, but rather than repeat it here, we decided to get off.

Next day we paid a call on the Portuguese Admiral, a small grey-eyed sailor, neat and precise, who received us with an old-world courtesy in a huge panelled room high over the harbour. He took us to the chart room and gave us some charts of the coast, so attractively drawn and coloured that we shall put them in a frame one day if we can keep them clean enough.

We made sail on 18 April, gliding up the long well-buoyed channel on the tide, bound for Inhambane a little more than two hundred miles up the coast. As we passed the light structure called Resinga da Xefina, the wind came dead ahead, and we decided to sail across to Portina da Inhaca on the south side of the bay. In the old days the ships that came to this bay to barter for ivory, used to catch sea birds on the low bush covered island on which the light stands, the Ilha Xefina Grande, 'large as geese, and so plump that their grease is used for the lamps and binnacles of ships.' We saw no sea-birds now, but there is a long point of sand, said to be growing, which stretches out from the light.

We anchored under the barracks on Black Bluff, in the shelter of the Baixo Chaimite, the passage being marked by one red buoy, but the black buoy that should have been marking the other side was missing. The wind was from the north, but we were well sheltered by the shoal. An old gaff cutter, a fishing boat with patched sails and a long bowsprit, tacked quietly up the channel between the shoal and the cliff, and occasionally a bugle sounded from the barracks above.

Next morning was still with mist and fog in patches hanging about over oily grey water. We left under the engine, and an hour later, when in the middle of the shoals and with the tide running strongly, the engine began to complain, and to my horror I saw that the oil pressure was right down. I stopped the engine, took off the cover, and saw that everything was swimming in black oil. I pressed the starter button and was rewarded by a direct hit with a jet of oil square on my anxious nose. As if in sympathy with our plight a light wind came from the east. We hoisted the main and *Tzu Hang* set off by herself as if she knew the way out of the channel, while we started the sordid job of patching a burst oil pipe and cleaning up the mess. 'That bloody image,' I mumbled, but I did not like to say it too loud.

By eight in the evening we had lost Cabo Inhaca light and at midnight we tacked offshore. By four we had the Limpopo light abeam, and when daylight came we could see the tops of the trees about its mouth. The grey-green, greasy Limpopo. Even out here the water was discoloured and sluggish as we passed the branch of a tree, floating sadly out to sea. Wind northeast, Force 4. We started to make good progress and by nightfall had 120 miles on the log.

There was a wonderful sunset. High above us the whole sky was covered by a light downy cirrus cloud, so that, as the sun set, from the horizon to the meridian, the sky flushed red, changing only in its intensity towards the zenith. We had noticed it on the last few evenings in Lorenço Marques. Tonight it was mentioned on the radio, and Beryl and I, together with the announcer, began to wonder what it might mean. However pleased shepherds may be, anything out of the ordinary bodes little good at sea. Little ships begin to wonder what is in store for them, and hoping for a quiet night we reefed the main and handed both the mizzen and the jib, although with a full crew we would have kept all sail.

When I came on my second watch at four in the morning the wind was much lighter, and an hour later we were virtually becalmed. The whole sky to the south was dancing with lightning and a line squall coming up towards us. With only a reefed main I waited for its arrival with equanimity, watching the lightning throwing cloud shapes into relief so that I could imagine all sorts of battle scenes, the roll of cannon, billowing smoke, and high-piled sails. Fifteen minutes later a light breeze came from the south, and the long roll of cloud was passing overhead, the lightning following close behind. 'Funny that there was so little wind with that squall,' I thought, and was then aware of a growing hiss of wind or rain approaching. It hit us with tremendous force, blowing, if I hazard a guess, at between 60 and 70 knots for a short time. *Tzu Hang* heeled far over, and there was a sudden crack from the sail and a frenzied thrashing and shaking. Beryl was up on deck almost as soon as I, and together we clawed the frenzied main down and then lay along the boom trying to stifle its thrashing until we could get some tyers on. The rain whipped our faces and the wind snatched our breath away and blew out our cheeks as we shouted to each other. As soon as the sail was safe we jumped below, towelled ourselves dry and left the wind to whistle in the rigging, although the main force of the wind had only lasted a few minutes. We then set the trysail and hove-to on the offshore tack while Beryl got down to a whole day of stitching. The sail had split from leech to luff about a foot along the boom, fortunately along a seam, although it had torn along the tabling at the leech. It was now four years old and had been exposed to all kinds of heat and sun and the stitching had weakened. We had it overhauled in Durban, but it was obvious that it needed completely resewing. The mishap foretold the end of the image, whom even Beryl began to dislike, although of course we did not like to say anything about it until we were safely in port.

We stayed hove-to for the night and next morning, after getting a good sight of Venus, found ourselves much further up the coast than we had expected. The wind had put the Mozambique current into reverse. Under trysail and storm jib we rattled off to the north. At ten in the morning we were twenty miles south of Point Barra, and by two we were rounding the point, the wind having eased. The reef sticks out half a mile from the point, and on its end there is an old wreck, still intact enough to look from a distance as if it is a ship at anchor under the shelter of the cape, shelter which I suppose she was seeking when she came to grief. We gave her a wide berth, watching the breakers spouting round her, but some tiger of a storm had dragged her out of their immediate reach.

Beyond the wreck there were two ships sheltering; a Portuguese frigate and a South African fishing boat from Capetown, manned by Cape Coloured who are said to make the best and toughest sailors of the whole coast. They were both southward bound and waiting for the wind to ease. We sailed under the stern of the frigate and on towards the big fishing boat whom we guessed would be in shallower water. Even she was in eight fathoms and after messing round for some time in search of shallower water we anchored ahead of them in seven, and let go thirty fathoms of chain. It was a restless anchorage, miles away from the low sandy shore that encloses the whole bay. A boat put off from the frigate and came towards us. 'Captain's compliments,' shouted an officer, 'and he would be most grateful if you would dine with him. We will send a boat to pick you up at six-thirty.'

At six-thirty we set off, bounding across the bay, while *Tzu Hang* shrank to the size of a toy ship, and the cat that we had left wailing on the deck hurried below to check the food-locker doors. We clambered up the grey weltering sides of the frigate and were led into a small wardroom full of clean and smartly creased young men, all of whom spoke English well. The weather? 'The weather is going to be good,' they said. The bar of the Inhambane river? 'No problem,' they said, 'if taken at the flood.'

We left rather late after a splendid dinner, with *Tzu Hang*'s light just showing in the distance. She hoisted us on to the deck with her roll, with an air of disapproval.

We left next morning before the frigate, who was bringing in her chain as we sailed under her stern to wave goodbye. We soon picked up the channel buoy eight miles north of Cape Barra. The waves were breaking on each side at the bar, but not in the channel. Inhambane is fourteen miles up the river of the same name, which flows northeast parallel with the coast and separated from the sea by a peninsula, of which Cape Barra is the northeast tip, and by a series of low islands, sandbanks, and mud-flats. There are two bars to cross; the outer of two fathoms over which the swell humps and rolls and sometimes breaks, breaking right across in bad weather, and a narrow inner passage over a bar of only one fathom, but where there is no danger from the swell. The forebodings of the *Pilot* are dismal; the shoals and mud banks are continually changing, and the position of the buoys and beacons is apt to lag behind.

We found the buoys without difficulty, but they did not conform to the courses or to the beacons on shore, and when we rounded No. 4 buoy and should have had a clear passage down channel, we found our way completely barred by breakers. We put about and sailed back to the last buoy to check our course again, but there was no way through. We felt hemmed in by shoals and breakers and uncertain what the tide was doing to us. We were tempted to withdraw to waters that we already knew and to put out to sea again across the bar but remembered the difficulties that must have beset early navigators without even a chart to help them, and so mustered a little more courage of our own.

On the beach there was a recognizable mark, named 'Pedestal' on the chart, with deep water close inshore; so, with breakers to port and on the beach ahead, in fact all around except for the passage by which we had entered, we headed for this mark. Presently a channel opened in the breakers to port, and we could see our way through, and far beyond to the small speck of the next buoy. We found later that No. 4 buoy, at the critical turning point of the channel, had dragged three hundred yards from its correct position. From then on there was no difficulty, and the wind was far enough in the east to allow us to sail all the way up the channel, and that was just as well, for the patch on the oil pipe was a very temporary affair, and the pressure was down again when I tested it.

It was a glorious sail. To port the mud-flats glistened in the sun, with here and there a small lateen sail showing as it threaded its way down some private channel. Beyond the mud-flats an occasional flash of white showed as some breaker curled and broke higher than the others. Further up on the port hand we could see the coconut trees on the Ilha dos Porcas and on the Ilha dos Ratos, but we couldn't see Inhambane even when quite close to it, as it was hidden by a fringe of coconut trees. To starboard the land was at first hilly with brown grass and green scrub growing in patches on the hill sides. Half way up the channel we could see Linga Linga point, on which stood tall trees, and the country beyond, lower and tree clad.

Presently the red roofs of Maxise, a small village on the opposite bank from Inhambane, appeared and a constant flitting of small sails across the river and finally Inhambane

itself from behind its screen—first the end of the pier, then the
clustering red roofs and finally the white clock tower of the
church, with the clock stopped at twenty minutes to ten. There
is little reason for a clock in Inhambane, and apparently little
reason in Maxise either, for the grandfather clock in the mission
house, the only timepiece of any importance on that side, was
stopped also. We sailed past the end of the pier that reaches out
three hundred yards across the mud flats to a T-jetty. A small
cargo ship arrives once a week and takes up the whole of the
jetty, but there is a place behind one concrete shoulder, where
the big Portuguese-type fishing boats jostle together while they
unload their catch or take on ice. This was too noisy and over-
looked for us, so we anchored in five fathoms a short way from
the pier, with just enough room to swing clear of the mud-bank,
which is covered with weed and sea-cucumbers, and where the
dugong come to feed at high tide.

There were always some Africans sitting on the stacked timber
or the piled copra bags on the pier-head, watching the tide
flow up and the tide flow down, only occasionally exchanging
a few words, spitting into the sea, and sometimes singing a little
falsetto song to themselves, as they gazed at the fishermen casting hopefully into the tide. Before the arrival of a ship they were
joined by a chattering throng of Africans, who streamed up the
pier for their entertainment, like sandgrouse to their dustbath,
and thronged the jetty as the ship drew alongside. Then there
was a mill of turning trucks, swinging derricks, and swirling
spectators, which reached a crescendo as the time for departure
arrived, for the boat having come up on one tide probably
wanted to go down on the other. There was a rush of eager
helpers to cast off her lines, and, as she drew away, the crowd
began to thin and disappear. Soon the pier was still and almost
deserted again. The only movement to be seen was the flick of
a fisherman's arm, or the leisurely movement of one of the tide-
watchers shifting from an upriver to a downriver stare. Beneath
them the tide swings up and down the river at up to four knots,
by far the most restless thing in Inhambane.

In the evening about the Jardim Vasco da Gama, at the
seaward end of the Avenida da Republica there is a *passeio*
under the trees. The Africans on foot, the Portuguese in expensive cars, looking pallid and well-manicured as if they never

exposed themselves to the sun or to manual labour, for these are the *functionarios* and this is the seat of government of a large district. As in Lourenço Marques we noticed immediately the friendly attitude of the Africans. This is a real multi-racial town, and we were often spoken to, usually in Portuguese to which we replied in Spanish, both sides understanding a little of what was said. When we mentioned this to Roy and Anne Tucker, two English people, whom we had the good fortune to meet, they said, 'Yes, they are friendly people. They think you are South Africans.'

'South Africans. I thought that they were supposed to be unpopular.'

'Good heavens, no. They all want to get down to South Africa. It's a sort of Eldorado for them. Good wages and shops to spend their earnings. When they come back they are "travelled" people and have something to talk about. And they like the South Africans who come here and spend a bit of money on their holidays.'

Roy Tucker had organized and built a cashew nut factory for Charles Spence's firm, Spence and Peirse, one of the oldest British firms in Portuguese East Africa. Before the invasion of Goa the cashew nuts were always sent to India to be processed in the factory there. When relations were broken off the firm decided that it would build its own factory and process them in Inhambane where cashew nuts grow wild all over the place. Roy came from India to set up the factory and it was already doing well. The heart of the factory was a Heath Robinson furnace, into which the nuts were poured and then passed through by a hand-operated worm gear. The nut has a virulent juice, which blisters where it splashes, but which the furnace disposed of. In more advanced concerns it can be extracted to make brake fluid. After passing through the furnace the charred husk is beaten off with a small piece of wood with a leaded end. This is done by hand as no one has yet devised a machine for husking cashew nuts. The kernels are then sorted, cleaned, and tinned for export. With all this sorting and husking a number of hands are required, three hundred in this factory, and I think that Roy knew them all by name and had a merry way with them, so that the girls were all laughing and rolling their eyes at him, as he led us down the benches.

We drove out to the beach and along to the wreck on the rocks and picnicked on the shore. The sandy road twisted erratically past coconut trees and cashew trees, past neat little native villages with separate houses, with a goat or a cow tied near, cooled by the sea wind, cleaned by the sun. 'Gracious living,' said Beryl, 'unspoiled by white hands.' The Portuguese may not have done a great deal for their people in Portuguese East Africa. I do not know. But they do not appear to have done them any harm, and my impression is that the African is happy to be Portuguese and more—a strange word to use—at home there than anywhere else on the East African coast. Perhaps it is the religion of his masters that believes all men to be equal in the sight of God. 'Of equal birth, but very far from equal worth.' Economically at any rate there were problems with the cashew nuts that did not altogether compensate the saving in shipping; in the Indian factories the women worked harder and were paid less than the belles of Inhambane.

We spent a week in Inhambane awaiting the arrival of a new oil pipe. Every day, all day long, the little lateen-sailed cargo-carriers and ferries sped backwards and forwards across the river, crabwise against the tides, and running up on to the beach at the end of their journey, where they stayed in little groups, the beautiful curve of their lateen sails fluttering loose in the wind. They looked like the butterflies that we had so often seen ashore, clustered trembling on some moist patch of sand, beside a jungle stream.

15 *Goodbye to the Image—
to Mozambique for Ann*

WE saw a lot of Roy and Ann Tucker during that week, and when they admired the image we offered it to them—rather diffidently as we were not sure whether it was a nice gift. They took it and their servant told them that it was a good image and would bring luck. 'Why do they want to give it away?' he asked.

'Because they have had too much bad weather since they found it.'

'But it brought them here safely, didn't it?' Before our arrival the Tuckers had lost their cat which they were very fond of, but they had seen or heard nothing of it for some time. The morning after the image was established in their dining room the cat returned. 'I told you it was a good image,' said their boy. The morning after that I asked Roy if all was still well.

'I suppose so,' he said, 'but a funny thing happened. We haven't seen a cat for weeks, and first ours turns up, and now another has arrived. I hope he's not going to bring a plague of cats now.'

When we last heard from them the image was still in favour and there was no mention of cats. I suppose that with two cats in Africa a plague of kittens is so inevitable that it wasn't worth mentioning.

As we set off down the channel we felt very glad to be rid of it and never have I missed an ornament less. Every time that we had ventured into the Mozambique channel we had hit a strong southerly and either because the wind was too strong or we were too cautious we had not made full use of it. Even the *Spray*, in the Mozambique Channel, Slocum said, 'suffered as much as ever she did off Cape Horn.' Now we were heading for Bazruto Island and Santa Carolina, called in Rhodesia

'Paradise Island,' a hundred and forty miles to the north, and since we were getting higher up in the channel, we no longer expected the winds to be so strong.

We climbed over the big swells on the bar with the sails slatting, but before we were round the marker buoy the wind steadied in the southeast. We made slow progress against the current, and by 0500 hours next morning were only fifty miles from the buoy. Then the wind began to freshen. By seven in the evening we had 127 miles on the log, and by eight next morning 200, but by position only 137 and rounding the northern end of Bazruto Island. The island had been visible at daylight looking exactly like a bit of the Libyan coast on a winter's day; the sky overcast, the sea grey and rough, the island a long dune above its cliffs, with the sand smoking away in the wind all along its crest. Since Bazruto is an island there is obviously a southern entrance through the few miles of shoaly sea that separate it from the mainland, but this has not yet been charted, and on a day like this long rows of breakers far out to sea guarded the secret of its shoals.

As we sped round the northern end of the island, close under the lighthouse, looking for the narrow channel leading south to Santa Carolina, we were able to see a large extent of white sand which was now uncovered, clearly marking the eastern side of the channel. The channel is not buoyed, but I expect that at high tide the sandbanks would still be visible from the colour of the water. Right under Cape Bazruto, her nose resting on the sand, one anchor astern and one on the bank, a big fishing boat was lying on the edge of a patch of clear blue water. We envied them their knowledge of the shoals that enabled them to find such comfortable resting places, but decided that we had better plug up the channel that we could recognize, particularly as we could now get a bearing on the tree-tops of Santa Carolina itself, which had just appeared on the horizon. We furled the sails and started to motor, but, although we had the tide to help us, we could only make two knots against the wind and sea. I decided to anchor before the tide changed on a shallow spit which crossed the channel half way to Santa Carolina. We found it with the lead and anchored on the far side, so that if the anchor moved we would be pulling into shallower water.

Even in five fathoms and with thirty fathoms of chain the strong southerly wind had kicked up such a steep short sea despite the protection of the shoals, that *Tzu Hang* behaved as if her chain was a whip that she was trying to crack. We tried all sorts of tricks to stop its thumping in the hawse-hole, and in the end shackled our forty-five-pound kedge anchor on to the chain and let go another ten fathoms. That stopped the unpleasant thumping immediately.

There we stayed quite comfortably, and for the next day too, as we guessed that Santa Carolina, which is a long thin island, running north and south, would give us little protection from the southerly wind. Also we were in no hurry to face the task of recovering all that chain. The best protection that we could find, when at last we mustered the energy to deal with it, was close off the northern point, from where we rowed in to a little beach backed by casuarinas. Santa Carolina, so horribly named Paradise Island, is a lovely little island, marred by a large sprawling hotel. It has long curving beaches, a variety of shore birds, trees, and honeymooners by the dozen, pink in patches, photographing each other under the casuarinas, and sometimes looking rather bored with paradise.

We were expecting a young tobacco farmer from Rhodesia, who had sufficient tobacco baled up to escape from his worries for a few days, to join us, and as soon as he arrived on the little ferry boat from Inhasson on the mainland, we set off for Bartolemeu Dias.

Twenty-six miles northeast of Cape Bazruto, a thin spit of sand, marked at its base by a tall line of wind-tattered casuarinas, stretches north to Ponta Macouvane. Within this strip of sand is the mouth of the Govura river and on the far side of the channel Ponta da Pedra, with tall trees growing on the shore there, too. On the east bank of the river some way up the channel once stood the port of Bartolemeu Dias. The houses have gone with a great wind and tidal wave, and the river has taken the wharves. Only if one searches can any trace of settlement be found, the foundations of a house in the bush or the remains of some old revetment on the river bank. It is still a secure and sheltered anchorage, as beautiful and wild as one could wish for. There must be many similar places where a yacht could find shelter along the Portuguese East African coast, backed by that huge, mysterious and largely uninhabited country, where one might meet an elephant only a short stroll from the ship. We were only able to touch the fringe of the possibilities of cruising there.

Bartolemeu Dias is a most fascinating place to visit—a difficult place to enter, between sandbanks and over two shallow bars, with the buoys, although good and in the right place, so distant one from the other that they are difficult to pick up. It is so deserted that you feel that it is a secret place that you alone have discovered. The *Pilot* as usual is gloomy about the dangers of shifting sands, but there is plenty of water in most of the channel, except over the inner bar where there is a depth of only nine feet, and as the tide runs at up to four knots it has to be crossed at fairly low water if you wish to take the flood up the channel. It kept us sounding busily until we were safely over.

As we approached the place that we had selected for an anchorage we saw that another yacht was already there, the *Walkabout* who had once sailed from Australia and was now owned by Jamie Marshall from Marendellas in Southern Rhodesia, whom we had met the year before. He and his family were living in tents and a bothy ashore. He had moved *Walkabout* from the dirt of Beira, and for the time being was keeping her in this clean, deserted anchorage, with two African boat boys to look after her. The Marshalls had flown in Jamie's aircraft—he was a pilot during the war—to Inhasson, and then had motored in the Land-Rover twenty miles along the beach at low tide to Bartolemeu Dias, such complex manœuvres for a short holiday being really nothing to the average Southern Rhodesian.

We went out to the end of the point in the evening to watch Jamie's son and one of the African boys casting into the breakers. The sky was dark with cloud whose edges were spilling, white as tattered towels on a line. The breakers were hitting the beach at an angle and seemed to race each other along the shore until their outer ends escaped round the point and rippled off into calmer water. The two young people, one white, one African, were casting beyond the breakers and pulling in some splendid fish from just outside, both completely happy and engrossed. They and the racing breakers made a joyful picture of movement against the sadly drooping sky.

Next day Jamie drove us to Inhasson. We slid down a steep sandy bank on to the beach and then raced along the wet sand, the wheels sometimes skittering through the ripples. For miles we saw nothing but deserted beach, but as we approached Inhasson we saw men pulling in a seine from far out to sea. The net is dropped from a row-boat perhaps a mile out to sea, the ends of the ropes attached to it being brought to the shore. It is then hauled in by hand by several pairs of men each with a wooden pole to act as a yoke, which they attach to the rope leading from the seine, and then straining against this yoke, perhaps six or seven pairs of men on each rope, they tread the sand slowly up to the cliff edge, and as each pair arrives they in turn detach the yoke and run back to the sea, wade out as far as they can and attach the yoke again to start their solid plod inshore.

There were several of these seines being pulled in, and one was being drawn by tractors—this concern was run by a Chinaman. Many fewer fish are brought in than they caught a few years ago, because the constant dragging of nets along the bottom has cleared it of weed that used to provide shelter for them. We saw one come in, mostly full of puffer-fish and another fish with excessively poisonous spines.

Mozambique is only 500 miles by the direct route from Bartolemeu Dias, but there is a considerable contrary current, and I knew that we would be lucky if we made it in under 700 by the log. In fact we sailed a little more than 700 miles before we arrived. We sailed on 12 May, leaving *Walkabout* careened on the sand to have her bottom painted. The glass was so low that as soon as we were over the bar we made haste to get offshore. In the evening the wind was light from the east, and the full moon came up through a haze that flattened it at its bottom, so that it looked like a huge pumpkin lantern with a greenish glow in the sky above. Sirius and Canopus were blazing as evening stars, and the Plough and Arcturus appeared like old friends that we hadn't seen for some time. It was good to see the northern stars again. There was a ripple in the sea as if we were on the edge of the coastal bank, and a strong south-westerly set from the current which we did not escape from for two or three days.

On one night during our passage, while an American astronaut circled the world above us, we saw such a glow of lights over the horizon that we thought a big ship must be approaching. Later several small lights, not running lights but dim little lanterns showing on and off like fireflies as they dropped behind the swell, passed or overtook us, moving so fast that, although we could not hear the sound of an engine, we knew that they must be very close. Although we never saw the ship over the horizon, we saw later that she was operating a searchlight, and concluded that it must be another Japanese fishing boat, working under arc lights so brilliant that the astronaut might have seen them, and that the dim lights about us had been her motor-sampans, that she was now collecting.

We had a splendid following wind to take us in to Mozambique, and at one time, hearing the distinctive rush of water that means *Tzu Hang* is sitting momentarily on top of a wave, Beryl and I hurriedly put our heads out of the hatch to find Ernest Howes, our farmer, his face alight with enthusiasm, sailing her as if she was his dinghy, with the wind almost alee. We were a week out from Bartolemeu Dias as we sailed between Ilha da Goa and Ilha da Sena, the one bare with a great square black and white lighthouse, the other tree-covered, and both with waves breaking on their coral reefs. As soon as we were through the passage, we headed for the great buttresses of the Fortaleza San Sebastião and, as we sailed under its abrupt walls, caught a glimpse of golden hair as bright as the sun on some old Portuguese helm, above the battlements. It was Ann who had come to Africa to take a second look at Roger Bate, another tobacco farmer whom we had met in Rhodesia, and to give Roger a chance to do the same.

They were both there, come to join *Tzu Hang* for her passage to Madagascar, from where they hoped to get a cargo ship back to Beira. They had seen our sail from the hotel, and had climbed on to the battlements of the Fortaleza to welcome us, as a long-awaited sail must have been welcomed so many times before. It was a most romantic rendezvous arranged many days ago, for which *Tzu Hang* was only one day late. *Tzu Hang* was weaving her spells, and it had a romantic sequel. We anchored a short way off an ugly iron extension of the old pier, which is made of whitewashed stones and built on great stone buttresses as solid and enduring as Vasco da Gama's monumental legs, athwart his pedestal on the sea front and looking towards Africa.

Mozambique is a dying port, but it retains an air of vitality. The large ships trading to northern Portuguese East Africa now use the deep water port of Nacala, as anything for the mainland unloaded at Mozambique, which is an island, has to be transhipped. In the early days of African exploration it was a secure, defensible base from which to trade was essential, but now it is an anachronism, and only the bustle of the coastal trade, by small coaster, by dhow, and by lateen-rigged boats, gives the port an air of clinging vigorously to life.

The streets of Mozambique are narrow, the shops filled with goods for the tourist trade. The African women are gay with coloured handkerchiefs on their heads, and the privately owned rickshaw, with a private man to pull it, is a status symbol. Portuguese soldiers drill within the walls of the Fortaleza as they have always done, the dhows tack silently except for the creak of tackle and the scuffle of bare feet, beneath the battlements, as they have always done, and still from boat to warehouse and warehouse to boat the African stevedores jog, naked and sweating under huge sacks of copra or maize which they carry on their heads, and transfer with a convulsive jerk of their neck muscles to another relaying head, so that the sack hardly falters in its course.

Roger persuaded a reluctant Ernest to drive the lorry in which he and Ann had arrived, several hundred miles over bad and deserted roads, to Salisbury, where they could more easily pick it up on their return from Madagascar, where we proposed to drop them.

'Very good of Ernest,' Roger said, after seeing him off from the little port to which the ferry ran, on the mainland, 'I thought that I had better not tell him about the brakes. That would have been too much.'

'Or of the door that wouldn't stay shut,' said Ann, 'but do you know what we met on the ferry coming back?'

'Not a clue.'

'The African Follies. They are coming to give a show in Mozambique. We've asked them on board. They have a lovely little man in charge of them. I think his name is Mr Mathys. Otherwise they are all Africans. They're coming at two tomorrow. They are simply huge,' she added with a delighted giggle. I can usually guess what has touched Ann's sense of humour and it may have been the idea of me surrounded by African belles that had done it now.

'They'll sink the dinghy. Can they swim?' I asked.

'They didn't look as if they could sink,' said Roger.

Only four turned up. Two fine Zulu girls, Maisie Radebe and Sheila Adams, and a Cape Coloured girl, Rosie, with beautiful eyes but features spoiled by prominent teeth. Roger was sent to fetch them, although he was no great oarsman, but it was a question of weight. He made the trip successfully, but on his second journey, with Rosie in the bow, whose slight figure provided inadequate counterpoise for Sheila in the stern, the dinghy kept ducking its stern, and Sheila's, under the water. They just reached *Tzu Hang* in time.

'Oh you poor girl,' said Beryl, seeing her dress all wet, 'you can't sit in wet things like that. We'll find you something to wear.' And she took her forward.

'Don't worry,' called Mr Mathys. 'She'll be quite happy in nothing. Won't you dear?'

Sheila returned in a moment. She really was rather big for any of Beryl's clothes and had chosen a large bath towel. 'Now what would they like?' Beryl asked. 'Coffee or tea or something to eat?'

'The girls would like whisky, if you can spare it, wouldn't you, dears? But I'll have a cup of good strong tea if I may. It's my stomach. It's in a terrible state. These people of mine. They're really good people you know, but I have to arrange every single thing, but everything. You have no idea the trouble that they can get into. I've got a real nice girl in jail now in Beira. She got married to a Goanese there and there was some passport trouble or something, I don't really know what it was all about, but she wanted to stay there anyway. We are hoping to work our way to Palestine where I've been promised some good engagements. We want to earn as we go, you know. Then I hope to take them to Europe. I've always been in the show business you know. My mother was a very well-known Jewish singer. You'll have heard of her. Its a wonderful life but you leave it. It's just one thing after another with this crowd.'

He lit another cigarette from the stub that he was smoking

and took a long draw through tobacco-stained fingers. He had a long intelligent face which was white and drawn, an effect that was enhanced by the fact that he was not wearing his teeth, which he only put in in the evening. He was dressed in white, with shorts that hung down over his knees and white stockings. I thought that he had a hell of a lot of courage.

'Miriam Makemba, you know. She was in my show, but they've got her in the States now. Making a pot of money too. Now they all want to join the Follies. Rosie here, she's got a good voice, and full of spirit, aren't you dear? And Maisie Radebe. She doesn't do much, but she doesn't need to. Do you, dear? She just stands about and wears some lovely things. She was a beauty queen. I've had three beauty queens in my show. Sheila there. She has a pretty voice. She and Rosie will sing to you if you like.'

Maisie in her blanket was sitting with Rosie's hand in hers, picking off the nail varnish and letting it fall on the floor. Beryl gave them some nail polish remover and then some polish, and while they busied themselves with their nails, they sang to us in between. Maisie sang the little Zulu song about the dung beetle that sweeps the paths clean, and the Zulu clicks came out like pistol shots. She then sang a beautiful lullaby. The moment she opened her mouth I was entranced by this big brown girl, however strange her presence at first seemed in the cabin.

We asked them how they liked Portuguese East Africa and what they thought of apartheid. 'I like it here,' said Maisie. 'You feel much freer here.'

'I don't,' said Rosie. 'I like apartheid. You know where you are. They don't like us and we don't like them. And another thing,' she added, 'if you buy a drink here you have to pay the same as the Whites. Me for South Africa.'

When they left we felt that it was we who had benefited, but the bottle of whisky was empty, although none of the girls showed a sign of where it had gone.

We went to their show in a hot tin hall and it looked as if their journey to Palestine might be partially financed by the Mozambique show, because the hall was crowded and the seats very expensive. The leading lady was what Mr Mathys described as 'pie-eyed,' in fact he was so upset that half way through he went to bed. The company were in tremendous spirits and obviously enjoyed the show as much as we did. It really didn't matter how pie-eyed they were, their wonderful sense of rhythm and tune carried them through. Maisie swayed about, bursting out of her gorgeous dresses, but never opened her mouth throughout the show. Rosie sang, her beautiful eyes flashing so that one forgot her teeth, and Sheila looked just the same as she did in her blanket on board, and sang as beautifully. Roger and Ann went to see Mr Mathys next morning to thank him, and found him as cocky as a sparrow in spite of his stomach, and drinking a martini while he shaved. He was still fuming about his leading lady. 'But you should hear her when she's sober,' he said.

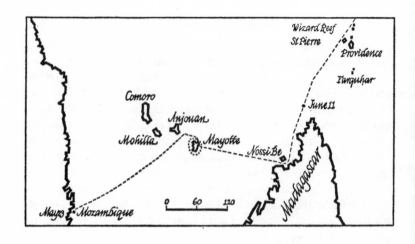

16 *To the Island of Mayotte*

HALF way between Mozambique and Cap d'Ambre, the northern tip of Madagascar, lie the Comoro Islands, thrusting green shoulders into the clouds, leaping with a white splash of spray like the porpoises that play around their shores, straight up into the skies.

The most northerly and the largest is the Ile Grand Comore, of 443 square miles. It is also the highest, with an active volcano smoking at 8,000 feet. South of the Grand Comore lies the smallest, Moheli, and east of Moheli is Anjouan, of only 143 square miles but with a peak of 5,000 feet. Southeast of Anjouan is Mayotte, the only island with a barrier reef all round and various refuges within. At its northeast corner, connected to the small offshore island of Pamanzi by a rock causeway, is the islet of Dzaudzi, separated from Mayotte by a narrow reef-studded passage. Here is the seat of government of the Comoros —as if the French, when they first established themselves in the Comoros in 1843, took good care, like the Portuguese in Mozambique, that their base could be well defended.

A weapon for the defence of Dzaudzi, an enormous cannon on a huge iron carriage, still stands on the summit of the hill opposite the Commissioner's office, staring open-mouthed and

silent over the many-coloured citizens of France, for the
Comoros are French Overseas Territory, and the mixture of
their races is phenomenal—Arab, Malagasy, Bantu, Indian and
European—their religion predominantly Mahommedan.

Jamie Marshall, whom we had met in Bartolemeu Dias, had
visited the Comoros in *Walkabout*, and had told us that above
all we must see Mayotte. He was going to send us a chart to
Mozambique, but the post in Portuguese East Africa or anywhere in East Africa, is not very reliable and we had sailed
without it.

We got away under sail on 23 May and tacked through the
pass under the walls of the fort, making a poor showing against
some small lateen-rigged boats that were doing the same thing.
They had a better knowledge of the tidal streams—that was the
reason I put forward, being unwilling to acknowledge that they
could possibly go better to windward than *Tzu Hang*. Once
outside, the breeze freshened, and we saw no more of our rivals,
making good speed on the starboard tack, closehauled for the
channel between Anjouan and Mayotte, 270 miles away, but
with a southwesterly current against us.

On the evening of the 25th we reduced sail to the main alone,
feeling that land was near, although as yet invisible. It was a
rough dark night, so dark and wild, with the feeling of land
about and of strong currents, that we might have been in the
Minches by the Hebrides, rather than in 13° South. At 0500
hours we had 305 miles on the log, well over our distance, but
no sight of land and a fresh wind with rain squalls still blowing.

As daylight came, a large mountain to port began to dis-
entangle itself from the murk, and soon we could see breakers
at the rocks at its foot, but it was some time before I was convinced that this was Anjouan. There is a reef that lies seven
miles from the island of Zamburu, off the northwest corner of
Mayotte, in the thirty-mile passage between Zamburu and
Anjouan. It was this reef that had been influencing me all night,
because I was certain that I could see Anjouan if I got too close,
but equally sure that we would not see Zamburu from seven
miles away. As a result of this caution we now found ourselves
right on the west side of the passage and we were faced with a
beat to make the pass through the reef on the far side of
Zamburu. We knew that beating against the current we could

not make the pass on this day, but hoped to get a sight of Zamburu so that we could fix the position of the reef and avoid another anxious night.

Anjouan disappeared in the grey haze that surrounded us, but we could not see Zamburu until it was nearly dark. By then we could lay the course, and after a time we hove-to with the island bearing southeast, three miles. Although there was no moon it remained clearly visible all night. Three miles north of Zamburu there is another detached reef, the Recife du Nord, and we stole slowly towards it throughout the night, so that at daybreak the island was bearing south, and we could see the waves breaking on the reef ahead of us. We passed it on the starboard tack and then went about for the entrance to the pass.

I had drawn the entrance through the reef and the passage to Dzaudzi again and again from the instructions in the pilot book, so that I knew the courses and bearings, the reefs and the rocks that we should try to avoid almost by heart. It is a wonderfully exciting thing to do, to enter a strange pass like this with a home-made chart. Everything went well and the obstacles appeared more or less where they were expected and were successfully avoided, but along the coast of Mayotte the wind came dead ahead, and rather than tack up the channel between the outer and the coastal reef, we decided to put into Longoni Bay, which now opened, green, still and inviting, on our starboard hand.

Inside the bay the coastal reef first looked like muddy water issuing from some mangrove swamps at its head, but Roger in the rigging called down that it was coral, and we skirted its edge until we reached the southeast corner of the bay, where we found a small arm clear of coral and wonderfully sheltered. Never was there a lovelier anchorage for *Tzu Hang*. The little bay, ringed by reddish gold sand, and grey weather-worn sandstone rocks, was backed by green jungle and topped by bush-covered hills, showing patches of coarse grass and crevasses of eroded red earth, that gave its colour to the shore. On a far beach a flock of tern was clustered, as if a sack of rice had been spilled there, and in our bay black and white crows hopped scolding about the rocks. The rest of *Tzu Hang*'s crew swam ashore while I rowed the cat to the beach in the dinghy. By the time I had arrived Ann and Roger had disappeared on a voyage of exploration, and presently we heard their laughter from the top of Kongoni point, a mile away across another arm of the bay.

It was so still that they could hear the cat complaining about the heat on the beach. Down an earth road that led through the trees behind the beach came a scuffling herd of cattle, driven by a Bantu in rags, who raised a tattered hat to Beryl as he passed, with all the dignity of a salute in Bond Street, but spoke no word nor turned again to stare. Other than this and a fish-trap across the head of the bay, we saw no sign of human habitation.

In the evening doves called along the shore. *Tzu Hang* lay as still as a boat in a bottle, and, in contrast to the urgent thrust to windward and the doubts and anxieties of the past two nights, all was peace.

We sailed next morning, but discovered as we left the bay that the wind was still dead ahead, blowing along the steep northern shore of the island. The channel between the barrier reef and the coastal reef is complicated by one or two detached reefs. In order to conform more closely to the sailing directions we handed all sail and used the motor. It was still impossible to conform exactly, as we were unable to keep the Morne H beacon in line with the summit of Zamburu on the bearing given. Either the beacon is not where it is supposed to be, or there is a compass anomaly here. The bearing of the beacon has already been corrected once in *Notices to Mariners*, but insufficiently.

It is only a few miles from Longoni Bay to Dzaudzi, with the green hills close to starboard and the swell humping and breaking on the barrier reef to port. Ahead lay the small Ile de Pamanzi, an old crater which the barrier reef joins, filled with sulphurous green water and surrounded by palms. As we rounded the northern shore of Mayotte the islet of Dzaudzi appeared, connected by its causeway to Pamanzi, and topped by the government buildings and the old cannon. A little further on we could see the passage between Dzaudzi and Mayotte itself, with discoloured water marking the reefs on each side. We anchored close to a short stone pier where some lateen-rigged boats were tied, beneath a little street of stone houses, a garage and some small shops. A ferry flying a huge tricolour came fussing in, stirred the sleepy village to momentary wakefulness, and backed out again with great *élan*. Roger went ashore for a haircut and when asked if he would have the French or the American style, he chose the latter and reappeared with no hair at all.

Our first visitor was Monsieur Rigolo of Rédiffusion Française and an enthusiastic yachtsman. He drove us to see the sights, which in so small an area were limited. First the airport, a grass strip on Pamanzi, lined by tall grass and running almost on the the reef itself. Then the war graves in the cemetery buried almost entirely in the same sort of grass. We climbed the wall for the gate was jammed as if there was no great demand on its use. We floundered neck deep in guinea grass, tripped over creepers and cacti, barked our shins on forgotten tombstones, but found no war graves. I had just about composed a letter to the War Graves Commission, when I heard that, though there had been some soldiers buried there during the war, their graves had been moved after the war. It seemed strange that the war had reached even to this little island, although there had been no actual fighting in Mayotte.

Having climbed the crater of Pamanzi, inspected the cannon on the hill, seen the cemetery and the airfield, and met the Commissioner himself, Monsieur Le Bec, we had just about done all there was to do on Dzaudzi. We left a visit to Mayotte on the ferry to Roger and Ann, who being young and attractive were quickly picked up by a Frenchman and taken to his farm, where he raised a number of children and grew vanilla and ylang-ylang, a flower from which a scent base is extracted and on which the economy of Mayotte remains comfortably balanced.

While this was going on Monsieur Rigolo, who had already persuaded Beryl and me to do an interview for Rédiffusion, came back for more. We were enormously flattered that our French had gone over so well.

'Very much enjoyed by all who heard it,' said Monsieur Rigolo in his persuasive way.

Beryl is not so gullible as I. 'You mean that our accent is so funny?' she asked.

'Yes,' he said, 'most amusing, and everyone wants to hear it again.'

From Dzaudzi we left under sail, beating out of the narrow channel through the reefs, one tack taking us past the pier on the southern side of the islet, where Monsieur Le Bec, Monsieur Rigolo, and their wives had gathered to see us off. The Commissioner, small and with a bird-like energy, was waving particularly to Ann, who had partnered him in a vigorous demonstration of the twist the evening before.

We beat south between the coastal reef and the barrier reef, and between various islets, to Amoro Point, on which are the markers for the entrance through the Bandeli Pass, the eastern pass through the barrier reef. Here there was a bay enclosed by the point and sheltered from the southeast wind, where we anchored. Its head was filled by mangroves and dark mud, its sides were steep, with tongues of black sand showing their tips here and there along a wall of volcanic boulders as desolate as a moraine. It would have been a gloomy place except for the green hills behind and the brilliance of the sun and sea about us. Entering it was like stepping into a small cave out of the sun.

We went ashore and found a path leading up the hill behind a fisherman's shack, the only dwelling. We climbed up the hill, passing a small cow that had made the path on the way, scrambled through some dense bush, and emerged on the ridge where the markers were for the passage through the reef. From the upper beacon we got a good view of the pass, whose waters looked deep and tranquil between the stained shallows of the reef and its lacy frill of breakers. Below us *Tzu Hang* lay as still as a sleeping duck on a pond. Seen from this height her masts looked higher than they are, and she herself appeared particularly lovely. The evening sun lit the pillared clouds which overtopped the mountains with a yellow light, brilliantly reflected in the black-bordered pool in which she lay.

We waited for the wind until after lunch next day, and then motored through the pass still without it. We motored for five hours and then stopped for the night. It came at last at midnight, and we had a quiet sail all next day, carrying our genoa through the following night, so that by daybreak we were in the channel between Nossi Be and Point Angadoke on the Madagascan coast.

Nossi Be is a hilly island covered with trees and ravines, whose beauty we had first heard of in Mauritius and Réunion.

It lies in a big hook of the northwestern coast of Madagascar, and is so surrounded by mountains, that its own mountain and the peak of Nosy Komba, an island just south of it, are at first difficult to detach from the wall of mountains behind. We are often asked which is the most beautiful place that we have visited in *Tzu Hang* and find ourselves tongue-tied at the memory of so many beautiful places and such a variety of scenery. It is impossible to compare a coral island and a Norwegian fjord, or Cully Voe with the Arabian coast, but Nossi Be ranks high with all of them. It had a quality of blueness about it. Blue hills, blue sky, blue sea and great blue distances so that an accurate colour photograph would be criticized by an expert for the wrong exposure.

We were bound for Helleville, the port on the southern side of the island. We came to anchor in its small bay between Ponte de la Fièvre, a bush-covered and rocky point, and the promontory on which Helleville is built. The bay is surrounded by reefs, but there is a red buoy to mark one side of the channel, and markers to guide you in, although cargo ships anchor outside. We have found in all countries where the discipline of 'imperialism' has been relaxed that the red buoys remain red, but the black buoys are red with rust, too. Nossi Be was still in the process of a transfer of power and the buoy was still covered with good red paint.

I cannot imagine a more misleading name than Helleville unless there is a lot going on there that we never discovered. It was a prim little village with one broad main street, with the same cannons that we had seen in the Comoros on high unweildy iron carriages. The last mark of the touch-hole cannon, out-of-date before they were used, and therefore sent to the colonies. From this street steep lanes ran down to the shallow harbour with a few small boats moored at its head.

'All is bad in Helleville,' said a furtive man, who sidled up to us in the street. 'Did you ever see such a place? No police and no President.' This seemed to be an excellent recommendation, but perhaps all was not good, for when I went to get our bread at the bakery there was a queue of beggars waiting for yesterdays stale scraps—something that we never saw in Africa. The island is now under Madagascar, but there was a French 'Handing Over' Office still in action.

Roger and Ann picked up a small steamer to take them down the coast in search of another ship to Africa, and ultimately to share the ups-and-downs of a tobacco farmer's life in Northern Rhodesia, where Roger was developing a new farm. Beryl and I, feeling a little lonely, turned our attention to crossing the Indian Ocean, close-hauled on the Southeast Trade and then with the Southwest Monsoon. A Norwegian steamer was anchored in the roads as we left, loading sugar and vanilla from lighters. We sailed through Lokobe Pass, between the green heights of Nosy Komba to starboard and the green forest of Lokobe to port, with Nosy Vorona light, like a Scotch castle, standing on a rocky island ahead. In the evening Les Quatre Frères, four small islands, appeared like haystacks in an empty field. A long lonely passage lay ahead, a wet one if it was going to be like our passage to the Seychelles, and behind us the hills turned away, wrapping themselves again in their deep blue cloak.

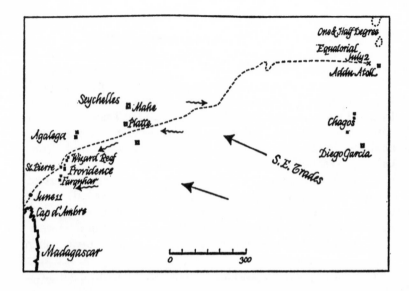

17 *Sunrise to Windward*

FROM Nossi Be to Addu Atoll, at the bottom of the Maldives, is 1,750 miles; from there to Dondra Head at the bottom of Ceylon roughly 600 miles. From Ceylon to the Nicobars and on to Penang is 1,250 miles, and from Penang to Singapore 360 miles: a total of 3,960 miles. And it was 7 June when we sailed from Nossi Be. From July to September there are no cyclones in the Indian Ocean, and those in the Bay of Bengal are tucked away in its top drawer. With the Southeast Trade Wind and the Southwest Monsoon we ought to find all the wind we needed. Allowing for stops at the Maldives, Ceylon and the Nicobars, two months should see us in Penang. Our only difficulties were likely to be the contrary equatorial current that we would have for most of the way, and the passage through the doldrums.

Our long-term plan was to take the Northwest Monsoon down the Java Sea, out of the Dampier Strait, up to Okinawa on the Northeast Monsoon, and so on to Japan. Owing to the

Indonesian policy of confrontation, it did not work out quite like that, but it's a poor plan that can't be altered.

To start with the wind was very light as we crept slowly northwards. First Cap San Sebastian pretended to be Cap d'Ambre, and when Cap d'Ambre did appear in the blue distance, it refused to sink below the horizon. The slow swell rolled in from two opposite directions, stirring the silken sea like the fingers of some great hand moving beneath a cloth. From the depths below us light was reflected as from the star in a sapphire, and poised there, stepped down in line ahead as if they were jet aircraft avoiding each other's slipstream, three sharks followed. They were sinister and streamlined, keeping their position in relation to our movement with a slow wave of their tails. Even Beryl, the most determined of shark-bait, who ignores shark if she cannot see them, was put off from bathing. Later on dark clouds gathered over Cap d'Ambre, hanging there motionless. One put out its thirsty tongue to the sea below, and the water leaping up to meet it was whirled out of the area of suction and fell back into the sea, so that the spout looked like some great shell that had fallen.

On 11 June we had made no easting against the current but had been set sixty miles to the north. The next day was squally, the sun coming up to windward right on the bow, showing its red rim as it broke from the sea, but thereafter giving us little chance of a sight till it was well up in the sky. Day after day it beckoned us on and turned to meet us again before we had reached the Maldives. We had made about sixty miles to the eastward and were approaching St Pierre, when I saw a great skua, a bonxie, the first that I had seen in these waters, beating his resolute and piratical way, low over the troubled sea. In the Southern Ocean I used to think of him as a bird of ill-omen, so rough and uncouth did he look beside the soaring albatross, an evil spirit; but now I like him, because he reminds me of the Shetlands, because he's such an obvious villain, and because he seemed to be a sign that we were off on our long step to the east.

We got a good fix in the evening, which put us seven miles west of St Pierre. Soon after dark we hove-to, hoping to make the landfall in the morning rather than attempt to pass it at night in the wayward currents of those seas. When I'm approaching a low unlit island with no moon, I always imagine that I will not be able to see it until I'm on it. Unless it is so low that it is impossible to distinguish its outline from the swell, or temporarily obscured by rain, it should be visible from a mile away, perhaps twice as far, even on a cloudy night, but unless a close approach is absolutely necessary, it is best to allow your courage to be overcome by your doubt, and wait until the morning.

Next morning the current had carried us out of range, and we never saw it. St Pierre is low and bare, except for a clump of casuarinas and the houses of the Guano Company on its northwestern side. It is steep-to, the holding ground is bad, and in twenty fathoms, so according to the *Indian Ocean Pilot* it is not very attractive, but we would like to have made the landfall, as it is impossible to be sure of your exact position in these waters for very long without a new set of sights, and the evening stars were often hidden. There was an impression of the whole ocean being on the move between and around the reefs, and sudden boils and overfalls might appear anywhere. We made sail again in the morning, but the sea was rough and the weather squally. Although we must have passed close to northward, we never saw the island.

Twenty miles to the east of St Pierre there is a long reef stretching north and south for twenty-five miles, over which at low water there is not even a boat passage.

Providence Island is one and a half miles south of the northern end, and Cerf Island, a sandy bay, lies at its southern end. This is an alarming barrier if a ship's course lies approximately in that direction, but twenty-three miles to the north there is another hazard, Wizard Reef, steep-to, one and a half miles by one mile, and drying at its northern end. None of these dangers are lit. We did not wish to give these reefs too wide a berth, as that would mean falling off to leeward, and wasting days while we recovered the lost ground, so we kept close-hauled and imagined that we saw Wizard Reef a dozen times, but the breakers that we saw always turned out to be tide-rips.

Luckily the stars were out in the evening, and I got a good fix, and according to my calculations we passed it early in the night, leaving it close to weather on our course. It was a great relief when at last we could look at the log, plot our course with a liberal allowance for every kind of current, and say to each other, 'Well now the Wizard absolutely must be behind us.' These last two days were the most exciting part of our passage, with that feeling of the whole sea in movement, simmering and sometimes boiling over, with strange voices that hissed and whispered in the night, with the night cry of sea-birds about us, and with reefs and islands lurking somewhere in the dark. Next morning the only sign of the islands were the Cape Gannets and Brown Boobies that came swinging over the sea with the sunrise, and by midday we saw them no more. These islands, and the islands of the Farquhar group close to the south, would have been well worth a visit, if only to see the birds, but for us with a long journey still ahead it would have been like an astronaut stopping at the moon, on his way to Mars.

A week at sea and only 500 miles on the log, but we were soon to win back, at least temporarily, our normal cruising average of 100 miles a day. During the following week we had fast wet sailing, although a contrary current detracted from our easting and set us ever towards the north. On 16 May we sailed between Platte Island and Coetivy and crossed our route of the previous year.

As always when sailing fast we were a special attraction to the porpoises. One morning I saw a porpoise, far in the distance, leap high out of the water and fall twisting back with a tremendous splash. As if this was a signal, as if one of them had shouted, 'Come on chaps, here's some fun—a sailing ship,' a whole pack of them turned and came leaping joyfully towards us from a couple of miles away. Some of them were jumping and spinning over and over in their excitement, and one walked the water on his tail like a hooked marlin. They were big, their bellies a rosy pink, and a distinctive dark line ran diagonally towards their tail, marking the limit of this colour. I have never seen porpoises quite like this before. One of them jumped out of the water at the bow as high as the lower crosstrees. I was standing at the bow and saw him coming up from the depths like a Polaris missile, and wondered what on earth would have happened if he had fallen on the deck or on the forestay.

There were flying-fish too, but nothing to compare with those that we saw in their hundreds on the way down from Socotra.

The cat did well enough. One night she was returning from her flying-fish patrol empty-mouthed when one sailed over the rail, hit the side of the doghouse with a loud thump, and fell fluttering into her claws. From then on, before going forward, she seemed to stop to consider whether these dangerous peregrinations were really necessary.

On 15 June we saw a solitary frigate bird four hundred miles from any reef or resting place. Frigate birds are shore based and do not rest on the sea. It is altogether exceptional, according to Harold Gatty's book, *Let Nature be Your Guide*, to see frigate birds as far away from land as three hundred miles.

We also saw another Japanese fishing-boat with one of its sampans in the water. Next day it passed us again, painted a greyish white, with its buoys, bamboos, flags and sampans, giving the deck a cluttered-up appearance, but it was well equipped with radar, D.F., and searchlights, and rolled off efficiently and powerfully on a course towards Penang. On one day we had the wind from twenty-nine to thirty-five miles per hour in squalls and were cut down to a reefed main. With reefed main and working jib *Tzu Hang* was doing seven knots, but as this was too uncomfortable we handed the jib, when she did two and a half knots. Later when the wind eased and we set the storm jib she did four and a half knots very comfortably, all close on the wind and unattended.

On the twentieth, with thirteen days at sea, we had 1,200 miles on the log and were battering our way through pouring rain and violent squalls, with much reduced visibility. We were approaching the northern limit of the Southeast Trade. In Latitude 2° 30′ South we ran out of the Trades and into the Doldrums. We had had a brief lift on the counter-equatorial current, but now found ourselves back in a contrary current again. Partly because of a fluky easterly wind and partly in the hopes of finding the favourable current again, we worked our way south, trusting that the Trades would reach out to us. They did on the 23rd, finding us still on the same meridian as when they had left us.

From then on, considering that we were in the Doldrums, we made fair progress with sometimes a Trade Wind sky and a light southeasterly wind, sometimes the wind in the east, and often the Monsoon swell jostling with that of the Trade Wind.

On the whole we had typical Doldrum weather, with dark squall clouds so numerous and arching so low and black over the sea, that it felt as if we were boating under the arches in the Roman reservoir in Istambul. For a few days we managed to hang on to our little branch of the counter-current, but it soon petered out, and we found later on that a westgoing current was setting as far north as the One and a Half Degree passage, north of the Equator. As we approached Addu Atoll we were carried even further to the north until we were across the Equator, and, when the wind shifted to the east, we were forced to tack to the south. It was then that we became plaintively aware of the current's strength.

We had heard Gan beacon for hundreds of miles, in fact we had first heard it on our way down from Socotra to Lamu. Now it was coming in very strongly at any time of the day with a narrow null point. On the evening of 2 July it was giving us a course that we could sail, so we decided to come in on the beacon to test my small radio direction-finding set in which I had never had any great confidence. We homed on the beacon until its red light appeared dead on the bow. Since then the D.F. set and I have become firm friends. Unfortunately it was some way away from the southern pass at which we proposed to enter.

We made our way round to the southern pass, tacking close in to the reef. Although the backs of the swells hid the breakers, the edge of the reef was clearly defined by the way that they humped up before breaking, showing a momentary transparency at their crests. We heard later that our course had caused some excitement in the R.A.F. control room, where they thought each time that we approached the reef, that we were going to try and ride the breakers in.

Gan is part of Addu Atoll, whose perimeter is split into various tree-clad or sandy islands, standing along the reef which enclose the lovely lagoon. There are two passes in the north and two in the south. Gan Channel is the easiest to enter as it is the most easily identified. Gan itself is purely an Air Force Base, which they were kind enough to allow us to enter. The capital of the Maldives is Male, the home of an intransigent Sultan. At the time that we were there the prosperity of Addu, due to the R.A.F. base on Gan, was causing the ruler to indulge in jealous animosity, for not only did he want the rent but some of their takings too. We were told by the Commander of the base that we would not have been very welcome at Male, and, before going there in a yacht, it might be as well to enquire about the existing situation.

As we approached the pass an R.A.F. crash-boat came out to meet us, heeled over by the curious crowd that had managed to jump on board before they left the pier. Anything new was exciting at Gan, and a yacht arriving caused visions of young blondes in blue and white striped jerseys and tight white pants to arise in the minds of bored airmen stationed in this girl-less Atoll.

'Is there anyone else on board?' called a still hopeful voice on the loud-hailer.

Beryl and I felt very conscious of our shortcomings.

'Only the cat,' she called back, 'I'm so sorry.'

They took it very well and made us welcome.

We had 2,300 miles on the log for this passage of 1,850 miles, the excess being caused largely by the contrary current. The counter-current, from which we had expected great things did not help us to any extent, and I believe that what we found was only a small eddy, the main stream being much further to the north. When we left Gan we found the west-going current still running as strongly—and as unexpectedly— as before. The Trade Wind, too, was more in the east than on our previous passage, forcing us to take a more northerly course than we had done the previous year. All things considered, particularly the Doldrums, we thought twenty-six days a very fair passage, and we had found it far from dull.

We were lucky to be in Gan at that time, because some Vulcans were flying non-stop to Australia and refuelling over Gan. The noise of the sea and the wind in the palms was shattered as the great white heavily-ladened Valiants roared upwards to their rendezvous, and once in a break in the dappled sky we saw a minute arrow-head cutting its way across infinity, blade straight for Australia, sucking fresh energy from another tiny arrow attached to it that would soon come curving back to the green ringed lagoon. Once a great white aristocrat of the sky came swiftly in, a Victor, and popped a parachute out as it rushed down the runway to slow its speed, and once a burly Vulcan snarled down. The mess was full of visitors, the jet pilots looking like county cricketers in the luncheon tent, at a charity village match.

I thought Gan a lovely place in which to spend a year, if I had been in the R.A.F., but I would have been in the minority.

'Drives you round the bend,' said one of its inhabitants. 'It's all right for the first three months and then you begin to think of an English pub or the girl friend, and you soon get a proper island stare. It's a wonder we're not all as crazy as those fellows you see walking across the gap in the reef up to their necks in water with an umbrella over their heads when its raining. You're the lucky ones,' he went on, 'you can sail off anywhere with nothing to do but enjoy yourselves.'

The Padre came on board and had a better appreciation of cruising: 'I can see what you're up against,' he said. 'It's this perpetual fight against squalor.'

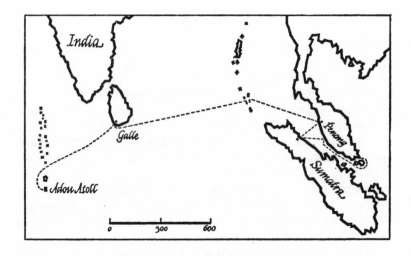

18 *To Galle in Ceylon and Nancowrie in the Nicobars*

We were due to leave Gan on 11 July, and so was a stately Shackleton of the R.A.F. and H.M.S. *Cambrian* who had also paid Gan a visit, and who had helped us with some tracings of the harbours that we were likely to visit. We were all bound for Singapore. The one, in spite of the doubts of the jet pilots, would arrive in a few hours, the other in a few days, and ourselves, last and least, in a few weeks.

'If you can be under sail by eight o'clock,' said the pilot of the Shackleton, 'we'll take a run over the lagoon and see if we can get a photograph of you.'

'The only reason that he wants to photograph you,' said his companion, 'is that he wishes to perpetuate the memory of someone slower than himself.'

We had to shift before leaving in order to take on water from the wharf, and by eight we were under sail with a light breeze just ruffling the surface of the lagoon. The Shackleton made one or two runs over us, looking as if it might take our masts with it, and then headed east for Singapore. We filled up with water at the pier and then sailed close past H.M.S. *Cambrian* as they were bringing their anchor in. They left by the southern pass and we by the northern. We caught another glimpse of her grey aggressive outline, beyond the barrier reef and framed for a moment between two green islets, as she altered course to the east while we were still only half way across the lagoon.

As we left the pass I noticed that we were being set rapidly to the west. I hoped that this was just an inshore counter current as the *Pilot* mentions a five knot current setting eastward in 1940 and says that the currents are predominantly eastward, but it covers itself with its customary caution by saying that there may be a considerable variation in the direction of the currents. With a light southeasterly wind we were able to set a course that should clear the southeast corner of Suvadiva Atoll comfortably, as the equatorial channel is forty-six miles wide, but even if the current was against us I knew that in these light conditions we would not reach the other side before daylight. Next morning the atoll, instead of being on the port bow, was on the starboard, and a two-knot current had carried us completely out of the passage in the wrong direction.

We decided to sail up the west coast of Suvadiva and to try our luck in the One and a Half Degree Channel, which is fifty-four miles wide and, like the Equatorial Channel, has no dangers. Again a contrary current carried us to the west and we found the far atoll again on the starboard bow. Then the wind came lightly from the southwest, and, with a little help from the engine and a little help from a favourable tide, we were able to overcome the current at last and found with relief the open sea.

As a result of all this we had spent the best part of three days, the crossings of the channels having been done at night, sailing close to the coral reefs and the green islands of the three southern atolls. The islands, linked by a barrier reef, form a necklace round each lagoon, and for the most part are covered with low green scrub, although a few are planted with coconuts. Much of the reef is under water and the whole of it is low, so that the coconuts stand out like a plantation in the winter prairie, and from a few miles off are all that can be seen. Close in, between the islands and over a mist of spray on the reef, are entrancing views of emerald water, as smooth as a sheet of glass, on which red or white sails glided.

Within the lagoons long narrow boats are used, with a large square sail made of horizontal cloths and preferably of different colours. They have a tall carved and painted detachable prow, shaped as if once it had been copied from a Viking ship. These are called *donis*, and the bigger boats, used outside the lagoons and which are also sailed to Ceylon and back, are called *bagalows*. We began to see them trolling in the channels, sailing fast, and rigged with a lateen mainsail and a small lateen mizzen.

On our fourth day we were virtually becalmed and still below the Monsoon. We continued to have nothing but the lightest of winds, if we had any wind at all, until the evening of 17 July, with cabin temperatures well up in the eighties. By now it looked as if we were going to make an all-time record in slow passages, but on this day the wind had freshened slowly, backing from north to west, and then veering again. A cloud bank grew to windward and by dark was hanging low over the sea and linked to it by sloping showers of rain. We ran on during the night, while the wind slowly increased and the overcast spread above us. At four in the morning we came into the weather with a bang. Wind Force 4 to 5 and gusting to 6 and 7, the night as black as the pit and solid rain that roared on the hoods of our oilskins so that we could neither see nor hear. The lightning flashed all round, blinding us and immediately blackening the night, while its stuttering cracks still rang in our ears. At the same time the flashes increased the luminosity of the compass face, which swam here and there in the liquid darkness, a hovering ghost swooping through the deluge, until *Tzu Hang* took shape again, our sense of balance was restored, and it dived to its customary place.

In the morning we were still swinging along, with black skies to starboard where the storm had gone, and a small chain of white cumulus clouds sailing across like swans on a dark pond. To port the sky was lighter, clean washed by the rain, with sometimes a gateway showing to a jade patch—an enchanted garden seen from a dusty street. It was a glimpse of the weather that was coming to us, and by the evening we were under clear skies, with the genoa drawing and a light northwesterly wind.

That was the one good day's run of the passage, until we

sighted Galle light, but it had broken the back of the journey, and on the morning of the nineteenth we found our way into Galle harbour. The big swell, rolling on from somewhere where the Monsoon was blowing strongly, was breaking on the shallows. These and the blue hull of the *Nellie Maersk* at anchor in the harbour, were our guides, for the buoys had not been painted and not all were there. Our first impression of Ceylon was one of disrepair, for the tugs and harbour launches in Galle harbour were equally dilapidated, and, although extensive alterations to the harbour were being undertaken, these basic signs of efficiency, new paint and good maintenance, were missing.

There were several ships in the harbour loading and discharging by lighter. Those loading were taking on tea and the cases were stacked high on heavy wooden lighters which were controlled by two men, each armed with a long pole with a disc at the end the size of a dinner plate that served as an oar —controlled in a manner of speaking only, as the wind caught them, and it was a miracle to us that they ever arrived at their destination. They swooped down on us and one came temporarily to rest on our anchor chain so that it looked as if we might go with it. The crew took this opportunity to offer us a case of tea—at a price of course—but Beryl and I were too perturbed to discover what this might be, or what the opportunities were of business in this line. As soon as they had revolved off our anchor chain, Beryl and I made haste to shift our berth a little further away from their drunkard's course.

Ashore the lighters were discharging grain. A long line of coolies waded to the lighter's side, up to their waists in water, and in turn each received a sack of grain on his back and staggered ashore. As the sacks were large and the labourers small, almost every sack was dunked in the water before it reached the shore. As the grain was almost certainly provided by foreign aid, no one seemed to be particularly concerned about it.

Our anchorage was a very uneasy one, and our official business through health, customs and immigration was thereby greatly accelerated. The port doctor only just regained his launch in time.

'You must come please to the hospital,' he said, as he began to recover. 'Not today because it is soon the afternoon, nor tomorrow or the next day, because it is the weekend. Come on Monday morning for a blood test for malaria.'

'But we are leaving on Tuesday, so surely you will not need it?'

'Oh yes, please. It is the regulation.'

'What about pratique?' I called, dropping the question of blood tests on a look from Beryl.

'Oh yes, please,' his voice faded behind the noise of the launch's motor. 'You may come ashore when you wish; it will be quite in order.'

Beryl and I stood on the foredeck to see them to the shore. Our second impression was that so little had changed. We had not been to Galle before, but after seventeen years we were back in the East. The grass ashore was freshly green after the Monsoon rains and dotted with goats, the bastions of the old Dutch fort standing grey and enduring above them. Here and there within the great walls that enclose the old port a shade tree towered that had seen the Dutch and the British come and go. It was the Dutch who had left the most enduring monument. From the shore came a familiar and indescribable smell, a compound of much, but with little that was pleasant about it, and yet to people who had spent many days in the East, a sweet nostalgic smell. The roads teemed with life. Taxis and lorries thrust their noisy and menacing way through dogs, chickens, pedestrians, bicyclists and bullock carts, and the only notable difference that we could see was that the bullock carts had rubber wheels.

We came ashore and were hailed by some Customs Officers sitting in a shoddy building under one of the great trees, by the arched entrance through the old harbour walls.

'Have you got any money?' we were asked.

Obviously one doesn't come ashore without money, but we were hoping to exchange it at the free rate, three times better than the bank rate. Obviously one doesn't explain that to a Customs Officer either. We asked him for the name of a bank where we could change our money.

'Not the bank,' he said in alarm, 'wait a moment and I will send you to a very reliable friend of mine, who will give you a much better rate.'

He produced a guide for us who led us along the narrow streets of the old town, and who almost immediately broached the subject of a private exchange transaction. He was interrupted by the arrival of the Customs Officer, who had changed into civilian clothes, at speed on a bicycle. He dismissed our guide and took us himself to a jeweller, where our business was rapidly effected to the benefit of all three parties.

The hospital, when we went there to get our blood test, with a cholera injection thrown in, was as crowded as if there had been an influx from a national disaster. The white dresses of the patients, their numbers, and the untidiness of the wards and passages reminded me of henhouses full of white Leghorns in moult. The nurses, small-waisted and in neat uniforms, flitted busily here and there. Some had been trained in Australia under the Colombo plan, and perhaps the little student nurse, who timidly pricked my arm, will one day be a martinet of a matron ruling the wards with discipline and asepsis. That is what they seemed to need.

Most of the port officials were eager to visit *Tzu Hang*, but the liveliness of our anchorage usually disposed of them. The climax was reached when the Chief Customs Officer brought his family to see us, all of whom were almost simultaneously laid low and suddenly appeared before my startled eyes, shrouded in a veil of rice. My remarkable wife was mopping and comforting on every side, but I was unashamedly first on deck at the sight of such an eruption.

I went to get my clearance the next day. Over the Customs Office was a black board with 'H.M. Customs' painted on it in white. Perhaps they liked it like that, or perhaps no one had yet got round to finding a ladder to remove it. I waited for some time to get my clearance, and in due course it arrived, showing that *Tzu Hang* of 15.08 tons burthen and carrying no cannon was in all respects ready for the sea.

'And what are your impressions of our country?' asked the Chief Customs Officer?

'It is very lovely, and I think that you are a very friendly people.'

'Is it not wonder,' he asked, 'that two great nations should part in gentility and love?'

The wonderful thing was to see their pride, not in any progress, for none was obvious, but in the fact that they were still managing more or less by themselves. There was even an inverted pride in their bankruptcy, which they had accomplished entirely by themselves. But I shall remember the nurses in the hospital who seemed to have stepped bravely into the future in spite of the tremendous task with which they were confronted. I shall also remember the friendliness and the eagerness of all whom we met, and the paragraph in the English language paper which said:

'DON'T WALK ON THE RAIL TRACK.'

'Announcements are being made at all railway stations in Sinhalese, Tamil and English, warning all persons not to walk on the rail-track because trains will be running in both directions on both tracks. With the introduction of the coloured light signals, which extend from Mount Lavinia to Polgahawela, it will be possible for trains to run in both directions on both tracks.

'It will be dangerous to walk on the tracks, therefore, because it will not be possible to know from which direction a train will come.'

The way out of a harbour is usually easier to find than the way in, and as we left we were able to check the buoys in greater tranquillity. Irrespective of colour the port-hand buoys were conical, the starboard-hand buoys on the way out had a square topmark. We had a good wind to leave by, and sailed past the *Nellie Maersk*, whose Captain had given us a blistering party the evening before. In a very short time she was a blue smudge against the background of the town, and we turned our bow towards Dondra Head with a fresh Monsoon wind to hurry us along. It hurried us to a good tune because forty-eight hours later we had over three hundred miles on the log.

Round Dondra head a stream of ships was passing, including an old Liberty ship, shambling along, and a fine modern tanker, the *Haikwang*, that hissed past us. That night the great red light on Basse Reef shone its clear warning. We gave it a wide berth and then drew away from the shipping lane, and had the seas once more to ourselves. We had a good passage, comfortable and uneventful, and only sighted one ship, southward bound from Calcutta. On the morning of the sixth day, with eight hundred miles on the log, we saw land ahead—hilly, jungle-covered, islands, seven miles away.

We passed north of Katchall; ahead lay Kamorta, close locked with Nancowrie, and to the north was Teressa. Green hills against low monsoon clouds, that dulled the coral sand within the horns of the coastal reefs. On many rocky points jagged teeth slashed viciously at the long monsoon swell, and on the grey cliffs above them creepers overhung and reached to the sea.

We passed by the narrow entrance of Expedition Harbour, because the pilot book warns that swarms of mosquitoes invade a ship that anchors there. Western Entrance, the opening that leads into Nancowrie Bay, between Nancowrie and Kamorta was soon visible. We were navigating on a tracing (from H.M.S. *Cambrian*) of the general chart of the Nicobars, but I had drawn a chart of the harbour from the *Pilot*, on a plotting chart, using a blown-up scale.

It was with pleasure therefore that we saw the waves breaking on the reef point, recognized the 'hole in the rock,' and even picked out a faded white paint-mark on a cliff, all of which were drawn on my plan and culled from the *Sailing Directions*. Easter Point and Alfred Point appeared, and successive beacons that had lost their top-marks and were rusty and bent. Rain squalls followed us into the harbour and blotted out the land-marks in quick succession, but I still felt that I knew it all well, almost as if I was a native, as a result of the laboured drawings that I had made during the passage. Lights go out and beacons decay, buoys change colour and are missing, but the land remains the same, and the sailing directions are usually given with reference to a recognizable landmark.

To starboard, through curtains of rain, we could see two small steamers, both looking as if they had been converted from sailing schooners, moored to a jetty. To port, as the rain passed, another jetty appeared with a few official looking buildings standing behind it. On the jetty was a green notice board, bright in fleeting sunshine, with 'Welcome' painted on it in white. This seemed to be the place to go to, but the coastal bank was shallow and steep-to, the depths outside were great. We anchored just on its edge, in poor ground, and our stern swung towards the pier, where umbrellas were sprouting like mushrooms as the rain came down again on a small crowd of watchers. We soon had our first boat-load on board. They were an anti-malarial team working in the islands. 'We have abolished malaria,' they claimed.

'What, abolished mosquitoes?'

'Oh no. That would be too expensive. We stop them biting.'

They were young, immensely enthusiastic, excited and amazed at everything that they saw. 'So between you you are, the captain, the engineer, the navigator and the crew,' said one of them, bespectacled and darker than the others.

'Yes, and the cat is the cook,' I replied.

His eyes almost popped through his glasses, he wagged his head and gasped with astonishment, 'It is all very wonderful.'

I realized, rather ashamed, that everything was so new and strange that for the moment he had accepted the cat's astonishing role. I had visions of endless tins of sardines for breakfast, lunch and dinner. 'Not really—I was only joking,' I explained to a great deal of laughter at his expense. I don't suppose he has been allowed to forget it.

Meanwhile another boat-load had arrived. The clerks from the Public Works Department office, the post office clerk, and sundry other small officials, so it only remained for the port doctor and the Customs Officer to arrive to complete the embarkation of most of the settlement. This was soon effected, and the two Nicobar boatmen climbed on board for their own personal inspection. They were small and mongoloid, as foreign to the Indians as a Finn to a Frenchman, a clean, tough and gentle people whom the doctor had a great admiration for. 'They are no trouble,' he said, 'even when they are drunk they don't fight, and when they are sick they give themselves to me with absolute confidence.' They looked as if they were Sherpas who had one day deserted their hills and taken to the sea.

We thoroughly enjoyed this invasion, thinking what fun it was to be back amongst Indians, able to talk their language, or at least one of them, and to enjoy their jokes. We talked to them of India, of which we, having had the opportunity, and seen so much more than they, until the doctor carried us off to tea, in a neat little house half way up the hill behind the jetty.

The Forest Officer came to tea. He had been educated at Dehra Dun, and Beryl pleased him by remembering it particularly for its jacarandas. He loved to talk about his work, about the trees and jungle animals that he had seen. They were experimenting in hardwood plantations here, a welcome change from most reafforestation that we had seen, which had almost invariably been quick-growing pines. The talk went on until dark, when the doctor showed us down the slippery track. The night was rich with a warm, sweet, jungle smell, and hundreds of small toads pounced on their shadows, as they hopped across the path in the light of his torch.

The next day we took *Tzu Hang* over to the Nancowrie side, and the Rani of this small island came on board. She was as elegant and agile in her sari as a bird and hopped on to the deck from the boat in which she was rowed out, with the greatest of ease and assurance. We heard that she had stood up for her people during the Japanese occupation, and that they had had a great respect for her.

Beryl wanted to get a tape-recording of some Nicobar songs, and it was arranged that we should go to the school next day and that the children would sing for her. They were all as polished and as best dressed as they could be, but the singing was as ghastly as any school song, and it went on and on.

'What are they singing?' asked Beryl with a sudden suspicion after a whole tape had been run off.

The Sikh schoolmaster, a very smooth young man wearing a brown turban, turned to her and said in his soft and unctuous voice, 'They are singing Indian patriotic songs about giving one's blood for one's country.'

'To the blood bank?' I asked, for in our day we did not teach children to sing songs like that.

'No. To the mosquitoes,' said the doctor.

Apart from the singing, the school was a most impressive place, so well ordered and so well staffed in such a small place. The games store had sufficient cricket bats, hockey sticks, and footballs to equip a whole school and several parents' teams as well. The school room was hung with posters showing the vast new industrial development in India since Independence: the dams, the steel works, the hydro-electric projects, but there was no mention of where the money had come from, nor of any of the great dams, the Sukkur Barrage for instance, that had been built before.

Our visit to the Nicobars that we had enjoyed so much ended in mild frustration. We returned to the Kamorta side where we were to lunch with the Forest Officer, but as we walked up the hill I was met by the Police Sub-Inspector, who asked me to come to the office. I sensed that there was some sort of trouble. At the office was the Customs Officer. He was the sort of officious petty official that one finds in every country, and whom no one likes.

'Excuse me, please,' he said, 'have you a landing permit?'

'I did not know the necessity,' I replied, 'and if there is one, surely you are the person to give it?'

'Then orders have come from the Andamans,' he told me with satisfaction, 'that you must leave immediately.'

'You had better show me the signal,' I said.

'If no Landing Permit order foreigners to leave immediately,' it said, and was signed by the Commissioner of the Andamans. I wondered what sort of message the Customs officer had sent to provoke this order. I told them that we would leave in our own time, when rested and filled up with water, and ready for the sea, and I told them to reply to the Commissioner and ask him to refer to a friend in Delhi in a considerably higher position than he was, if he wanted to know more about us.

'But orders come from above,' said the policeman, pointing at the sky. 'We are only small men. What to do? What to do?' In order to save the policeman embarrassment we agreed to stay on board until further instructions had arrived. If we had expected any trouble or if we had been up to any mischief, we would not have come to Nancowrie but gone instead to one of the sandy and attractive little bays on Katchall or some other island. They would never have known that we were there, nor, if they had, could they have visited us, as they had no launch available.

Next morning the policeman arrived to say that our stay had been referred to the Foreign Office at Delhi, but we had lost our taste for the islands and decided to leave anyway. Beryl started to give the bewildered policeman a lecture on 'small people' taking some authority instead of cluttering up the air with radiograms, but seeing he was shaking with the malaria that had been abolished, gave him some anti-malarial pills instead.

The charming doctor came sadly on board to say goodbye. Beryl had given his little wife a red folding umbrella from Paris, since when it had never left her hand. 'Would you mind signing this to say that the umbrella was a free gift,' he asked diffidently, 'otherwise the Customs Officer may make some trouble.' The policeman, wrapped in a blanket, was out in a small boat to thank us for our co-operation, as we sailed down the channel, and the red umbrella blossomed like a flower amongst the trees on the hill. We forgot the abominable Customs Officer, and felt again a surge of affection, mingled with exasperation that any people so nice can be so bloody annoying at the same time. It was the sight of the signal calling me a foreigner that had really piqued me. I should never dream of calling an Indian a foreigner, and we thought that to be ordered to leave immediately was un-Commonwealth behaviour and, since there were no means of enforcing the order, stupid as well.

A fresh wind. The islands were soon left astern and *Tzu Hang* leaned towards a new landfall.

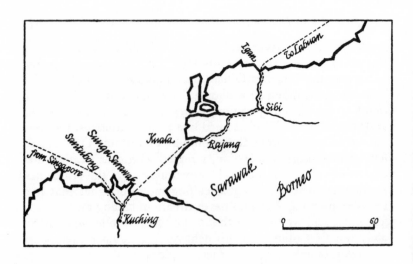

19 *Down the Malacca Strait*

WE left Nancowrie with a fresh Monsoon wind that held for
two days, until we ran out of wind altogether. We sighted the
Bhutang Islands, off the Malaysian coast, on 5 August, after
spending another two days flirting with puffs of wind from all
directions, and being joggled about by the remains of the
Monsoon swell. There was a splendid moon that night, and the
islands showed up clearly. We had a gentle and steady breeze
at last, a soft, sweet-smelling breeze, blowing from the southeast, and we slipped along in calm water, the calmest that we
had had for many a day.

The islands grew steadily taller and more distinct in the
moonlight until we could see the deep-water channel shining
between them, but instead of beating through it we decided
to make two long tacks to windward, hoping thereby to gain a
more restful night. The wind dropped during the night, but
only for a short time, and by daylight we were passing the
southern end of the islands, where fingers of rock thrust suddenly
out of the sea. The early morning sun, peering hazily over the
mountains of the mainland, lit their wet flanks in a golden
light.

All that day we approached the mainland, watching the hills and ravines take shape, their colours intensifying until a thin white line of breakers appeared, bright against the black rocks, with red gold beaches in between. We came in south of the island of Lankowie and sailed up the islet-studded coast. So delicious a coast it seemed from out there in the cool breeze, a siren coast, with here and there small beaches enclosed by rocky points, and dark shadows overhung by green. In the shadows one could lie, or better still two could lie, in the cool sand, snuggling into it, pushing up a mound with one's feet, and watching the white sand-crabs run up and down with the ripples until the heat had gone out of the day. These lotus dreams were suddenly cut short by the appearance of a row of bamboo stakes ahead of us. Out came the lead in a panic, only to find that we were still in six fathoms. Later we came to welcome these stakes which guide the fish into traps and run out to the six-fathom line, or stand on six-fathom or shallower shoals. Near them we knew that we could always find good anchorage in sticky mud and in comparatively sheltered water.

There was a slight haze, and this, or the shallow sea, was responsible for a greenish light typical of these waters while we were in Malaya. To think of them brings back immediately a picture of this haze, of the long lines of stakes marching out from the shore to the platform above the trap, of the dim mountainous jungle behind, and of the tree-covered islets that sprout so abruptly almost anywhere in the sea; of the whole wrapped in a soft green light, the colour as delicate, the lines as lightly etched, as in a Chinese painting.

At supper time we were almost becalmed close off a light-house called Kq Yao, which sprang out of a jungle-covered point like a jack-in-the-box. From down below we could hear a clamour of frogs, but on deck nothing. There are various fish noises that can be heard through the skin of a boat, and we decided that the frogs must have been a shoal of fish round us. We were to hear them like this on several other occasions—but always fairly close to the shore.

Next day we made good progress along a low coast of mud-banks and river mouths, with occasional islets as round as footballs floating on the sea, and presently out of the haze there appeared the outline of Pulao Penang. By noon a fresh wind was blowing and we beat up towards the anchorages, finding the channel well marked and easy to pick up. In the man-of-war anchorage a cruiser, two destroyers and a minesweeper were at anchor, their awnings rigged taut, their paint new, and their brass shining. We thought that they were British until we made out the strange flag on the jackstaff and discovered them to be Indian.

We sailed past them, but as the channel became more crowded and large ferries ploughed their unrelenting way across our course between Penang and the Kota side of the harbour, we handed our sails and threaded our way under power towards the railway pier and the coastal traders' anchorage, where a number of small vessels jostled for room as they swung with the tide. It was a most uneasy place, with all kinds of traffic going in all directions. At one time we were called on deck by the shouts of three sailors who were painting the stern of a small freighter called the *Ulu*, the swing of the tide having placed the plank on which they were sitting almost over our bow. We let go some more chain but there was no hope of recovering the anchor from under the *Ulu* until the tide had changed.

Penang, even at the hottest time of the day, was as busy as an ants' nest. Chinese shops crowded on Chinese shops, their doors agape for the traveller. Beryl was soon ashore with the laundry bag. She also carried a Shan bag and a plaited straw bag from Mozambique. This was empty, ready to receive our most immediate necessities, fresh bread being the first. The Shan bag was full, and if it had been turned out on some astonished merchant's counter, as frequently happens when the shopping list is missing, it would have been found to contain a small crescent wrench, a stainless steel screw, a couple of shackles, her purse, something that had been missing for ages and perhaps the shopping list which always seems to be the most elusive thing in her bag.

Beryl had a friend in Penang, Sjovald Cunninghame Brown, whom she had first met in Malaya on her way to Australia at the beginning of the war. He was then in the Malayan Civil Service and had helped Beryl—and Clio—to climb Mount Omei. Clio was only five months old and had climbed in an old-fashioned way, her cot slung on a bamboo pole, on the shoulders of two Malays.

The war had come to Singapore soon afterwards and Sjovald, who was in the Royal Navy Volunteer Reserve, after many adventures, was finally captured off the south coast of Java, while trying to help some Navy personnel to escape from that island in a sampan. He survived a terrific smash-up in a Japanese driven lorry, a torpedoing in a prison ship when most people crammed below decks were drowned, and a long spell on the railway in Sumatra, from which fewer returned than from the equally infamous line into Burma. He came back at last to his work in Malaya, and when the time came for him to retire, he decided to stay on in Penang in order to continue to help those with whom he had spent so many happy years. He must be the busiest man in Penang, and though we have met others who have returned to the countries in which they spent their service, in order to repay some of the good that they had gained, there can be few with such ability and such a gay talent for helping others. Both he and Beryl were looking forward to this meeting, and Sjovald particularly to seeing Clio, the finished article, whom he had launched on her first adventure twenty-two years before.

Beryl telephoned him and he overtook her in the street, walking like a hill woman and now loaded with her shopping, the despair of every rickshaw cyclist. 'I would have known you anywhere,' he said.

'That was because you only saw my back view,' said Beryl, leaving him momentarily at a loss for a gallant reply.

In view of the trouble with Indonesia we had decided not to take the easier way on from Singapore on our way to Japan, which in the time of the Northeast Monsoon is down the Java Sea and out into the Pacific by the Djailolo Passage, by the northwestern tip of New Guinea. Instead we were going to take the more direct route, and more directly into the teeth of the Monsoon, up the west coast of Borneo and through the Philippines. Before doing this Beryl wanted to see something of Indonesia, and Sumatra was just across the way. If Sjovald could come with us to Sumatra we need have no fear of getting into trouble, for not only did he speak Malay fluently, as well as several other eastern languages, but he was also the French

Consul and could charm Neptune himself if the need arose.
Beryl broached the subject immediately and Sjovald, who is
always ready for any adventure and particularly, since he is a
Shetlander, if it has something to do with the sea, was ready to
come with us. Lest it should appear that he has no faults, we
soon found that it was impossible for him to pass any outlandish
person without a few minutes chatty conversation in Malayalam,
Telugu, Hokkien, or Tamil, the most difficult of all and the last
language left in the cupboard when the rest were dished out,
except perhaps the Bushmen's.

We moved *Tzu Hang* a few miles further up the channel to
Glugor, where there is a good place for yachts to lie away from
all traffic and a Navy pier to land on. Clio arrived, her legs
longer, her dress fashionably shorter, than anyone else on the
aircraft, full of talk about Bangkok, where she had made a
brief stop on her way out, and a false assumption that we were
up-to-date with her news. In a short time we knew that *Tzu
Hang* would take her in hand and alter this strange, smartly
dressed, and glowing person into something that we were more
accustomed to.

A few days later we set out. The day was perfect except that
there was no wind, but in spite of this three or four junks were
sailing ahead of us, drawing ahead on a freer course, their great
sails collecting what wind there was until we felt as if they had
collected some of ours too. We drifted across the Straits, with
an occasional burst of speed as a rain squall swept over us, and
in one of which the end of a crosstree broke off and we found
the wood to be rotten. We were able to set the shroud up again
in a groove, cut in the broken end, which served well enough
until we got to Singapore.

On the morning of the second day, being now in Indonesian
waters, we hoisted the Indonesian flag on one spreader and the
French flag, in honour of our Consul, on the other. Shortly
afterwards we saw a large sampan with a number of fishermen
fishing with handlines over the side—our first contact with the
enemy—and we went up to speak to them. Sjovald unloosed
a flood of Malay, while Beryl, Clio and I awaited an answering
spate of welcome, but it was received with a deep and suspicious
silence. Sjovald tried again until their distrust subsided and they
were all answering and volunteering information. Reassured

by this success we continued on our way, until we saw a number of masts and funnels on the horizon, marking the entrance to the Deli River.

There were several ships awaiting wharfage at Belawan, but since the tide was favourable we sailed through them, and entered the river between low mudbanks and mangroves. The channel was well marked, the buoys and markers in good order, and there were numerous fishing stakes extending right to the edge of the deep water to help us keep our course. We were able to sail all the way, with a short tack here and there, until we reached the wharves which stretch for a mile along the south bank. A little further on we anchored in a shabby stretch. A small canoe-like fishing boat with a large square sail made entirely of patches glided past between *Tzu Hang* and the dreary mangroves. I do not know whether I expected endless questions, annoying officials, police guards or pistols, but certainly I did not expect that no attention would be paid to us at all. We had an early tea, and then Sjovald and I went in to investigate, tying the dinghy to a small river gunboat with a home-made look and a two-pounder gun.

We eventually found a Customs Officer, but as it was past three o'clock and all offices were closed, he did not know what to do with us. He wore his cap on the side of his head and his manner was off-hand, but Sjovald persuaded him to ring up the Immigration Officer, and we were told to take a taxi to the Immigration Office and from there we drove to wake the Port Doctor from his afternoon sleep. They were friendly, and we were told that we might come ashore without any further inspection.

As yet we had not broached the subject of changing our money, for it was absolutely essential for us to get the free rate of exchange if we were to do anything in Sumatra. This had to be handled with great caution, but one of the officials suggested where we should go, and it was obvious that no one expected us to be stupid enough to change our money at the official rate at the bank. Once the exchange had been satisfactorily and furtively effected, feeling considerably better off than we had been for some time, we hired a taxi to drive us up to the Toba Lake, high in the hills above Medan.

It would be hard to find a less attractive place than Belawan. Mud-flats, mosquitoes, heat, pariah dogs, and a general tawdriness provide most of the disadvantages of the East with few of its advantages. Added to this there is an unpleasant feeling of being in an occupied country, for there were odd truck loads of Javanese soldiers raising the dust. The men wore jungle green, jungle boots and helmet liners of American pattern, if not of American origin, and most of them were armed with a wicked-looking automatic rifle which had a Russian look about it. As these were the same type of soldier that we were already engaged with in Borneo I looked at them with hostile interest.

The road on to Medan, and Medan itself, is flat and uninteresting. We passed the ink-spattered British Consulate, and went on to see the American Consul, whose home and office up till then had not been subjected to brickbats and hostile slogans. He arranged for us to stay in the house at the Toba Lake, which they rented for American personnel to escape to, when they needed a breath of fresh air to cool their exasperation.

We set off again, enjoying the luxurious feeling that we were running on petrol which, at our rate of exchange, cost us fourpence a gallon. The country began to improve. We drove through some small and not particularly unkempt rubber plantations, and then through the well-ordered Goodyear estates, then still under American ownership. We also drove through a large dry rice project that the Russians had undertaken. How often must Americans and Russians, busily wooing emergent nations, look at each other with understanding and a great and forbidden longing to get together and discuss their prodigal and indifferent hosts!

We came to Siantor and walked down the crowded street to inspect from outside the jail in which Sjovald had been locked up by the Japanese. It would be hard to remember a jail with nostalgia, but it was obvious that his memories were not all bad, and I expect that it was the comradeship that he remembered more than anything, as we walked down the outside of the high stone wall. There is also a zoo in Siantor, but it is better not to visit it. It was well laid out, and in the time of the Dutch must have been beautifully kept up. Now it is littered with paper, with the animals living in squalid dejection, in several cases with large untended wounds. I wondered if any of them, like our driver, remembered the 'good days.'

Our driver, growing bolder as he left the periphery of soldiers and officials behind him, told us what he thought of his present overlords and what he thought of President Sukarno's treatment of the local Chiefs and Rajahs. If the Indonesians were trying to infiltrate into Malaysia, here it seemed was fruitful ground for the Malaysians to infiltrate into Indonesia. From our very brief and superficial view it seemed that the soldiers and officials were usually Javanese and liked their posting no better than the Sumatrans liked their presence in the country.

Presently the hills shook the jungles from their shoulders and emerged as coarse grassland and scrub-filled ravines, with the huge Toba Lake spreading its octopus arms among them. The air was cool and fresh, sweet with the smell of mist on wet grass and of wild flowers, a welcome change from the torrid stuff at sea level. Here also were a different, freer people, living in a different sort of house with steep thatched roofs extended at each end to form gables, and decorated by elaborate wood carvings along the eaves. The houses stood on posts, the corner posts being carved with long-headed faces.

Our house, a modern one, above an arm of the Toba Lake, was owned by an old Dutchman, tall and deaf, who himself lived in a house next door on a site quarried out of the cliff below the road, where he grew orchids for pleasure and operated a private still for profit. He had spent his life in Sumatra, first as a planter, then operating his own taxi firm, which he had continued to operate during the war. When the Dutch left he had stayed on and become a Muslim, although possibly a not very devout one, and an Indonesian. Under his round Indonesian hat his predatory black eyes alternately hooded and unveiled over an aquiline nose. He looked like some old vulture about to regurgitate as he prepared to deliver himself of a flood of repressed thoughts, but always checked himself for fear of some other listener.

'That's another thing,' he said, 'my house being below the road level. I don't think they'd notice.'

'Notice what?'

'If they turned against foreigners. But then I'm an Indonesian.'

'If who turned against foreigners?'

'If the British attack Indonesia, then the Sumatrans might

rebel. Then who knows?' He rapidly became incoherent and went off, stoop-shouldered and mumbling angrily.

He brought us his photos to see. The old days with fancy-dress dances at the club, picnics and fishing parties and the model T Fords. Then there were photos of himself and his taxi drivers in taxi service uniform, and there they stopped. He recognized that Sjovald, as an old eastern hand, would not quail at the thought of alcohol before breakfast, and took him off next morning to see the orchids and sample the products of his still. Sjovald came back to us rather flushed and in need of coffee, having sampled Toba Gin, Toba Gimlet, Toba Heering, and Martini Toba, all with the same fiery foundation.

A few days later we were back in *Tzu Hang* and heading out of the Deli River. We had had our trip to Sumatra just in time as with the declaration of Malaysia the Indonesian policy of confrontation had been stepped up, and we might not have been allowed to enter or, if we had entered, to leave without some form of unpleasantness.

We recrossed the Malacca Strait in much the same way as we had crossed it, on our way to Lumut at the mouth of the Dindings River, but with a little more help from the wind.

We crossed the shipping lane during the night, a constant stream of traffic in both directions, which kept the helmsman busy and made the watches pass quickly. It was lovely to watch the long necklace of red and green and white lights drawn through the dark hands of the Straits. There were ships whose lights grew steadily taller and taller as they approached, until they towered above us, who passed us with a deep thrum of power and a hiss of water glowing green at the bow and dancing white under the light at the stern. There were ships who came throbbing through the night with great heartbeats, so that it seemed as if the whole ship must shake at every pulse, and there were ships showing only a single mast-light, which took a long time to meet or overtake us, whose engines sang an uncertain song in cracked old voices.

Next morning we were ten miles north of Pulao Berhala with a long low roll of cloud coming across from the Sumatran side. We had a fresh wind from the south, and were sailing nicely with a Messageries Maritimes ship passing us to starboard. I watched her enter the squall, and as she did so the smoke from her funnel, which was blowing towards us, was ripped away from her starboard side and dragged into the squall, into which she in a moment disappeared. We got the mizzen down as the wind switched to the north. *Tzu Hang* heeled to a strong gust as the cloud came over us, and the rain poured down, reducing visibility to a few yards, flattening the sea and stinging our faces as the yacht surged forwards. We wondered whether the ageing stitching on the main would hold, and whether there were any other ships near, as we rushed through the rain. I could not have had a gentler warning of how a 'Sumatra' behaves, but it turned out that I was no wiser.

We passed north of Pankor Island on the following morning, still in the haze that moderates all colour and gives a delicacy of outline to all that can be seen—a spur with dim trees above, a small round islet, a fisherman in his sampan. Bit by bit, as we approached the mouth of the river, the haze cleared, unfolding slowly a panorama of island, jungle and hill; but to begin with it offered us the simplest monochromes, each perfect in delicacy and line.

A mile or two up the river we anchored off Lumut in a strong tide. Lumut was one of the earliest treaty settlements, and was a lovely contrast to the drab port that we had left, being quiet and green, with something of the atmosphere of an English village about it. We stayed here only a day or two and then set sail for Singapore after saying goodbye to Sjovald. He stood waving on the wharf but as we drew away turned to address one of the men standing there in some strange tongue, so that we knew he had found a temporary distraction from any sorrow that he may have felt at leaving *Tzu Hang*.

For most of the way down the coast the tides set at a rate of one to two knots and a little faster round the more prominent capes or in narrow channels. In the light wind conditions that now prevailed we expected to anchor when the tide was against us—if there was an anchorage available. There was usually one somewhere near. We took the channel south between Pankor and the mainland with a fast tide running in our favour, and were rewarded by the sight of a Malayan-Chinese fishing village on the starboard side. The whole village was on stilts in the water, with boardwalks running along the front to which many fishing boats were tied.

By the time that we had reached the Sembilan Islands the tide had changed, and we anchored close west of Pulao Lalang. Beryl and Clio took the cat ashore, but I stayed with *Tzu Hang* as it was an unpleasant anchorage on a rocky shelf where the chain growled and grumbled. I could see them, and from this distance they appeared to be three youthful figures, for the cat went scurrying in short dashes ahead. When they returned it was dragging behind, its protests against the heat, the distance and the speed of the walk sounding above the noise of the waves on the beach even as far as *Tzu Hang*. We were glad to find that when the tide changed the anchor came up easily, and we were soon on our way.

Next day we found no suitable anchorage but passed many fishing stakes, single bamboos with a palm frond tied to the top, leaning to the tide and sometimes almost entirely submerged by it. Sampans were tied to some of them, the fishermen using handlines to catch the fish attracted to the eddy round the stake. By dark we were in sight of the lighthouse on One Fathom Bank. Two hours later it was bearing east, but then we had to tack across the tide and were unable to improve our position. About midnight I noticed a dark cloud coming up from the south and supposed that it might be a 'Sumatra,' which the *Pilot* warned might blow up to sixty knots, and I took down the mizzen as a precautionary measure. I had just counted seven ships coming towards us round the lighthouse, when the wind dropped as the cloud approached. Suddenly it came back with a wallop from the opposite quarter, and Beryl and Clio needed no call to being them on deck. Between them, while I struggled with the helm, they brought down the cracking jib and got it safely stowed below. *Tzu Hang*, immensely eased, starting sailing herself again under the full main.

'Don't you think that we had better do something about the main?' asked Beryl.

'No. She'll be all right now,' I said.

They started to go below but suddenly the wind hit again with double its former fury. *Tzu Hang* heeled to it like a Finn and then the whole track ripped from the boom, leaving all the strain on the clew. In a moment this tore out taking the bottom cloth with it for the length of the foot of the sail, and our whole

main, less the bottom cloth and the clew, was left thrashing in
the wind like a Tibetan prayer flag on a mountain pass.

The rain pricked like a fall in a gorse bush as we struggled to
get the flogging sail down. Beryl and Clio lay on the boom
dragging the sail in foot by foot and stuffing it under their
bodies until they could get a tyer on, while I heaved on the luff,
for *Tzu Hang* had fallen across the wind and the sail clung to the
shrouds as if it would never let go. All the time I thought of the
seven ships coming our way. We could not see a yard beyond
the ship. As soon as one of us could be spared we switched on
the bright masthead light, so that we had a tent of light about
us lighting our wet struggles and the myriad splashes that leapt
momentarily from the pitted sea. It lit Clio's wet hair and her
eyes sparkling with the struggle and the excitement, while I
wondered how anyone could enjoy a show like this. Presently
all was secured, and we were able to start the motor and make
off as fast as we could go for One Fathom Bank, where we
would be safe from the traffic. The rain thinned, the light
reappeared, and soon I found the bottom with the lead. We
anchored in five fathoms. The squall was over and we turned
in.

The lighthouse on One Fathom Bank is a grey stone Victorian
affair, like the clock in the square at Mahé in the Seychelles,
and is about half way between Penang and Singapore. We
left the bank in the afternoon with our small loose-footed trysail
replacing the main, expecting to anchor off Port Dixon about
sixty miles away. It was midnight when we picked up the Pulao
Arang Arang light which marks the entrance to Port Dixon, but
there were no lights of a port beyond, although we could see
lights about six miles away down the coast. Most cautiously we
approached this sleepy city, but although the light came closer
there was no outline of the island or the lighthouse from which
should have been flashing. Suddenly we were upon it and I
could see that it was a buoy. We knew nothing about buoys
here, so, we turned about and retraced our steps till we thought
it safe to continue down the coast. It turned out that the buoy
marked a new and deeper channel to Port Dixon, newly surveyed and marked, and too new for the corrections in our
Malacca Strait Pilot. The tide was now against us, so it was daylight before we were off Port Dixon. By then it had turned in

our favour, so we decided to go on to Malacca and by lunchtime had anchored in the roads two miles away from the town. Beryl and Clio now refused to go on until they had seen the town, and there we spent the night.

Early next morning we moved close inshore, but there was still a formidable distance to row. The two of them started off against a strong headwind and a cross-tide, so that it was soon obvious that I would only meet them again some way down the coast. As I considered this I leant against the lifeline, which had been slacked off to launch the dinghy, and Clio, who was rowing and saw me collapse, and that I was hanging overboard upside down, voiced the same idea to her mother. Luckily I still had a leg entwined round a stanchion and was able to haul myself back on board, while Clio and Beryl were picked up by a Chinese fisherman, returning from the sea in his outboard-engined sampan. He towed them to the breakwater, and then up the river between rows of Chinese houses to show what a strange catch he had made, and Chinese turned out on both banks to laugh and wave.

We left on the tide in the evening, stalking slowly through calm water beneath great pillared clouds, and came to anchor by the Tanjong Tohor fish-traps before daylight. On clear nights, even without a moon, these fish-traps can be picked out without glasses, and as they usually burn a lantern on their end, the five-fathom line is picked out by a row of dim little lights, half a mile or a mile apart.

We made another stop at Pulao Pisang, where a fresh south-easterly wind kept us a day or two at anchor, below a lighthouse and within sight of the shipping in the Straits, and from there we made our last stop on Long Shoal, at the entrance to Selat Sembulan. Next day we sailed through Keppel Harbour and anchored off the Royal Singapore Yacht Club, but, in spite of their friendliness, it is not a good place for a deep draft yacht to lie, as the anchorage is too far out, with the usual problems of getting ashore in dry clothes, and where *Tzu Hang* herself was under constant threat from tugs and lighters. While we were there we had the additional threat of a large illuminated dragon, towed by a tug and accommodated on six junks, which breathed fire. It was in celebration of Malaysia day.

We moved on to the 'Red House,' the Navy Base Yacht

Club, and found ourselves once more in the hands of the Navy. *Tzu Hang* has met with so much friendliness in different parts of the world that there are few places that we can remember without a warm feeling of gratitude for someone's unexpected kindness. We have no right to expect it, and least of all perhaps from our own sort of people amongst whom we are not particularly odd and no sort of novelty. How very nice it was to meet it to the nth degree at the Navy Base. H.M.S. *Lion* hauled out our masts, H.M.F.A. *Retainer* replaced them. We leant *Tzu Hang* against the Red House to paint her, and the dockyard did various minor repairs for us. Captain Geoffrey Pearce, the Chief Engineer there, who seemed akin to the Rock of Gibraltar, and Elisabeth, his warm-hearted wife, opened their comfortable home to us. Whenever there was something to be done there were young and able hands to help. It may be that Clio and Romilly, a Canadian girl who had joined her, had something to do with this. If Beryl set the trap, perhaps it was they who baited it.

CLIO left us in Singapore and set off with Romilly on an over-
land trip to India. They intended to travel as cheaply as possible by third-class train and local bus. Clio talked about
camping out, and Romilly, who could afford greater comfort,
happily agreed. They had persuaded a friend, a Submarine
Officer, to drive them as far as Penang.

'You'd better look out,' Beryl said to Clio, 'I'm sure he's a
snake.'

'What on earth do you mean, Mummy? He's a very nice
man.'

'Pardon, Miss, my name is Snake,' hummed her mother,
slightly out of tune.

'Of course he's a snake,' I put in. 'They all are. At least they
were in my day.' I remembered various visits of H.M. Warships
to distant stations, and the way their officers marched off—
temporarily—with our girls, 'Especially submariners.'

On the day they left we watched them loading a dilapidated
car at the back of the Red House. The sun shone on the Monsoon clouds already gathering in the east. It was sticky and still
and brilliant, good to be young and starting off on a journey,
when every sparkling moment lingers in delight. The Snake,
as he was now called between ourselves, had thought of everything that could be needed on the expedition. The last of the
camping kit to be loaded was a long rope, too weak for towing.

'What is that for,' I asked him.

'That's a snake rope,' he replied. 'You put it round your camp
to keep the snakes away.'

We burst out laughing, but the Snake had given me a look
out of the corner of his eye that made me wonder just what
Clio had passed on to him, and who was going to laugh the
longest in the end. Snakes or no snakes, our worries as to the

girls' ability to look after themselves, the likelihood of their being attacked by some fell tropical disease, or of being snapped up for the white slave traffic, were all loaded into the car with them and disappeared with it round the bend in the road, between the green grass, the whitewashed stones and the palm trees.

Beryl and I sailed a few days later, on 11 November, with a poppy twisted into the forestay, bound for Kuching in Sarawak, about four hundred miles away. Kuching, the principal of the three towns of Sarawak, lies twenty miles up the river called the Sungei Sarawak, which has two entrances, the Muwara Tebas and the Santubong, which joins the main river after about fifteen miles. The Santubong entrance, which is navigable at high tide for craft of *Tzu Hang*'s size, is rarely used. It is the nearest to Singapore, and if we used it successfully, we could come back down the main stream, only retracing our steps, which Beryl is always averse to, for a short distance.

In our staid and elderly way we also experienced some of the excitement that shone in Clio's eyes, for we also were going to a new country that we hadn't seen before, and our excitement was enchanced by the imagined possibility of a brush with the Indonesians, if we went too close to their shores, or disturbed some infiltrators in the river mouth.

It was a typical day at the change of the Monsoon, with the dark clouds hanging over the Rhio Islands, the sun brilliant on green shores and red earth. The fish-traps marched out to meet us for the last time, like long columns of infantry awaiting evacuation from a beach, and an R.A.F. crash-boat that had done the same trip in twenty-four hours motored up to wave goodbye. *Tzu Hang* moved so slowly that it seemed as if she was part of the steamy, heat-stilled seascape, in a silence broken only by the noise of an aircraft running up its engines at Changi and by the hum of the crash-boat disappearing at the head of its wake, which shone black and silver in the oil smooth sea on either side.

After a time a hiss sounded across the bay, and a sudden wind sucked us into a grey veil, sending us blindly scurrying and slapping through the water, while the rain cascaded off our sails. After half an hour we lay still again, the decks steaming, and the main and genoa emptying and filling with a loud crack as we rolled. This was to be the pattern of our journey across to Sarawak.

On our first night, still close to the Rhio Islands, and within the arbitrary twelve-mile limit imposed by the Indonesians, for a sailing ship cannot be too fastidious about this sort of thing, a darkened patrol vessel appeared. Whether it was Malaysian or Indonesian we could not tell but it circled us stealthily in the darkness and then lay alongside. Suddenly it illuminated us with its searchlight. Beryl and I sat breathless and still in the cockpit, in the brilliant light which shone on *Tzu Hang*, and left all else in blackness. There was complete silence except for the slapping of the water between the two close hulls and the burbling of a powerful engine. We were uncertain what to expect next, but suddenly the light went out, the note of the engine changed, and as our eyes became accustomed again to the darkness we were able to make out the dark shape drawing rapidly away.

'Well,' said Beryl, with some relief. 'I wonder who that was!' Indonesians, I thought, and was glad that they hadn't questioned our position too closely. The Malaysian patrol craft at that time all had British officers in command, and they would surely have wished us good night or a good voyage.

The passage across to Sarawak was made on squalls only. They came towards us spilling a white cloth of cloud over dark recesses, whisked us briefly and wetly on our way, and dropped us casually a few miles away from where they had picked us up. At night we took down all sail, lit a lantern, and rocked comfortably on the unpopulated sea. In Northern Borneo the Monsoon was already blowing freshly, but although when we left Singapore it was expected momentarily, it still lingered in the north.

On the eighth night of *Tzu Hang*'s slowest and least tiring trip we loitered for the night close off Tanjong Datu, on the southwest coast of Borneo, on the border between Sarawak and Indonesia. I wondered on which side the lighthouse stood, which showed white against the tops of great trees. Beneath the forest the rocks stood sharp and dangerous, bare from their constant struggle with Monsoon seas. Again we heard the strange creaking of fish about us, or were they frogs on the shore two miles away?

Next day we were off early. As we closed the coast in the bay beyond Tanjong Datu, the hills in the hinterland stood up like islands in the sea, but the low coast through which the rivers meander as indeterminately as an Essex road, was still invisible. Taking our bearings from the hills we rolled our way across the shallow discoloured waters of the bay, until we discovered the point which concealed the river mouth, behind a long hilly peninsula which formed the eastern side of the bay. There were rocks and shoals to be avoided, but we found them all, and soon slipped past a white, deserted, police post overlooking the river entrance, and into a sheltered stretch, with Santubong mountain on the peninsula behind us and a long straight stretch of river ahead.

Nothing is more thrilling than to come into a river from the sea, a river whose entrance is unbuoyed and unspoiled by man. Suddenly there is security, and bird song, and the knowledge that nothing very serious can happen, and it is all your own. On each side stretched mudbanks, bare for a few feet and thickly covered with nipa palm above the tide-line, so that whatever went on beyond was completely screened from the river. Sometimes a small creek opened a channel, a tunnel for canoes, through the low arching leaves of the palms, waiting for exploration. And what sort of river-dwellers would we find, we wondered, if we had the time to explore? Almost immediately a long black canoe came hissing out of one of these side entrances, a 'longboat' driven by a Johnson outboard engine. Its bow was lifting and a wake creaming astern where a man crouched. Four slender women sat in the canoe, each with an umbrella to protect their delicate complexion from the sun. As the sun was sinking all umbrellas were lowered to one side, and they, and the eager way in which the man and women leant forward as if they were thrusting towards some adventure, made them look like Viking shields along a Viking boat, as they flew past us.

We did not get very far that night, as an oil-pipe burst and had to be repaired. As I washed and scrubbed myself all over on deck after almost bathing in black oil I noticed that the mosquitoes were biting. As soon as I could I pulled on a shirt and went below. I was itching all over.

'The mosquitoes on deck are ghastly,' I told my disinterested wife, who was reading a book and cooking at the same time. I rubbed and scratched and twisted and complained.

'Aren't you making rather a fuss?' she said, 'I haven't noticed any.'

'Look at this,' I shouted, pulling off my shirt indignantly.

'Oh dear,' she said, 'didn't you remember that you have an allergy to that detergent you were scrubbing yourself with?'

Darkness came, the tide talked against the planking, and *Tzu Hang* had turned her head to the sea as if she preferred to rest that way. She lay there absolutely motionless, and as the irritation had gone I slept as soundly as if I had been ashore.

Next morning we were off before the end of the ebb in order to have better control at a difficult bend where two rocks were marked. The chart was too small for accurate navigation, but it served well enough, and we passed the place where the rocks were shown without noticing a ripple. The banks closed in on us. We held dead centre in the straight stretches and veered towards the concave bank on the curves. The danger is that the helmsman tends to concentrate on one bank and, while keeping a comfortable distance off one side, finds himself suddenly uncomfortably close to the other. We reached the Sungei Sarawak without any trouble, although we touched the mud momentarily on one bend.

Once in the Sungei Sarawak the traffic increased. Longboats sped past, each with a Johnson engine, and more ungainly river boats, usually under control of a Chinese and loaded with vegetables or other merchandise. The country was more open, and houses appeared on the river banks and sometimes through the vegetation a glimpse of a green field of rice, or of a rubber plantation. Notices to mariners appeared also, nailed to trees or on poles. 'Rocks,' they said, and one, more verbose but no more explicit, said 'Rocks Hug This Bank.'

'Who hugs this bank?' I shouted to Beryl, nerves twanging. 'We or the rocks?' It was too late for an answer as we were shooting up on the tide, and I took it correctly that it was we who should close the bank.

Shortly afterwards we arrived in Kuching, a small town along the river bank between a lovely little Chinese temple at one end and the Government Buildings and a mosque at the other. We were about to anchor off a landing stage, where a path led to the Astana, the white building that was once the home of Rajah Brooke, and from where he used to cross every day to the Government offices, when we were hailed from the Customs House and directed to a small pier on the opposite side. As I walked down the river bank to report to the Customs, delicious smells came from the numerous little restaurants amongst the crowded Chinese shops on the street that runs along the river. All the buildings done in the Brookes' time were solid, enduring, and in good taste. They had left a pleasant atmosphere behind them and we heard continually the phrase 'In Rajah Brooke's time,' always spoken with a sense of nostalgia for something picturesque that was missing, particularly the old personal contact of the people with their ruler.

The first Brooke had arrived in 1839 when Sarawak was the southern province of the Brunei Sultanate. The Malays and the Land Dyaks were then in revolt against the oppression of the Sultan's Viceroy. Brooke brought about a settlement and was rewarded for his services by being installed as the Rajah of the territory that is now known as the First Division of Sarawak. Another two generations of Brookes followed, paternal and autocratic, and the boundaries were gradually extended, trade developed, piracy and head-hunting put down.

At the end of the last war, after occupation by the Japanese, the last Rajah felt that he could no longer rule the country after the old fashion, and that he required far greater resources to re-establish it than he could command. The country was therefore handed over to the British Crown. Colonial Government ceased in 1963 when Sarawak became part of the Federation of Malaysia.

The Sea Dyaks and the Chinese each account for about a third of the population, the Malays a sixth, the Melanau, the Land Dyaks and other indigenous tribes for the other sixth, but the economy of the country, as in most of Malaysia, is in the hands of the shrewd and mercenary Chinese. Without a strong disinterested power in control, these racial differences, so easily exploited, are the root of trouble in Malaysia, and this little twig of a country, which could be and has been, so happy and prosperous, is spinning in the flood between the great vortices of Asian unrest.

Should America and Britain withdraw their influence and

power from South East Asia, Sarawak and North Borneo would come under the control of either Indonesia or the Chinese, and if of the latter they would be reverting to a situation that virtually existed some hundreds of years ago. Ultimately, unless a full-scale war re-establishes our authority in the East, this is what will happen.

We moved down next day to the new port which was almost completed. A splendid lay-out a few miles below Kuching with long wharves to take seagoing ships, and all that anyone could wish for in warehouses, roads and offices. Lucky little country to get a gift like this! The only point that no one agreed on was why such a port should have been built where it is. Another mile by road to Pending would have put it within reach of much bigger ships with greater space for manœuvre and a three-fathom approach at all tides, rather than one of seven feet at low springs.

We left on 23 November, and as we left a friend called down to us.

'Dreadful news today! President Kennedy has been assassinated!'

With the same sense of shock that numbed all decent people in the world that morning, we slipped down the river, passing a British minesweeper on her way up, swinging round a bend, her ensign at half-mast.

We took the regular route out by way of the Muara Tebas, bound for Sibu, 116 miles away—sixteen to the outer bar, thirty across the bay to the Kuala Rajang mouth, and seventy up the river. Directly we were over the outer bar we made sail. The rocky headland which separated us from the Santubong entrance, up which we had entered, lay to port and to starboard the long low coast of the bay, curved away with here and there a tall clump of palms or rubber trees showing like small blue islands across the shallow sea.

We raised Jerijyeh light at nightfall and anchored two miles south of Rajang, on the south side of the river mouth but with both banks showing dimly through the dark. Soon the tide was talking away, lulling us to sleep, a sleep only slightly disturbed by one or two violent rain squalls, which hammered on the deck and set the halyards tapping against the mast. We had plenty of chain out, and the anchor was in good mud, so we only turned over and thought it good to be in shelter and not struggling with sails and sheets.

We were off at daylight as the tide slackened and passed the S.S. *Cardiganshire*, loading from a lighter a few miles up the river, just before it forks. We took the right fork, and, as it narrowed and we left the big ship behind, the tide strengthened. We seemed to slip so quickly up to the bends that there was barely time to appreciate all that each revealed before we had left the succeeding stretch.

We both felt a sense of great excitement at the thought of the long river journey ahead, enhanced by the closing, secret banks, the swift brown flood, the newness of it all. Beryl was at the helm and I was below when a longboat, driven as usual, by a Johnson outboard engine, came fuming up from astern, with an Englishman, John Parkinson, fitting his launch like a cigar in a cellophane wrapper, under the awning. He was agent for the Glen Lines and paid us a short visit. As he arrived, Beryl, overcome by the Conrad-like atmosphere of stream and jungle, looked down the hatch and called to me:

'A white man is coming!'

On deck we exchanged some of the usual remarks that Englishmen make abroad about England and the Willard-Smiths who were last seen at the Gold Cup three years ago, and after, as it were, lifting our legs at the nearest palm tree, he left us to perform a similar duty with the Captain of the *Cardiganshire*.

Presently we anchored in a narrow stretch. The character of the banks was already beginning to change. The trees were higher and more varied than the nipa palm stretches at the mouth. The tide slid down from their roots leaving dark brown corrugated banks. *Tzu Hang* sank lower and lower between them. A night heron sat motionless on a rotting log amongst some reeds beside us, and small flocks of white paddi birds came flitting up the stream towards a low-tide snack-bar that they knew of. John Parkinson and the S.S. *Cardiganshire* might have been a hundred miles away and the river deserted except for the flicker of bird and insect life amongst the trees and reeds on its banks.

We were off again after tea, passing Sarikei, where a number of small steamers had tied up. Their Chinese crews gave us a wave and shouted to us to join them as we passed. They were tying up for the night, but as we had a good moon we hoped to make use of the tide while it lasted.

The night fell cool as the full moon climbed into the sky. *Tzu Hang*'s engine hummed away and the banks slipped steadily past. Sometimes a light appeared on the bank, sometimes the sound of voices came across the water as the moon shone on a longhouse roof, and sometimes a tree trunk slid along our flank and rolled in the wake behind. We came out into the Muara Payang, which leads down to another entrance from the sea and the night was clear enough to allow us to pick up the beacons on the bank, which showed the channel. Mile after mile with the swift tide and the reaches of the river unfolding—not a boat to be seen, nor any sign of life now, for what there was seemed to be resting. At last at midnight, when the tide turned against us, we anchored, and from somewhere near came the sound of a man's voice singing and the little notes of a single-stringed instrument. Beryl and I stood silent on the foredeck, almost breathless with wonder. The water whispered in the reeds at the shore. There was the chatter of a nightjar and an owl called. Then there was nothing but 'The waters wap and the waves wan.' Never had we made a more romantic journey.

We were awoken at daylight by the song of birds, and I lay in my bunk listening to them. A monotonous tonking that brought back the Indian jungle, mynahs scolding, and a bulbul of some sort just above us. It was time to be off. We passed Binatang with some pretty laughing girls washing clothes on the bank—their skins pale, their burnished hair tied close to their heads. We passed one or two longboats driving under their outboard engines, and eventually came to the main river on its way to find another broad and shallow outlet to the sea. There are dangerous sand-spits on either side here but with good beacons to show the way over. As we got into this stretch we were joined by a number of small cargo boats. We were passing rubber plantations now and several large saw-mills. Here the wealth of the country flowed. A great black squall roared over us as we approached Sibu, but we held on and anchored off the Residency, whose tree-shaded grounds came down to the river's edge.

We rowed ashore to a wharf on the river a little higher up. As we did so, a platoon of Gurkhas left in two longboats in pursuit of some reported infiltration of guerillas. They, too, were leaning forward—there must be something about a long-boat that makes one do this—with rifles and automatics across their knees. At the same time another platoon returned down-river, looking as tired as these hardy men can ever look, after a long and frustrating patrol.

We were fortunate in that a famous woman war correspond-ent was paying the Gurkhas a visit and was flying next day to see the troops in their outpost positions, in a helicopter. As I had had the honour to fight with Gurkhas, and Beryl too had been with them with her mobile canteen in the Burma war, room was made for us also.

We were flown by one of the Navy helicopters under the charge of a splendid bearded Commander from a little tented camp in the bush, some miles from Sibu. The Commander's confidence and enthusiasm seemed to radiate through the camp. Beards were very much *à la mode*, some of them twisted into the likeness of helicopter blades so that men looked as if they could take off under their own power. It reminded me that morale is never a question of the availability of 'Coke' or beer, but of a job worth doing, being done well.

We flew over the creased green tablecloth of the forest, broken by occasional patches of dry paddi and by the long dark line of the river, which showed here and there the white scales of its rapids, and yellow sand-bars. The pilot swung us down with superb élan on to tiny clearings clinging to the edge of the hills, where a white mark had blossomed momentarily to show him in.

Although I was once used to jungles and to jungle warfare, these great forests with their tenuous river communications seemed particularly strange, dangerous, and secretive. But they were in good hands. After twenty years the calibre of soldier and officer, Gurkha and British, was as good or better than ever. Here were the experts—this was their life. They were living under war conditions, always on the alert, always in pursuit or on patrol, and only limited in their endeavour by a frontier behind which the enemy could safely retire, without even the need to conceal his camps. The overriding impression was one of efficiency and enthusiasm, and it is only because of this efficiency that the situation has been kept under control.

That evening in the mess at Sibu, the war correspondent was telling us of her adventures in different parts of the world. She was dressed in a green battledress, one leg crossed over the other trousered knee, a cigarette in her lips and a glass in her hand. With the humility of experts at their job, the officers round her were listening to her tales.

'Algeria,' she said, 'that really was something. Compared to that this is Boy Scout stuff.'

A silence fell. The Colonel, finding himself in the rôle of Scoutmaster, politely excused himself, and the others soon drifted off to twice-read papers or to their rooms.

Next morning, having already written her report, the war correspondent left.

'I don't know what has happened to the Colonel today,' she said to Beryl. 'He seemed so nice yesterday, and I can't get a word out of him today.'

Beryl, whose father, brothers, and husband were all soldiers, and who perhaps knew soldiers better than the reporter, said nothing either.

The Resident, a big man, one of the few remaining and much respected 'Rajah's men,' who had spent a lifetime in Sarawak, arranged for us to stay a night in a longhouse. One afternoon we left *Tzu Hang* busy collecting a raft of river débris on her anchor-chain, and sped away in a longboat which was carrying a Government clerk back to his house on a visit. He was to act as interpreter and all that we were required to provide were numerous bottles of beer.

It was one of the longhouses that we had passed on our way up, about a hundred yards long, built on piles, with an open veranda on one side, from which ladders led down to the river bank. At one end a small stream ran down to the river. Here there was a platform to which longboats were tied, and from it a bamboo walk led to the veranda. This was also the wash-room and bath of all the inhabitants. Inside the longhouse there was a communal room running the whole length of the house, and facing this a long row of single rooms, so that this longhouse was in fact a row of single-room flats with one indoor and one outside veranda, and a communal bathroom in the river.

It was a sophisticated longhouse. Breasts, except for those of the very old and the very young, were covered, and when two girls were persuaded to dress themselves in the 'visiting' clothes of freer days, the effect was spoiled by cotton bras beneath the silver ornaments. In a basket at one end hung some smoked heads, but they were there more as a concession to visitors as curios, than as a mark of present prowess. In fact the need of the longhouse as a protection against raiders had gone, and their use was falling into a decline. Presently they will disappear, for raiders are no longer armed with spears, and a limited dispersion is a better safeguard against mortars and automatic rifles. Something that will disappear with them is the friendliness of this group living. Dogs and children wandered up and down the inside veranda, babies were slung to rafters, and anywhere a circle of men and women formed to sit on the floor and gossip.

That evening a blind minstrel arrived, wandering to sing songs of old times and of great fights and heroes. He sang of modern times too, making the song up as he went along.

'What are you singing of now?' Beryl asked.

'I am singing of you. How beautiful and adventurous you are. How rich and generous,' he replied.

Three hours later he was still wistfully harping on the same subject.

The noise was appalling and he sang 'each song twice over' for Beryl had brought her tape-recorder, and each song had to be played back. After hours and hours we managed to withdraw to the Headman's room and lie down, under a picture of the Queen and the Duke of Edinburgh, amongst numerous women and children and pinging mosquitoes. Outside, until the last bottle of beer was finished, the grunts, moans, and wails continued, an operation for which there was no anaesthetic.

There is another way out from Sibu, particularly if one is bound for the north, by the Kuala Igan, which takes off from the point at which we were anchored and leads fifty-five miles to the sea. This would avoid our retracing our steps, but it had the disadvantage of a shallow bar (four feet) which opened right into the Monsoon wind that was now supposed to be blowing.

We left Sibu on 29 November. We had a chart of the first two or three miles, which leads down to an oil installation, and we had a chart of the bar, but for the remaining fifty miles we only had the word of the *Pilot* which says that in 1879 there were depths of between two and twelve fathoms in the river. The only hazards that we met were one or two long-tows on their way to the saw-mills near Sibu, floating logs, and patches of green weed. In a way the Igan was even more fascinating than the Rajang because it is less known. We anchored for the night well down the river in another wonderfully secluded and silent stretch. The weed collected on our anchor chain, the shadows of the clouds slipped slowly across the reach, and the lightest breath of wind came down the river, promising, we hoped, an easy passage of the bar next day.

We took the tide in the morning and passed close to a fishing village on the right bank, within the curve of the river mouth. It was shallow water here with a long spit of sand in mid-stream, but we were on to our chart now. We anchored on the outward end of the spit, just beyond a fish-trap which is used as a bearing mark for the crossing of the bar—in line with a dead tree. There are many dead trees, and we never found the right one. As the tide ran out and we looked anxiously towards the bar, we could see the waves were breaking right across. They were still doing so at high tide, when the time came to face it, but not so frequently as before. We took our bearing from the fish-trap, watching a set to the westward, and hoped that we could find a patch free from breakers, although our route ahead seemed never quite clear of them. Presently *Tzu Hang* began to buck over the swell. Waves were curling and breaking on each side, and one broke right at her bow, which she rode without a splash on the deck. A mile of this and her motion eased. We were over. We set our sails to a light breeze, but we did not complain about this, since it had let us over so easily. We were lucky to find that the Monsoon was only heralded by its swell and was by no means established. We found ourselves sailing again on the wings of squalls by day and on the land breeze by night. It blew more steadily than the sea breeze, which the squalls always interrupted.

On 4 December before daylight the Labuan light was in sight. We had passed the great oil flares at Tanjong Baram during the night. Now we were sailing to a light wind offshore, over a calm moonlit sea, with cloud to the north and the swell from the still delayed Monsoon rolling in. South of us there was a dark low coast, to the east a great pile of black cloud, and to the northeast a distant mountain, Mount Kinabalu, showed against the first red glow of the morning. More immediately ahead was a splatter of dark islands, and Labuan light winking away. A lovely morning it turned out to be as we sailed slowly towards the harbour and time for a swim, toppling over warm blue depths, before we started to worry about details of navigation in the harbour entrance. After one or two shifts in search of a suitable berth we anchored between the wharf and the oil jetty on the edge of a shallow bank, backed by a sandy beach and some tall casuarinas.

I went ashore to the Harbour Master's office and found a tall man outside, fitting himself into a small English car. He had a dour Scots face and the mark of a sailor about him.

'Are you the Harbour Master?' I asked.

'Yes,' he replied with an uncompromising look.

'We've just come in, in that white yacht,' I explained.

'You're anchored in a prohibited area,' he said. 'Where are you from?'

I told him and he began to thaw, his cold blue eyes becoming friendly and interested. I soon found out that he too was looking forward to doing one day the same sort of thing that we were doing. He came on board and charmed us with his knowledge-able interest in *Tzu Hang*. As he told us of his wish, he asked if he could bring his wife, Mary, on board. 'I'm no so sure how she is going to take to it,' he confessed.

'Bring her to lunch tomorrow,' said Beryl, 'and we'll start her indoctrination.'

It was a good beginning. Next morning the sea was calm. A light breeze chased the flickering cloud shadows across the awning over the deck, and rustled the tracery of the casuarinas against a dappled sky. The harbour launch, glistening in dark blue and polished brass, came alongside, and the Harbour Master, in a smart white uniform, handed his lovely and well-dressed wife on to our deck. He did it with obvious pride and some wonder that he, the Harbour Master of Labuan, could produce someone like this for us to meet. Not only was she lovely, but she was good fun, too. We felt that this was more like Cowes than Labuan, and when they left, hoped that we might have helped him on the way to his dream ship.

A few days later we arrived back from Brunei. It was dark and as we anchored a gusty squall swept over us. At the same time a flashlight signalled from the beach, and a great voice boomed across the water—'*Tzu Hang*, ahoy.'

I rowed in and found the Harbour Master on the beach asking us all to dinner, but as we had been given a leg of lamb in Brunei and had no refrigeration I persuaded him to come on board instead. After a few drinks Beryl suggested that Mary should join us and that they should have dinner on *Tzu Hang*.

'A very good idea,' said the Harbour Master, ignoring the rain. 'Shall I take the dinghy now and persuade her?'

'And I'll come and help you,' I said, eager to see something more of Mary and knowing how courage fails on a warm hearthstone. We rowed in through the rain, beached the dinghy, and stumbled over the driftwood on the beach in search of the Harbour Master's car. A few minutes later we arrived at his house.

The lights shone out from the big room on to a curtain of bright raindrops and over wet flags and green grass to the rocks by the sea shore. Beyond, a red light in the channel blinked solemnly, warning adventurers to stay at home. Mary had changed into a blue dress, had lit a cigarette and poured out a drink. She had put Brahms *Requiem* on the radiogram and perhaps for the first time that day was feeling cool, relaxed and comfortable, her elegant legs stretched out in a long chair, when two wet roisterers burst in. Gone were the visions of a peaceful evening as we urged her to come out to *Tzu Hang*. After one or two mild protests she picked up an umbrella and came out with us to the car. The Harbour Master glanced at the umbrella with disapproval. Umbrellas are the mark of a landsman and have no place on boats.

'There's a shorter way to the dinghy,' he said, as he parked the car on a grassy track which led through the casuarina grove, beside a small stream. The rain was falling harder than ever. The Harbour Master strode on ahead while Mary and I slipped and stumbled after the flickering flashlight.

'Oh,' she called, 'are you sure this is the right way?' Her shoes were already wet through and muddy, but the Harbour Master's thoughts were on great adventures in small boats, and a slight stiffening of his dim back was the only reaction to such weakness.

'Couldn't we go back and try the right way?' she asked hesitantly, but the light danced on. Suddenly there was a gasp and a splash followed by a cry of dismay. For the first time the light turned to illuminate the path for us and discovered Mary, sitting in the stream, and still holding the umbrella over her head. It was too much. Suddenly the seaman took charge and the voice that had met a thousand emergencies roared out, 'For the Lord's sake, Mary. Get off that bluidy bum—and put that umbrella down.'

Mary was a good sport, but I felt that that wasn't the last word to be spoken on the night's doings. Some weeks later a man in the same service said to us, 'I hear you've ruined someone's wonderful dream.'

On the way up from Labuan, along the west coast of North Borneo, *Tzu Hang* called at one or two small tree-covered islands. In Brunei we had picked up Marguerite Glennie, who was coming as far as Jesselton with us. She was dark-haired and petite, and found strange little things that we would never have seen, shells, flowers, insects, and life in rock-pools, like an inquisitive little bird. Her husband, who was in charge of the fighting there, flew over us in the morning on his way to see his scattered soldiers.

Every morning Kinabalu, the highest mountain in South East Asia, stood clear to the northeast, its blue serrated ridge above the white clouds which covered green ridge and valley below. By noon the whole mountain was hidden. We found a safe place in Jesselton behind a T-jetty to leave *Tzu Hang*, so that we might go and climb it. She was in company with the grey Philippine smugglers' boats, which were anchored stern to the sea wall. They each had an inboard engine and up to four outboard engines, which could be hung as required on a wide transom in order to outdistance the Philippine patrol boats. The crews looked tough and cheerful, and we were told that we had nothing to fear from them. On the northeast coast beyond Sandakan there were genuine Sulu Sea pirates who preyed on the coastal trade. These were definitely dangerous, and we had no intention of going into that area.

We set off in a police Land-Rover for Kinabalu and as Marguerite's husband was protecting the country we only had to pay for the fuel. Jesselton, like Labuan, was almost entirely destroyed by bombing during the war, and there had been a flurry of building that was still going on. A modern block of flats had been built above the harbour, and the shops were loaded. Amongst the British whom we met, there was a feeling of enthusiasm. They were almost all busily engaged in trying to help the small country stand on its own feet within the Federation of Malaysia. As we drove through the countryside and saw the paddi standing high in the fields, the crowded markets, and the timber on the hills, it seemed that they were doing it very effectively.

Everywhere in Malaysia there is this feeling of progress, a feeling that it all might work if only . . . if only Britain or the responsible members of the Commonwealth stayed there in sufficient strength to see that it did. With such a varied mixture of races, of such different degrees in development, with such great distances and such fragile resources, continuity and cohesion can only be supplied by some strong unifying force. To whom then the Empire?

The road soon shed its tarmac and, growing steadily narrower and rougher, set off into the foothills. We climbed up and round spurs and saw it doubling back on the opposite hill. We climbed over bamboo-filled ravines, passed little cottages clinging to the side of the hill, edged our way round a new landslide, and halted at a village market where we drank black coffee and sweetened condensed milk, carefully poured so that it lay black and white in the glass in two distinct layers. Soon we were driving through the cloud itself and stopped at a small roadside store where the porters were supposed to be waiting. To old eastern hands there was no surprise to find that they were not. We shook the dust off our clothes, breathed in great gulps of this cool mountain air, and set about finding them. We collected four. Two men and two boys, each with a tall cone-shaped basket into which our food and kit were loaded. The Land-Rover took us all a little further up the road, which was being cut out of the hill on the way to a radio station, and from the road head we set off up a jungle trail, climbing for a couple of hours to an ugly group of tin huts and steel towers on a cleared shoulder of the hill. Amongst them the grey cloud trailed its fingers and stretched out to cover the deep ravines on either side, the mist-wet roofs dripped, and a few members of the Post and Telegraph Department gloomily awaited their relief, as imprisoned as if they were in a dungeon by the strangeness of their surroundings and quite unable to find relief in some new interest.

We camped in an empty room and set off early next morning while the mountain was still clear above us. The path, little more than a game track, twisted up through the dripping trees, and the cat, who accompanied us, enlivened by the coolness of the morning, dashed half way up their trunks. This display of energy soon exhausted her, and we took it in turns to carry her across our shoulders. Soon the mist rose from below to enfold us, and we saw no more of the mountain that day. We camped in the Paka cave at 10,000 feet and set about getting a fire to burn. When eventually the smoke had cleared from the cave and our eyes had stopped running we could look out from our eyrie, through the riven cloud and over the creased green hide of the hills, to a pale and glassy sea.

We were off early, leaving the cat to fend for herself, and carrying lanterns made from candles and food tins. Their dim lights danced and flickered between the close short stems of the scrub jungle as we scrambled and sometimes crawled under the branches, until we came, with the daylight, out on to moss forest, and finally on to slabs and slopes of bare rock. It was a great hump-backed whale of a mountain, lying half awash in the forest and there was only an occasional scramble on the way to the summit, but there were some impressive faces and the two subsidiary peaks as sharp as asses' ears for mountaineers to climb one day. At our age, on a mountain that in our youth we would have been up and down in a day, glorying in the sheer physical exertion, it was sufficient to reach the top.

Back at the camp there was no sign of the cat. We called and listened, but there was no reply other than the mocking of the waterfall beside the cave. Eventually we found her, seething with indignation, secreted in a prickly bush. Unlike Beryl and me she finds going downhill easier than climbing and walked the whole way down to the radio station without assistance. Next day we hobbled stiffly to the road and down to the sea again.

We left Jesselton on 30 December, bringing up a bicycle on our anchor chain, complete with three-speed gear and a generator for its light. It wasn't in very good condition, so I dropped it in again, feeling as if I was disposing of evidence that might have been required by the police. Outside the true Monsoon wind was blowing. It was the wind that would take us most of the way to Japan. *Tzu Hang* seemed glad to meet it as we shortened sail and started to beat up the coast. We sighted Mantinini Island about ten miles away just before dark. The jib and mizzen were brought down and *Tzu Hang* allowed to sail herself under the main against wind and current. This was running much stronger than I had expected, and daylight showed that we had lost ground during the night.

There are two islands, each consisting of a steep jungle-covered ridge about two hundred feet high, connected by a long reef on which there is an islet standing like an upthrust thumb. Both provide shelter in this Monsoon, but on the bigger there is a small fishing village, and we could see some of the grey smugglers' boats there. They use this island as a halting place on their way to Palawan, and as they were far removed from the law, we thought it better to leave them to themselves and went behind the second island which was deserted. We sailed in and anchored when the shore seemed very close, and yet when it came to rowing in or swimming we seemed a long way out. Behind the beach and over the ridge the wind was singing a new song in the trees, while above them hundreds of frigate birds hung as if suspended from the sky.

We set off again next morning, beating against a strong wind and current, and cracking the skin on our fingers from the unusual struggles with the sheets. We were almost late next day at the pass between Cape Sampamangie, the northern tip of Borneo, and the island which lies just off it. The current was running very strongly here as we made short tacks to clear the reefs on either hand, and it was almost dark before we were out of the bottleneck. We turned down towards Kudat in Marudu Bay, very glad to be through, and *Tzu Hang*'s motion wonderfully easy after the windward beat. Lights of fishing vessels began to come on in the bay, trawlers from the Philippines, and presently Kudat light blinked out from behind the headland where it had been hiding. We shortened sail to allow the moon to rise and presently sailed in to the harbour and anchored off a promontory below the Commissioner's house.

Michael Pike was the Commissioner, whom we found next

morning, young and athletic and smouldering with suppressed energy as he listened to the pleas of a line of the local short-turbaned Kadazans at his office desk. It was obvious that he lived for the time when he could be out and on tour about his province, and his energy found its outlet when he drove his Land-Rover, leaving his villagers looking like an advertisement for motor fuel, their heads turned this way and that, or when in the evening he swam in a fast crawl far beyond the reef. He and his wife opened their house to us, and from its veranda we could look down on *Tzu Hang* riding at anchor in the bay.

At Kudat, also we met John Edwards, originally from Nottingham, who had become a Colonel in the U.S. Army during the war after having been turned down by the Australians owing to an old leg injury. Now he was in charge of the Philippine trawler operation in Marudo Bay and sometimes at odds with Michael Pike about fishing boundaries. He was a lone adventurer full of courage and humour, and he needed it all. He told us of Ursula Island off the east coast of Palawan, where no Philippine would stay the night because of the noise of Spanish ghosts, the clank of armour and the clash of swords —an island, Beryl and I decided, that we would have to visit.

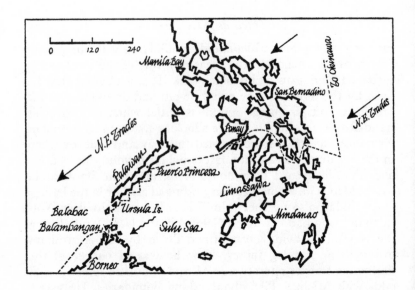

21 *The Last Long Leg*

IT was 11 January and the Northeast Monsoon was now blowing steadily in North Borneo and across the Sulu Sea. The ocean current of the Southwest Monsoon had long ago been set in reverse, and the waters of the Sulu Sea were pouring into the China Sea at the average rate of about a knot. Our object was to get to windward against the current while still in the milder latitudes, so that by the time we reached between ten and fifteen North, where stronger winds prevailed, we would be able to lay an easier course on one long tack for Japan.

We could not make to windward immediately because of the pirates of the Sulu Sea, but up the east coast of Palawan the Monsoon does not blow too strongly and later we could make use of the weather shores provided by the Philippine Islands until we broke out into the Pacific. The best way out for us, because the land offered us protection until the last moment was through the Surigao Strait, the great San Bernardino Strait being wide open to the northeast. Once out of the Surigao Strait the angle of the shore would enable us to heave to in safety in the event of winds of gale force, and—biggest attraction of all—it was the strait by which Magellan had entered.

To begin with, through the islands and currents on each side of the Balabac Straits, between North Borneo and Balabac and up the east side of Palawan, we would be in waters that are not always accurately charted, where lights are not always lit, and where a rusting hulk on a reef is too often visible to the anxious seafarer. We hoisted sail in the darkness early on this morning and slid out past the lighthouse, very well aware of the beginning of a new adventure, nor had we to wait too long before we had almost too big a taste of it.

Tzu Hang soon began to take shape with the coming daylight and the lights of the Vila Flor Company's trawlers out in the bay to fade. There are a number of islands and islets just north of the Northern tip of Borneo and south of the Balabac Strait. *Tzu Hang* sailed up between Balambangen and Banguey and entered Luk Barabok Bay on the eastern side of Balambangen. The island is uninhabited, the bay deserted, and our chart was drawn in 1844. It is full of reefs and shallows, but the tide was low, and with the sun behind us we could see the discoloured water of the shoals. We anchored near a long sandy beach, well protected from the wind and sea, and took the cat ashore. Behind the tall casuarinas that lined the beach there were salt flats and the tracks of wild pig and mouse-deer.

We left before daylight on a half-tide, favouring a one-and-a-half fathom patch rather than the port side of the channel, where I had seen the sea breaking on shoals on our way in. Beryl was at the helm while I conned the ship from the bow, watching the mizzen mast against a dark point astern to ensure that our bearing did not change and looking out at the same time for dangers ahead. I could see the faint white line of breakers well to port and was just about to alter course to keep parallel to them, when with a dull crunch *Tzu Hang*'s bow rose and then stayed still. I looked over the bow and saw appallingly close under the water the shocking ulcered outline of the reef.

I looked again as I hurried aft, hearing Beryl repeat in dismay, 'We're aground!' The mizzen was still in line with the point which was beginning to show more distinctly. With the engine

full astern *Tzu Hang* slid off, but such was the shock of running
aground when I believed that I had plenty of water, that I felt
uncertain as to our position. I sounded and found five fathoms.
Sounding carefully we crept ahead, closer to the breakers and
found no more dangers.

It was the one-and-a-half-fathom bank that we had run on
to, shallower and more extensive than in 1844, but on the way
in, since it could be clearly seen, I had not bothered to check its
position and depth too closely. It had given us a bad fright, for
there was no means of finding help if we had stayed hard
aground, and it made us wary of entering bays at night, in
these coral and badly charted waters. *Tzu Hang* had scraped
a few barnacles off the bottom of the keel, but there was no
sign of damage.

The gloom that oppressed us as a result of this accident was
soon dispelled by the sailing that followed. 'You don't want to
worry about a little thing like that,' *Tzu Hang* told us, as she
heeled to the wind and thrust forward to the pass between
Balambangen and Banguey, between Tiga Shoal and Rifleman
Rock, with everything brilliant in movement and light, with
spray flying at the bow and white horses everywhere, a reddish
brown reef, a bent and rusty iron beacon, a long spit of white
sand and seabirds wheeling.

Once through these dangers we could lay a course for Cape
Melville on Balabac, but not for long, as all the Sulu Sea was
pouring through the Strait and we were carried to the west
until we had to beat in short inshore tacks to clear Cape Melville Lighthouse. We were almost up to the narrow reef-
enclosed Clarendon Bay when night fell, but our nerves, still
shaken by the morning's grounding, wouldn't stand an attempt
to enter, so we hove to for the night. The light, which was
supposed to have a range of twenty-four miles, was so dim that
we could hardly see it at five, and Comiran light was not lit at
all. It was a sign of the decay that marks the emerging nations.
The light bore west, then north, then disappeared altogether
as the current carried us out into the China Sea. By the next
evening we had recovered our lost ground and were once
again approaching Clarendon Bay when we saw a Philippine
patrol boat boarding a suspect fishing vessel about five miles
up the coast.

At the same time it saw us and as soon as it had disengaged from the fishing vessel, it came lurching towards us, with large black moustachios from over-age diesels rolling away over the sea on either side. It was an old U.S. corvette and, after threatening us with hideous indecision as it swung first to one side and then to the other, turned up alongside and asked us from where we had come. As his ship was to windward the captain could not hear my reply, so he swung her to port, turned a complete circle and crossed astern of us, while we continued sailing fast on the port tack. He then came up close on the starboard side, angling across our bow. This forced Beryl, who was at the helm, to squeeze *Tzu Hang* up into the wind to avoid a collision. We ought to have gone about, but it would have looked as if I was trying to avoid him, and I could not believe that he was going to continue on this course. This, however, he did, and suddenly the jib and main began to flutter, and *Tzu Hang* lost way. I ran forward too late to fend off, and the pulpit struck the iron side. We pushed off as best as we could while the patrol ship slid past us. Something caught in the jib, the sheet carried away, and his tatty ladder, stowed outside the rail, hooked in the shrouds. If *Tzu Hang* had not been rigged so strongly we would have lost the mast, but instead it was the lashings of the ladder that carried away and it was left swinging wildly as the ship drew off.

I called after them some proper sailor's language, believing that the damage was worse than it was. Beryl came up to help me secure the jib while we changed the sheets. 'If only they'd not try and be efficient,' said Beryl, 'and just be themselves, they might be all right.'

The patrol ship stood off—out of earshot—until it saw we were able to hoist the jib again and then went off on its own riotous business. We met them later in port, and paid an official call to make friends, but everyone was ashore except the captain, with whom we drank many cups of black coffee.

As a result of this delay we were again unable to get in to Clarendon Bay and had to resign oursleves to beating all night up the unlit channel between the island and the reefs six miles to the eastward. Next morning we sailed into Calandorang Bay and the untidy little village of Balabac, where fat pigs rootled under the houses and where we met a pretty girl and a young man carrying a little pig under his arm, smartly dressed and looking as if they were off to a christening. We also met a Customs Officer.

He came on board *Tzu Hang* and drank our whisky. 'Do you know American Mrs Wilson?' he asked. 'She have one helluva big yacht. Every time she come she give me a case of whisky.' He looked round hopefully. 'That all the drink you got?' he asked.

'Yes, but it's for you,' I replied, bowing to the inevitable. 'You must take it with you.'

It wasn't enough. Next day he called us into his office and asked us to pay a large amount for harbour and port dues. We told him to refer by telegram to Iloilo, and as we had no facilities for drawing money in Balabac we would pay there. This silenced him except that he asked us not to mention our visit to Balabac to any of the authorities in Iloilo.

We sailed from Balabac in search of the Ghosts of Ursula Island through the Nasubata Channel, on the north side of Comiran Island where turtles come in great numbers to lay their eggs. This part of the Sulu Sea is scattered with banks and shoals which take their names from ships that have either reported them or grounded on them, and their positions are often doubtful. We sailed along the edge of Argyll shoal where a British barque of that name was lost in 1892, and could see the bottom clearly. The following morning, after an anxious night surrounded by some real and many imagined dangers, the tops of Ursula Island's trees were right on the bow.

We anchored on a patch of sand, shining clear blue amongst the darker coral, on its western side. As we anchored, flight after flight of pigeons were leaving for the mainland of Palawan a few miles away. We rowed ashore, beached the dinghy, and found a path which led through thick underbrush to a small pit in the centre of the island, as if fishermen sometimes dug for water, or even treasure, there. The tall close-growing trees reached a hundred feet up to the sky and the wind sang in their tops. A few pigeons that had remained behind made a strange moaning cry, and there was an occasional clatter of their wings. The cat led on ahead, unaware of any supernatural aura. She was delighted to find such a deserted island, and cocked her head at the bird noises, calculating the chances of a meal of squab. This was not a time for ghosts, and we went back to *Tzu Hang* to catch up on our sleep.

Some time in the afternoon we heard the cat complaining on deck and decided later that she was trying to tell us that the dinghy had gone, for when we came up in the evening we found the painter hanging slackly at the stern and no pin in the shackle. I had changed it the day before and had not wired up the pin, so could not blame the loss on the ghosts. We took off downwind in pursuit but after several miles, having seen no sign of it, turned back for the island. We anchored with the returning pigeons, and since it was soon dark and we felt disinclined to swim ashore, slept soundly on board and heard nothing of the ghosts of Ursula Island.

We left on the 18th and sailed into an anchorage behind Malanao Island, near Puerto Princesa, on the morning of the 22nd after a rough struggle against wind and current. This passage was perhaps the most difficult stretch of the voyage as it was dead into the wind and into a current that was running up to one and a half knots against us. It was like the passage along the Arabian coast, and as we came back to the land on the starboard tack it often turned out to be the same headland that we had seen before. From Puerto Princesa across to the southern tip of Panay, *Tzu Hang* would not be so close to the wind, and from then on until we reached the Pacific we would have the shelter of the islands.

Malanao was low and green, covered with mangroves, with here and there a fish-trap standing in the shallows, and at night fishermen's flares burning. The coast of Palawan close behind was low and green also, with tall mountains some way inland. We did not go ashore but sailed next morning through the narrow pass and fast tides into the long inlet and up to Puerto Princesa where we tied temporarily to a T-jetty. Close off the jetty there was what had once been a good-looking freighter on the reef. She had already been salvaged off a reef outside the bay, but was determined to end her days on one. She was the fourth ship that we had seen abandoned on a reef in these waters.

Beryl returned from a shopping trip ashore with Bud de Vries, an American missionary, who moved us down to an anchorage below his house, which he and his pretty wife, Ginny, made us use as if it were our own. With his help we had a replacement for the dinghy built—and blessed—in his garden. Bud took his work with great enthusiasm and energy. Life was a game and God the Captain of the football team. Before starting off in his car we had a short prayer rather on these lines, 'Lord, I'm going to hit eighty on the bends, please keep Your eyes open.' He had built a large motor-boat which he took as far as Panay loaded with Baptists. He had a large station wagon, a sixteen millimetre movie camera, a fine new house. 'Truly the meek shall inherit the earth,' said Beryl. I had never come into close contact with missionaries before, and the thing I liked about these was that they so obviously enjoyed what they were doing.

We left on the evening of 28 January with the Puerto Princesa light, which Bud de Vries told us we would need a flashlight to discover, blinking a dim goodbye. Away for Panay. We stole out on a beautiful evening, genoa set, the moon a great lantern in the east, Venus and Jupiter racing together like two yachts to harbour low in the west, and Sirius blazing in the south. Next morning our course had improved, and it looked as if we would be able to hold the same tack all the way and clear all the dangers. We averaged just under five knots for the passage with a one-knot current against us and made Naso Point early on the morning of 31 January. There the wind left us in a most unpleasant sea, amongst a school of whales, with the currents racing down each side of Panay and meeting just off the point.

We gave Noga Island a berth of half a mile, as it has an extensive reef, and as soon as we could recognize the church in Aniny village, we sailed in to anchor. This was a new country. Palawan had been covered with tall trees, but these hills were bare, with dry brown grass and patches of bush, and steep ragged hills down which in the evening we could see a man driving a bunch of cattle. A sandy beach with tall palm trees partially hid the church and village. On the beach a number of outriggers were drawn up with plaited palm-leaf sides extending the edge of the dugout shell. Nets were hung on frames along the beach, and women waded offshore with a fish net. A man came out to us in a single seater outrigger as light as a feather, controlled with a flip of his paddle. 'Where from?' he asked in English, and then the remark dear to all yachtsmen when they have made port, 'Much wind last night!' We had been down to storm jib and well-reefed main, and we heard that one of the fishing boats had gone missing. A few weeks before a boat had also been caught offshore and had eventually reached Palawan, but once they had been blown out there was little hope of their being able to sail back.

Our impressions of the Philippines had got off to a bad start. Balabac had been a depressed little place and the brush with the patrol vessel had not helped. Now they were improving. These people were desperately poor, but they were laughing and friendly and made no attempt to beg. The men were wonderful seamen and the girls handled a boat as well as the men.

We spent a day there and left before daylight the following morning, getting away to a sudden offshore gust just as the anchor came up, and we were soon sailing fast in a short wet sea. After a hard beat all day, during which we made only twenty-two miles in the right direction, we saw some fine outriggers anchored close offshore. We sailed up to them and then found that they had their bows on a shingle beach, and as we could not find a reasonable depth to anchor in, even close to them, we turned about and resigned ourselves to a night at sea.

The outriggers were splendid ships, about seventy feet long, with a lovely curved prow, and with the spread of their floats as wide as the ship was long. They had a small mast from which the outrig was suspended, and none of these ones appeared to carry any sail. They all had engines and a cluster of lights at the bow. They were gaily painted and varnished, usually painted blue and white, and the masts red or red and white. As evening fell, one by one they put to sea, and soon a great row of brilliant lights spread across the channel. As we tacked, sailing faster than they were cruising, our tack crossed the outside of the line, so that we found ourselves sailing ahead of the brilliant array, feeling like a flagship with a squadron extended behind. Presently our ships turned about as the tide changed, and soon they were marked only by a glow in the sky to the southward.

We tacked on up the western shore until we reached the long sandspit that splits the Iloilo channel, and there we decided to anchor. We sailed in towards the western shore, sounding as we went, and at the same time trying to discover the meaning of a light that was moving on or near the beach. It turned out to be a fisherman detaching his petromax light from a beached boat, but it had so occupied our attentions that it was only then that we noticed something to starboard and through the glasses discovered it to be a boat tied to a row of fishing stakes. We were sailing under the main alone, and put about as quickly as possible on to a reverse course, and now saw lines of stakes on both sides between which we had sailed. We cleared these and then saw more stakes ahead. This was too much and we anchored in six fathoms finding in the morning that the new stakes were on the sandspit and that we were on the starboard side of the channel.

We crossed the bottom end of the spit next morning in order to use the main channel on the eastern side. A yellow sailing ship with a red sail, a small cargo carrier, beat up with us, but we were faster than she was, and her captain, making a race of it, cut across the spit. He was a little early and grounded so we left him still further behind.

The wind whistled down the channel, which looked like a broad river and was covered with whitecaps. We beat up in short tacks under the cliffs on the starboard side, until Iloilo River was open, when we shot across the strait and plopped into its sudden stillness. We tied up to a wharf for a short time, fending off a crowd of bystanders, and then, finding that the Customs House was further up the river, moved up and anchored below a bridge above the main traffic—too late to avoid losing a spring which holds the backstay not in use to the shrouds. This had been filched from under our eyes. Although this was our only experience of theft in the Philippines, it must constitute one of the disadvantages of sailing there, for we were continually warned about it.

The Philippines are a great cruising ground, as there is always a weather shore, plenty of wind, and there are all kinds of interesting straits and passages and an immense variety of scenery and anchorages. The people are very friendly and gentle, almost too friendly, as in the villages they are all water-borne and from the moment of arrival until dark a yacht is besieged by visitors, by little tappings on the hull by insistent little cries of 'Hello Poppa, hello Momma!' which I found very hard to bear for long with a smile, and not too often, but often enough to be annoying, of 'Cigaretto, cigaretto.'

We were not in the wealthy areas and met no landowners or whatever is the aristocracy of the Philippines, and with the exception of the commercial port of Iloilo, only visited small fishing villages, and often only a few houses in an otherwise deserted bay.

From Iloilo there were two ways to reach the Surigao Strait. One was north of Leyte and down through the fascinating San Juanico Strait, ten miles of extremely narrow and reef-encumbered water. We first intended to go this way, but experience with unlit lights and missing buoys made us decide against it, especially as we would have arrived there in the middle of the spring tides. The other way was to go south of Leyte to Limassawa, the small island where Magellan first landed, and then up the west coast of Dinagat.

We set off from Iloilo on 7 February, sailing by day and almost invariably anchoring by night—most interesting navigation, good hard sailing, and lovely exciting anchorages. Our first objective was Canas Bay where we proposed to spend the weekend. It is a small bay on the coast of Panay, surrounded by coconuts and hills, with one or two small villages on its shore almost pushed into the sea by the hills behind, and always a sailing ship in sight. These sailing ships are the chief delight of the Philippines, usually outriggers and often two-masted, with a Joseph's coat of patched sails. Under most of the houses in the villages a fighting cock is tethered to one of the posts and a pig or two to the others. Once we saw a cock being rowed out to a match away from home on an anchored salvage ship.

At this time we relied on a powerful missionary radio station for our weather reports. 'Winds of five to fifteen miles an hour shall prevail,' boomed a voice every morning, as if it was the voice of Jehovah himself forecasting. Our ventimeter, which is certainly not given to overstatement showed a wind of thirty miles an hour one day in the Visayan Sea, as we listened to the forecast, and we wished the forecaster in a place that he seemed confident he'd never see.

Our last halt where there was any chance of getting some stores was at the bottom of Leyte, at Maasin, which has steamer communication with the rest of the islands. We anchored well off the pier, but when I asked whether we were clear of the steamers, I was told 'It all depends on the Captain.'

From Maasin we sailed to Limassawa. We anchored on the western side, but Magellan's boats had anchored on the eastern, so we walked over the hill to see the spot. There was a cross and a bronze plaque at the place where Mass was first celebrated, but the original cross had been removed. The village was swarming with attractive brown children who, as everywhere else in the Philippines, escorted us wherever we went. All the young people seem to wish to be schoolteachers, and in every village there are two or three of them. The education seemed to be well looked after, but the problem is not a mere population explosion, it is an atomic burst, and what will happen to all the education, when the fish and the land run short, Heaven only knows!

From Limassawa we beat up the west coast of Dinagat and made our last anchorage in Layauan Bay. The entrance was as narrow, steep, and wooded, as many near our home in British Columbia, and a grey day and rain made us feel as if we were there. Inside was very different, with a coral reef dropping off into deep water. It happened that the local councillor and a number of dignitaries from the nearest town had come by boat to discuss the necessity for another school for the two families that were populating the bay. They all shouted instructions to us, quite unaware of the requirements of a yacht of *Tzu Hang*'s size. As soon as we were anchored they all came on board and we handed out oilskins to them in a sudden downpour. These they took as gifts, but we were off to cold waters and had need of them. Somehow we had to recover them and it took force to do so, and the person who put up the strongest resistance was the councillor himself.

On Monday, 24 February we set sail for Okinawa. The crucial point of our journey, the beat out into the Pacific had arrived, and at 0145 next morning, as we cleared Homonhon Island, we felt the first long Pacific swell.

To a yacht like *Tzu Hang*, who has made several long ocean passages, that first long swell, so different from those of inland waters, must feel like a homecoming. Beryl and I felt our spirits lift with it. 'Did you feel that?' we called to each other in excitement. All night the light wind held and the clouds slid across the face of the moon, but by daylight, the sky was covered and the land so obscured that we could not tell whether we had been set north or south of the entrance to the Strait. During the day the wind freshened and by the evening was blowing gale force in squalls. Eager to get well offshore we had carried too much sail for too long, and once again the mainsail had split right across on one of the longer seams, where the stitching had not been renewed. We let *Tzu Hang* sail under jib and mizzen on the port tack, heading south east, as the northerly tack would have kept us too close to the shore.

All next day Beryl stitched away while *Tzu Hang*, with her tiny trysail, worked her way out against a strong monsoon. Next morning Beryl was still stitching while we tacked to the north. The Monsoon had eased, but clouds covered the sky and we could not get a position. On 28 February, we set the main and sailed to the north under clearing skies. At noon I knew where we were. We were sixty miles south of the entrance to Surigao Strait, but seventy miles offshore; the current had taken us a long way south, but at least we had a good offing and could sail in the right direction. Our troubles were not all over, as Beryl rolled herself in her blanket and turned her face to the wall, her energy suddenly drained away. I saw that something was wrong and felt her flushed cheek. We take our health at sea so much for granted that I was surprised to find that we had a thermometer on board. Her temperature was 103°. I began to imagine all sorts of terrible things.

'If you're thinking of turning back, that'll really kill me,' she said, 'I think there are some red pills in the medicine chest, I'll take those.'

It was lucky that they were red, and the pills of tape- or round-worm in cats, of which we had sufficient to dose a tiger, were white. They were in a box labelled 'To be taken before dining with natives,' but Beryl thought that they were suitable for any infection. After three days she had recovered, nursed by good, gentle *Tzu Hang*, who sailed herself to windward, in spite of rough weather, as quietly as she could.

With Beryl once more her old vital self the enjoyment of sailing returned. *Tzu Hang* sang her song and plunged and shook herself and blew like an old sealion on his way to the nurseries. Sometimes we changed a jib and sometimes rolled a reef, but that was all that she asked us to do. Always we shared the watches with her, watch and watch, not on deck for she did not require it, but reading or even dozing below, ready if needed.

On the morning of 12 March, I put my head out of the hatch at about 4 a.m. and saw to my surprise the lights of Okinawa blazing on the port bow. Twenty minutes later they were disappearing over the horizon on the port quarter and I realized that they belonged to one of those huge Japanese tankers that are as long and as brilliantly illuminated as a city street. Luckily I had kept my landfall to myself and it wasn't until later in the day that Okinawa appeared ahead of us. We hove to for the night under the steep cliffs from where the last of the Japanese soldiers defending Okinawa are said to have thrown themselves into the sea.

Next morning the F 105's tore down the strip beside the shore and split the quiet sky like an axe on a cedar log, curving away into the clouds. *Tzu Hang*, in strange contrast, white sails still and leaning gently to the wind, came silently and unobserved into Naha Ko. For the first time I found myself being interviewed by a square-shouldered and square-jawed C.I.D. man.

'But Captain,' he said, scratching his shaven head, 'I just don't see how you got in.'

'Sailed in.'

'But how come nobody saw you?'

'Perhaps nobody was looking.'

'If only you'd gone to the civilian side,' he said, 'we wouldn't be in a spot like this.'

It was easy enough to change sides and with everyone doing their best to help we were able to overcome official barriers and stay for a few days. Meanwhile, we had tied to a floating crane whose captain, a small grizzled man in neat khaki and wearing a cap covered in gold leaves, came on board.

'I was brought up the hard way,' he told us. 'I was an Alaskan fisherman for twenty-five years. I believed a man had to work hard to earn his bread as my father taught me. Then the war came and I wised up. Man—what a break! Government service. That's the way to live. Look at me now. Clean hands, all the money I need, a house in California, and the biggest voyage I make on this crate is to the other side of the harbour.'

A tall engineer, a sailor, but a Colonel in the U.S. Army,

was particularly kind to us during our stay, because he also, the founder of the Yacht Club, had always hoped to do what we were doing. 'The trouble is,' he said, 'I can't afford it. I'm paid so well in this job that I just can't pack it in.'

When Beryl and I sailed away, impressed by the sight of so much military power, overawed by the luxury of the clubs, our digestions overloaded with huge steaks and too much beer, the least well off in all that affluent society, we thought that we were still the richest.

On 24 March, we found ourselves when daylight came sailing along the coast of Tanega Shima, one of the islands close off the southernmost point of Japan. White breakers foamed on tide-ridged rocks below steep eroded slopes. On the slopes and on the ridge above were pines, those particular pines of Japanese paintings. Soon a spray of sunshine would break through to add a little colour.

'Come on!' I called to Beryl, whom I heard below busy with breakfast. 'You must stick your head out. It's just like a Japanese picture.'

'Of course it is,' I heard her say, but she did put her head out. 'Aren't we rather close inshore?' she asked.

Ahead of us off the point of the Island I could see a number of small fishboats trolling. They were in a tide-rip and motoring fast through the troubled water. *Tzu Hang* was sailing fast too, doing about seven knots. We held on through them. There was only one man in each boat, their heads muffled against the cold, paying no attention to *Tzu Hang* and preoccupied with their work. Suddenly I saw them again as I had last seen them in tatty khaki caps twenty years before, uncouth and unshaven, and even now a fisherman wearing one of those same caps was coming in towards us. As he passed I thought that if he didn't reply to a wave, I wasn't going to enjoy Japan. I stood up and waved. Immediately he stepped aft and waved back in reply, and his face, between a green muffler and the old khaki cap, split in a toothy grin.

That night we were in Kagoshima Kaiwan, beating up towards Kagoshima, and a bitter wind was whistling down the bay. There was little sleep for either of us, for after our ocean passage the waters seemed constricted and full of traffic. *Tzu Hang* rushed across the bay and no sooner had one of us gone below than there was a call from the deck that it was time to go about again. A last night and nearly the end of a journey, and my heart went out to my love sitting at the helm, indistinct in the darkness, whose every movement I knew so well, and who carried the greater load so lightly. I did not envy any man in his bed that night.

Next morning Sakuraijima was blowing great clouds of smoke at the head of the bay and presently we could make out a line of ships at anchor outside the breakwater. The ensigns of three Japanese frigates dropped in reply to our salute and, like a small colonel taking his place at the head of his regiment, we sailed between the ships and anchored in front of them. Since none of them had sailed as far as *Tzu Hang*, that was the right place for her to be.